ALTERNATIVES TO VIOLENCE PROJECT

MANUAL
for
Second Level Course

Revised 2005
By the Education Committee
Alternatives to Violence Project / USA

1st Edition – 1982
2nd Edition – 1990
3rd Edition – 2005

ISBN: 978-0-941758-06-2

©Copyright 2005 AVP/USA, Inc. All Rights Reserved
The Alternatives to Violence Project/USA Inc. is a 501(C)(3)
Nonprofit corporation formed to support the needs of local
AVP groups throughout the United States. Anyone engaged
In offering training in conflict resolution is hereby granted
the right to reproduce this document in small quantities for
their own non-commercial use, without prior permission.

This manual is the product of many dedicated, talented and generous AVP people who have created and contributed to the exercises and ideas that it contains, and to the others who have done the organizing, typesetting, formatting, copy reading and editorial work. All of their contributions count, not only for its intrinsic value, but for their love of AVP and their desire to enhance its presence in the world. We wish to acknowledge them here with deepest gratitude.

This manual is published for the use of volunteers serving as team members and coordinators of workshops conducted under the sponsorship of the Alternatives to Violence Project/USA.

Other readers are advised that the material in the manual is based on a particular philosophy and a set of carefully structured group dynamics, without which the program outlined here simply will not work.

For this reason, the use of the name AVP for workshops and programs not approved and sponsored by Alternatives to Violence/USA, Inc., whether utilizing this material or not, is strictly prohibited.

Published and Distributed By:

Alternatives to Violence Project/USA, Inc.
AVP Distribution Center
1050 Selby Avenue
Saint Paul, Minnesota 55104
1-888-278-7820   manuals@avpusa.org

All orders and inquiries should be addressed to the Distributor.

TABLE OF CONTENTS

SECTION A: **Introduction**
- Preface A-3
- The Way We Do Things A-4
- Therapy and AVP Workshops A-5
- Touching as Part of AVP Training A-6
- Working as a Team A-8
- Feedback A-10
- Resolution of Conflicts in the Workshop A-12

SECTION B: **Agendas**
- Introduction — Format of a Second Level Workshop B-3
- Guidelines to Agenda Writing B-4
- Agenda Worksheet B-5
- Planning Guide B-7
- Exercise Times B-9

SECTION C: **Transforming Power**
- Transforming Power in This Workshop C-3
- Transforming Power: On Violence C-4
- Transforming Power Talk C-5
- Transforming Power Short Talk C-6
- Transforming Power—What Makes it Work C-8
- Transforming Power Mandala C-9
- Transforming Power Guidelines Related to the Mandala .. C-10
- Transforming Power Talk Using the Mandala C-11
- Transforming Power Indicators C-12
- Guides for Being Open to Transforming Power C-13

SECTION D: **Exercises/Techniques** (in Alphabetical Order)
- Section Contents D-2

SECTION E: **Role Playing**
- The Boxing Ring E-3
- Role Playing—Variations on a Theme E-5

SECTION F: **Talks – Explanations**
- Opening Statement F-3
- Anger F-4
- Anger, Fear and Taking a Stand F-6
- Communication F-7
- Empathy F-9
- Fear F-10
- Forgiveness F-12
- Forgiveness — Removing Obstacles to Forgiveness F-13
- Making Friends With Conflict F-14
- Power F-16
- Stereotyping F-18

SECTION G: **Gatherings, Light & Livelies, Closings/Affirmations**
- Section Contents G-2
- Gatherings G-3
- Light & Livelies G-6
- Closings & Affirmations G-18

SECTION H: **Resources – Index**
- Resources H-3
- Index H-5

SECTION A

Introduction

Preface

The Way We Do Things

Therapy and AVP Workshops

Touching as Part of AVP Training

Working as a Team

Feedback

Resolution of Conflicts in the Workshop

PREFACE

Welcome to the newly revised Alternatives to Violence Project Second Level Manual: the 2005 Advanced Manual for Facilitators.

As AVP's creative conflict resolution workshops grew in the last quarter of the twentieth century, from area-wide to nationwide, the need for a second level of workshops to complement the ongoing basic workshops was recognized. A second level manual was developed by the members of the AVP Education Committee, facilitators all, with new depths of understanding gained from years of experience with old exercises and experimentation with new ones. As AVP has become a worldwide program, we have been enriched by the flourishing of ideas from facilitators around the world. Input from prison inmate facilitators has always deepened and enhanced our knowledge. Now, as facilitators have continued to use variations and to make additions and deletions, and as suggested changes in recent years have come to be widely accepted and used in workshops, the Education Committee has realized the need for a full revision of our second level manual. This, our 2005 AVP revised Second Level Manual, is the result. Some talks and exercises have been improved, some omitted, some replaced. Most material from the Supplement has been included.

A primary focus in this revision has been to enhance and simplify agenda preparation. Variations of methods for choosing a workshop focus topic are included, as well as new sample agendas. In deciding changes to the manual, we kept in mind the AVP goals of bringing people of all cultures, levels of education, and walks of life into the circle of facilitators.

Transforming Power has always been and continues to be the heart of AVP. Thus we, the volunteers, the facilitators, approach workshops with the certainty of the Inner Light as the guide coming through us, not from us. Facilitators and participants are always learners and teachers to one another, even when an occasional near failure or real failure presents itself. "Trust the Process" is still our motto. We continue affirming and reaffirming one another in a loving spirit.

We can continue to maintain our contact with one another through our international network and through AVP-USA at http://avpusa.org.

THE WAY WE DO THINGS

In the earlier edition of the manual, we included several AVP techniques in this section. In this revised manual, the "Exercises" section is renamed the "Exercises and Techniques" section, and the following techniques are in alphabetical order along with the exercises:

Brainstorming (look for the specific exercise as a sub-title of Brainstorming)
Concentric Circles
Consensus (look for the specific exercise as a sub-title of Consensus)
Dialogue (See Claremont Dialogue)
Fishbowl
I Messages: Another Approach
Journal Writing
Letter to Myself
Listening
Query Writing
Reflection (see Guided Reflection — Alternatives to Violence)

THERAPY AND AVP WORKSHOPS
There is a difference!

It is extremely important to remember that AVP is not a therapy program and that AVP facilitators are not qualified to act as therapists.

Sometimes, a participant feels comfortable enough to share some extremely personal experience and/or asks the group for help in solving an extremely important moral dilemma. When such sharing goes on, it is important to:

- acknowledge the intensity of the feeling.
- affirm the speaker for being so brave.
- thank the speaker for the gift of trust he has given the group.
- ask if any participants who have so far been silent want to respond.

The facilitator(s) then have choices to make:

If the moral dilemma is presented early in the workshop, suggest that it be written as an "unanswered question." If this is done, it is VERY important that it be written in a way that does not specify the problem or the speaker, since C0's or others might read it.

The leader might express regret that this problem cannot be confronted and resolved here and now, but that often things happen afterward that might be of help. Other members might come to the speaker later to help; and the speaker might also later find that putting his feelings into words has helped him with his own problem.

It may happen that a particularly needy and assertive participant might make undue demands on the group's time for dealing with personal problems. It may then be necessary, for the sake of both the individual and the group, to point out that the AVP is not a group therapy program and its leaders are not psychotherapists and not qualified to conduct group therapy sessions.

An example of what appears to have been a successful handling of a moral issue occurring in advanced prison workshop was when a participant shared that he had learned that the man who killed his father might be coming into the same prison that he was in. He felt obligated to kill the man, but was obviously struggling with this obligation.

The facilitators said that this was a question that needed a lot of thought, and suggested that they put it on the "unanswered questions" sheet (which they did in code). In the final session, after the group had been together for three days, they brought the question to the group.

One of the other participants said to the man: "You said that your father loved your mother, right? You said that you are the only child left to your mother, right? You said you are up for parole in five years. Well, what would your mother want you to do?" The man answered, "She'd want me to be able to come home." The other participant persisted, "Then what would your father want you to do?" The man answered, "He'd want me to go home and take care of my mother." The other participant brought it to a close, "Then whenever some guy is goading you to get this guy, you just tell yourself what your father and mother would want you to do." The man with the problem had found his answer.

TOUCHING AS PART OF AVP TRAINING

The Alternatives to Violence program has as its objective to help people find other ways of dealing with the conflicts in their lives than through resorting to violence.

The central theme in AVP is something we have chosen to call Transforming Power. This is the power that is available to us all to change (transform) what might be a violent or destructive situation into a nonviolent (win/win) solution. The basis of Transforming Power is an appreciation of one's own self-worth and a caring attitude toward all other people. This requires an ability to separate out feelings toward another's behavior from feelings for that person.

In AVP workshops we seek to teach these concepts not by lecture or reading but by giving participants in our workshops hands-on experience so that they teach themselves by actually living and feeling the concepts we are trying to pass along.

To help people feel the importance of caring for one another, we have many exercises that expose participants to these kinds of feelings. From the very start of the workshop, we emphasize instilling and reinforcing a sense of self-worth, building community, and developing trust within the group. The exercises AVP uses to accomplish these goals involve sharing life experiences and life goals, and honing communications skills.

Communication between individuals is not simply verbal. It takes place in other ways as well. Behavior, body postures, facial expressions, hand and head gestures, and physical touching (hand on shoulder, pat on the back, hugs) are all equally eloquent forms of communication as words. Listening, too, can be a creative act of communication. Sadly, the importance of some of these forms, particularly touching and listening, is not well understood.

One of the most common causes of violence on the streets seems to be the unspoken but powerful need for personal space. We all feel that a certain part of the space near our bodies belongs to us, and we feel uneasy if it is trespassed upon. Most streetwise people, including most prisoners, are especially sensitive about this.

If anyone invades their space, they are likely to feel so threatened as to justify using violence to protect themselves or teach the invader a lesson. This feeling is intensified if the other person (especially a stranger) touches them. Part of AVP's effort from the beginning encourages them to realize that touching is not necessarily hostile, that it can be a communication of good will and caring. To this end, AVP exercises are designed to gradually accustom participants to accept friendly touching as an expression of acceptance and fellowship, free of hostility or sexual aggression.

In a prison, even more than in most places in our society, touching is an act that is easily misunderstood, with potentially explosive results. AVP's approach is to begin with simple activities such as standing in a circle holding hands. This is a rather strange and initially uncomfortable experience for prison inmates not used to this type of intimacy. Games are played that involve even closer body contact. One such game is the human pretzel, where two participants volunteer to leave the room while the rest of the group, while holding hands, twist themselves into a tangle by moving and stepping over hands. The volunteers return and try to untangle the group without having anyone let go of hands.

Other forms of touching that are routinely experienced during a workshop include such sharing as shoulder rubs and hugs. A more intense touching exercise is the Trust Lift, usually used toward the end of a workshop when (and only if) a group has developed a sense of community and trust strong enough to justify the perceived risk that it involves. In this exercise, an individual lies down on the floor, and eight or ten participants position themselves around him or her and slowly lift the person up above their shoulders and over their heads. Then the person is slowly lowered down to the floor. Throughout the exercise the person is rocked gently, as in a cradle, to calm anxiety and bring on a sense of peace and trust.

Equally profound, and even less well understood, is the importance of listening as a form of communication. Most people have much experience of being talked at; the experience of being really listened to is very rare, and very precious. Violence often is the result of frustration at never being heard, and can often be defused, and turned into a satisfying human encounter, by nothing more than an act of creative listening. AVP has therefore developed many exercises which help individuals to test their capacity to listen, to practice and improve this skill, and to learn by experience the power of this seemingly simple thing to do.

In an AVP prison workshop individuals learn caring for one another. This is so even though the prison environment tends to be hostile to such an attitude, and even though the majority of participants in any given workshop have never met each other prior to its opening session. In any environment, but especially in this one, the experience is rare and profoundly moving. It teaches by personal experience that it is possible and satisfying to be caring toward another individual, even though this may be a person with whom we disagree. AVP builds on this experience in every workshop through role plays that challenge participants to use their new-found communication skills, and their sense of community and Transforming Power, to solve potential conflict situations.

The intensity of the AVP workshop builds a strong sense of community arising from a shared experience. Participants often get a sense of a completely new way of living their lives, built on trust and consideration for one another. The AVP experience stands in sharp contrast to the daily realities of the prison environment, and the difference usually finds expression in a great reluctance on the part of participants to have a workshop end. The AVP experience and the potential for individual change stands or falls on the extent to which participants feel a genuine sense of caring from the group leaders and from the group as a whole.

*From a letter by Stephen L. Angell, AVP Administrator,
to New York State Correctional Officials*

WORKING AS A TEAM

The AVP Manual provides directions for team-building, for developing an agenda for a workshop, and for leading specific exercises. This sheet is to deal with the "why."

All of the written directions are guidelines — structures that will provide an "anchor" that you can use to start from as you develop your individual style. The complicating factor is that as you develop your individual style, you have to remain conscious that you will ALWAYS be working as a member of a team. When you deviate from the structure of an exercise that the manual provides, you need to share your new approach with your team so that they do not think that you simply are confused about directions and step in to "help" you, resulting in confusion for all, including the participants.

You are NEVER leading an exercise alone; you may be giving the directions and you may have "center stage." But you are never alone. So, how do team members work as a team, supporting and aiding the team member leading a specific exercise, rap, or discussion without getting in the way? The way the team makes decisions BEFORE you start the workshop is important:

1. Together, the team develops the overall theme or goal of the workshop. In an advanced workshop, this means deciding the process by which the participants will choose the focus topic.

2. Together, the team develops themes for each session. These session themes are sequential "steps" toward the goal or theme or objective of the whole workshop.

3. Together, the team chooses exercises (learning experiences) which will help the participants achieve awareness and understanding of each of the themes of each session.

What this all means is that, the members of the team ALL know
   a) WHAT they are doing
   b) WHY they are doing it
   c) HOW they are doing it

Some "rules" that help the process along:

1. Post an outline of the entire workshop with the objectives for each session.. Go over them with the participants so that they understand where you are headed, and why the answers aren't coming in the first session, but will emerge gradually.

2. Refer to that outline of session objectives as your team prepares the specific exercises for each session. When you include an exercise, you must know what the participants are supposed to get out of it, and the discussion questions you put forth after the exercise is concluded should be designed to draw that understanding out of the participants. You should also know what TP guides relate to the exercise.

   Once your team has decided on the exercises for a particular session, and you have worked together to revise/adapt them for the specific objective, you decide who is to facilitate which exercise. As facilitator of a specific exercise, you are not only responsible for knowing the WHAT, WHY and HOW of the exercise, but also for working out with your other team members as to what part(s) THEY play during the exercise YOU are leading.

3. Decide what help you need from the other members of your team. Is it
    a) to take part in the exercise so that each participant has a partner?

    b) to act as observer of one of the small groups working on a task?

    c) to sit next to someone who has trouble following directions or staying on task?

    d) to be prepared with some "leading" discussion questions so that if the discussion gets bogged down, they can push it in another direction? (Example, when brainstorming what violence is, and participants seem to be naming only physical violence, to ask if violence can ever be other than physical.)

    e) to pass out pencils, record comments on a posted sheet of paper?

    f) to keep track of time, and signal you when the discussion should be brought to a close?

Remember: No member of the team is ever "on vacation" at any time during a workshop. Everyone is responsible for the group at all times. One person may be center stage while giving directions, but all other members of the team are constantly alert, ready to step in (with a question, not a correction, if possible) if the person giving directions fumbles or forgets an important part, and, during the exercise, everyone is "tuned in" to what is happening in the process of the exercise and the discussion afterward.

Example:
The importance of the team being "tuned in" was brought home to a team of facilitators by a participant. They had noticed that first day that there were a few men who seemed to be competing with one another by using "big words" during discussions. They had also noticed the second day that three of the Spanish-dominant participants had brought Spanish/English dictionaries. What the facilitators hadn't done was "put two and two together." A participant approached one of the facilitators during the break that second morning and asked if he could speak to her alone. He asked her if she had noticed the dictionaries. Then he explained to her that the Spanish-dominant participants had brought them because they were feeling intimidated during discussions by the men who were using vocabulary they could not understand.

The facilitating team was able to correct the situation, thanks to a sensitive participant. The lesson remains for all facilitating teams: When one is busy handing out materials or giving directions, other members of the team must be listening and observing.

Unless a team member is specifically assigned the task of becoming a participant, s(he) should avoid acting as a participant, specifically in discussions. We DON'T provide the answers — we provide leading questions that will stimulate thought so that the answers come from the participants. During discussions, facilitators should reframe their comments to become questions that move the participants to think in a new direction. You may think that you have the most wonderful insight on the subject — it is your job to think of a question that might lead one of the participants to have that same insight.

We DON'T become so involved in the topic being discussed that we lose sight of our responsibilities as facilitators: these are to hear what is coming out of the group discussion and be prepared with a question, to observe who is participating and who is not, and to watch the time and communicate to the facilitator leading the discussion if it needs closure.

REMEMBER!
Don't hesitate to close a discussion while it is still lively. You can ALWAYS come back to it. If there are unresolved issues, make a point of writing them in question form on the "Unanswered Questions" sheet. You then have time as a facilitating team to discuss what exercises or other shared experiences might help provide answers.

FEEDBACK

Giving feedback and learning from it is a component of much of what we do in AVP. It is part of our task of helping one another do as good a job as possible. Many exercises require it. Each workshop session should be followed by a clinicing session in which each team member gives feedback to the others and receives it from them. No one is "the expert," and no one is exempt from the need to improve. However, neither giving nor receiving feedback is simple: There is an art to both.

Giving feedback:

1. Start with strengths. Specify exactly what was positive. Never forget to praise. Strengthen one another by letting people know that the good things they do are recognized.

2. Then move to things needing improvement. Again, be specific. Remember TP Guideline about reaching for that good in the other person; that "good" in this case is the shared vision that this workshop be the best it can be.

   - Speak only with awareness of the value of the other person and of the difficulty of responding constructively to criticism.
   - Describe behavior rather than labeling it. Be objective rather than judgmental.
   - Offer a possible way of improvement, a concrete suggestion. Speak in a tentative rather than a dogmatic manner. Do not impose a suggestion.
   - Ask for reactions to the suggestion. Give room to accept, refuse or modify it.
   - Stick to the basic problem, and do not get involved with complex descriptions of the history of the problem or anticipated negative reactions of the other person.

Receiving feedback.

1. Remember that we all have much to learn and can always improve. It is even possible that we may be wrong. So can our critics; but even misguided criticism can nonetheless be helpful. At the very least, it can tell us that we were ineffective with that person at that time, and thus lead to a more effective approach.

2. If A gives B hostile or misguided feedback, B should remember that the feedback says at least as much about A's opinion of himself as it does about his opinion of B. If you are B, try not to take it personally.

3. Each person is the final judge of what is valuable in him/herself, of what cannot be changed and what must not be changed. Criticism directed at what is best in a person must be rejected. On the other hand, some things are just too difficult to change. We all have to accept much imperfection in ourselves and others. Let's try to learn to live with it.

Criteria for feedback in exercises (or situations) that call for assertiveness where it may be difficult:

1. **Verbal behaviors**
   - Were statements direct and to the point?
   - Were statements firm but not hostile?
   - Was consideration, respect, and recognition given to the other person?
   - Did the statements accurately reflect the speaker's goals?
   - Did the statements leave room for escalation?
   - If the statements included an explanation, was it short rather than a series of excuses? Was there sarcasm, pleading, or whining?
   - Was the other person blamed for the speaker's feelings?

2. **Nonverbal behaviors**
   - Was eye contact present?
   - Was voice level appropriate, loud enough but not yelling?
   - Was it expressive, not flat?
   - Were there pauses, so as to avoid making the other person feel crowded?
   - Did the person speak confidently, without nervous gestures or inappropriate laughter?

RESOLUTION OF CONFLICTS IN THE WORKSHOP

Strong feelings aroused in a workshop need to be given recognition and space. Occasionally conflicts may arise between participants, or between participants and facilitators. (Serious conflicts between facilitators usually need to be resolved privately in a clinic).

A conflict that arises in a workshop is a golden opportunity to model and demonstrate non-violent conflict resolution in the present. It moves our process out of the theoretical and into the practical and immediate, and can have a powerful impact. The most important thing is never allow a group to leave a subject that has aroused them without finishing their exploration of it.

There are a variety of ways to openly resolve these conflicts and air feelings, including, Claremont Dialogue, Fishbowl, Think and Listen and You Said/I Said all of which are in the Exercise Section. Shorter, simpler methods are listed below.

Minicounseling ("Mini's') (Dialogue in Pairs)

A method of doing this that allows the team to move on to the rest of the agenda without too much loss of time is called Mini's. Put the group into pairs. Then tell them that each will have five minutes to say whatever they feel they want to say about what has been happening in the workshop. Don't spend time structuring the experience. Let them speak as they want to speak, only making sure that each one speaks and feels heard by the partner. When both have spoken and been listened to, return to the large group and briefly discuss whatever needs to be discussed.

Uninterrupted Time in Groups

Some exercises are capable of arousing strong and disturbing feelings in participants, and there may be a need to give further closure to the discussion of the topics arising from them. If so, do one of the following:

1. Gather the whole group together and give each person time to speak, without evaluation or response from other speakers, of whatever seems most important to the participants about the topics raised in such exercises: Let people speak as long as they need to in order to unburden themselves.

2. Or divide into smaller groups and follow the same procedure. Reconvene in large group and let each small group report back the gist of what was said in that group.

Agendas

SECTION B

Introduction
Format of Second Level Workshop

Guidelines to Agenda Writing

Agenda Worksheet

Planning Guide

Exercise Times

INTRODUCTION

Format of Second Level Workshop

Second Level Workshops in the Alternatives to Violence Project (AVP) have a standard form, as follows:

Part I. Building Community, Setting Goals, and Group Decision

With any AVP workshop, success depends greatly on building community within the group. People need to get to know one another and feel comfortable working together. They also need to recapture a sense of some of the thoughts and experiences they had in their Basic Workshop. Usually, they will not all have been in the same Basic. Some will know each other and some will be strangers. Community building, therefore, far from being omitted, must be given all due attention.

The concept of Transforming Power also needs to be reintroduced. It is the foundation of this workshop, as it was of the Basic. People will expand their perception of it during the workshop. Like breathing, it doesn't have to be part of consciousness all the time, but it must not be absent.

People will be looking in some depth at their individual goals and thinking about exploring some that seem important to them for this workshop. They will then work to put them together with the goals of others. The group will come to a decision on a subject or set of subjects which will become the focus of Part II of the workshop. The experience of making a group decision in a way that leaves no one out is an important part of this section.

In some cases, the focus has been decided in advance. If so, the team will still need to help people explore their goals within the focus.

Part II. Focus on Subject Picked by Group

The group will pick a topic on which to spend major effort (usually three sessions). This topic is usually one that gets in the way of nonviolence; something that has meaning and creates difficulties for the group, such as anger, fear, power, communications, man-woman relationships and others. The list of focus topics has grown and is still growing in response to the expressed needs of AVP workshop groups.

The focus topic(s) for the workshop may be chosen in many ways: through a Gathering; through one of the four "Choosing the Focus Topic" exercises or "Consensus: A Five Exercise Process," all in the Exercises and Techniques section; or by the team in advance of the workshop. This last way may be helpful if you are doing an second level workshop with participants who have already participated in one.

It is important that each session in the workshop have a goal or theme so that the exercises have a sequence that leads the participants through awareness and understanding to confronting issues relating to the focus topic. In the sample agenda we have provided, we have a suggested goal for each session. *It is helpful to move the second to last session into some kind of healing or resolving stage.* The final session is the summing up and bringing the workshop to a close.

GUIDELINES TO AGENDA WRITING

As we all know very well from our experience of the Basic Workshop: each group is different; each team is different; each workshop takes on a life of its own. AVP agendas, far from being written on stone, should be written on water. They should be fluid, changing their flow and even their channel in response to the needs of the group. Second Level Workshops provide an opportunity for this fluid response.

There are several ways to develop a Second Level Workshop. First, some facilitators choose a focus topic before-hand, and volunteers can sign up for the workshop if the topic is of interest to them. More often, the group chooses a focus topic.

On the following pages, you will find a **SAMPLE AGENDA** for a workshop where groups chose the focus topic. It is designed to be copied and filled in as the workshop progresses. Following the sample agenda is a **PLANNING GUIDE** which will suggest exercises appropriate for a variety of focus topics.

Of course, very experienced facilitators will adapt these suggestions in creative ways, including having groups develop their own community agreements, including the entire group in the In Common exercise, or using Bean Jar as a consensus exercise without the facilitators knowing the "right" answer. In Section D, see *Consensus: a Five Exercise Process*. Creativity is encouraged as experience with the workshop over time develops confidence.

The following guidelines may help to keep things functioning effectively:

- The basic technique of agenda construction in an AVP Second Level Workshop is to include in each session some of the basic AVP ingredients: affirmation, community, communication, etc., building as the workshop goes along.
- Keep the agenda going with the flow of the group's feelings, problems and growth. This means that:
  a) The agenda of every session should be made up in the light of the group's evaluation of the previous session, and should in some way address any concerns, problems or complaints expressed or implied in that evaluation.
  b) The team should lead up to any exercises that are likely to be emotionally demanding or "heavy," by first using exercises that are lighter, introductory, and/or affirming.
  c) No "heavy" exercise should be scheduled in such a way as to leave the group in an uncomfortable emotional space at the end of a session. Allow plenty of time to deal with whatever feelings may be aroused.
  d) No agenda item is so important that it should not be sacrificed to accommodate any issue or concern that manifests itself, however unexpectedly, and be as of immediate and serious importance to the group. It is the team's job to help the group work on whatever it needs to address, not to superimpose its own agenda. To force the team's agenda on the group, instead, is a prescription for failure.
  e) Having a few "fillers" in mind is a wise plan. Sometimes an exercise one expects to take 30 minutes only takes 20. Advanced planning is always helpful when deviations arise.
  f) Bear in mind that a Second Level group has probably been sufficiently empowered by previous AVP experience that it will feel entitled to take more charge than it had previously done over the conduct of the workshop. This may manifest itself as rebellion, but let it happen. It is a growth experience, and it means that AVP is succeeding.

AGENDA WORKSHEET

SECOND LEVEL WORKSHOP   Name _____   Date _____

SESSION 1: COMMUNITY BUILDING

Welcome and brief introduction of facilitating team

Opening Talk, including explanation of how this workshop is different from the Basic workshop.

Agenda Preview

Introduction of Participants: My name and something I've used or thought about from the Basic Workshop

Community Agreements: *(Review ones from the Basic and open it to additional suggestions)*

My Adjective Name (or Name and Gesture) and Why I Chose It

Light and Lively:

Community Building Exercise:

Evaluation

SESSION 2: REINTRODUCE TP AND CHOOSE WORKSHOP FOCUS-TOPIC(S)

Agenda Preview

Gathering: Something I want to get out of this workshop is ...

Review of Transforming Power *(see Transforming Power in this Workshop in TP Section)*

Exercise *(Guided Reflection or other exercise to raise awareness of choices, goals)*

L&L:

Exercise to choose the Focus Topic *(see exercises listed under Choosing a Focus Topic)*

Evaluation

Note: if you need short exercises in the first two sessions, see the exercises under brainstorming and consensus.

SESSION 3: AWARENESS OF THE FOCUS TOPIC(S) – HOW DOES IT AFFECT ME?

Agenda Preview

Gathering (Something on the chosen focus topic(s):

Exercise:

Exercise:

L&L:

Exercise:

Evaluation

Suggestions for Session 3: Brainstorms, Getting in Touch, Concentric Circles, Listening.

Agenda Worksheet

SESSION 4: EXPERIENCING THE FOCUS TOPIC(S)

Agenda Preview

Gathering:

Exercise:

L&L:

Exercise:

Evaluation

Suggestions for Session 4: Include a deeper experiential exercise, like Masks, Sculpting, Dots, Speakout, Perceptions Based on Partial Knowledge.

SESSION 5: INTEGRATING THE FOCUS TOPIC(S)/MAKING CONNECTIONS

Agenda Preview

Gathering:

Exercise:

Exercise:

L&L:

Exercise:

Evaluation

Suggestions for Session 5: Role plays, Escalator, Let's Go Swimming, Tangram Dog, Facts/Feelings Person.

SESSION 6: APPLICATION TO MY LIFE – PROBLEM SOLVING OF PERSONAL ISSUES AND EMPATHY

Agenda Preview

Gathering

Exercise:

Exercise:

L&L:

Exercise:

Introduce Affirmation Posters to be posted and worked on during breaks

Evaluation

Suggestions for Session 6: Review of I-Messages, In His Shoes, Magic Carpet, Values Clarification, Empathy Talk if you haven't used it with Speakout.

SESSION 7: SUMMARY, REFLECTION, REAFFIRMATION

Agenda Preview

Gathering:

Exercise:

Where do we go from here?

Complete affirmation posters

Evaluation, Graduation, Affirmation Closing

Suggestions for Session 7: Lifelines, Goals/Priorities part 2; Magic Carpet, Contract with Self.

PLANNING GUIDE

EXERCISES FOR BEGINNING SESSIONS

Community Building
Adjective Name with
 Gesture (L&L – Sect. G)
Concentric Circles
In Common
My name is and I like to...
 (Gatherings – Sect. G)
Three Question Interview

TP Review
Transforming Ourselves
TP Mandala Experiences
TP Reverse Mandala
Transforming Power
 Quartets

Choices & Values
Choices
Choosing Focus Topics
Values Clarification
What's in My Circle

EXERCISES AFTER SESSION 2

For Any FocusTopic
Brainstorming
Brainstorming: Web Charts
Breakthrough
Bumper Stickers
Concentric Circles
Consensus Exercises
Crossover
Facts/Feelings Person
Fishbowl
Getting in Touch
Group DaVinci
Guided Meditation
Guided Reflection
How Do You Feel When..
Inclusion
Journal Writing
Letter to Myself
Life Beliefs
Life "Bios"
Lifelines
Mini News & Goods...
 (Gatherings - Sect. G)
Picture Paints....
Picture Perfect
Picture Sharing
Query Writing
Think and Listen
Values Clarification

Anger
Body Imaging
Buttons
Dealing with Put-Downs
Escalator
Escalator Variation—Anger
Exploring Roots of Anger
Grief
I Messages
In His Shoes
Injunctions of Childhood &
 Life

Masks
Processing Anger
Projection
Rumors (L&L Sect–G)
Sculpting
Three Questions on
 Oppression

Power
Assertiveness
Carefronting
Contract with Self
Dots
Injunctions of Childhood &
 Life
Let's Go Swimming
Masks
Personal Space
Power Grab
Power Inversion
Sculpting
Symbols of Power
Territory
Three Questions on
 Oppression

Forgiveness
Dealing with Put Downs
Forgiveness
Forgiveness Quadrants
From Another Point of View
Grief
Guided Reflection on
 Forgiveness
In His Shoes
Injunctions of Childhood &
 Life
Magic Carpet
Three Questions on
 Oppression
Whispered Affirmations/
 Forgiveness Circle

Fear
Aliens (using fear)
Body Imaging
Concentric Circles
Escalator Variation—Fear
Getting in Touch
Personal Space

Communication
Acknowledgment Process
Active Listening
All Aboard
Assertiveness
Buttons
Carefronting
Claremont Dialogue
Dots
Escalator
Four Part Listening
From Another Point of View
Goal-wish Problem Solving
I Messages
I Want/I Want
In His Shoes
Inclusion
Injunctions of Childhood &
 Life
Let's Go Swimming
Listening I Statement
 Combination
Masks
May I Share Something..
Parallel Construction
Perceptions Based on
 Partial Knowledge
Personal Space
Rumors (L&L Sect–G)
Tangram Dog
Tinkertoy Dog
You Said / I Said

Relationships
Acknowledgment Process
Active Listening
Assertiveness
Buttons
Carefronting
Contract With Self for Future
Dealing with Put-Downs
Dots
Facts / Feelings Person
From Another Point of View
Goal-Wish Problem Solving
Grief
Human to Human
I Messages
I Want/I Want
In His Shoes
Injunctions of Childhood and Life
Masks
Perceptions Based on Partial Knowledge
Personal Space
Power Grab
Power Inversion
Projection
Sculpting
Three Questions on Oppression
You Said / I Said

Stereotyping
Dots
Fairy Tale Theater
From Another Point of View
Getting in Touch
In His Shoes
Labels
Let's Go Swimming
Masks
Perceptions Based on Partial Knowledge
Picture Paints a Thousand Words
Power Grab
Projection
Sculpting
Speakout
Three Questions on Oppression
Who Says I Am

Transforming Power
Assertiveness
Body Imaging
Carefronting
Contract with Self for Future
Dots
Goal-Wish Problem Solving
Grief Exercise
Human to Human
I Messages
Personal Space
Power Grab
TP Mandala Experiences
TP Quartets
Transforming Ourselves

Resolving Conflicts
Active Listening
Assertiveness
Buttons
Carefronting
Dots
Escalator
Goal-Wish Problem Solving
Grief
Human to Human
I Messages
In His Shoes
Lets Go Swimming
Masks
Personal Space
Projection
Sculpting
Territory
Three Questions on Oppression
You Said / I Said

Empathy
Anatomy of an Apology
Empathy
Fairy Tale Theater
From Another Point of View
Human to Human
In His Shoes
Projection
Speakout

Planning for the Future
Assertiveness
Buttons
Carefronting
Choosing a Focus Topic – Goals/Priorities, Part 2
Contract With Self for Future
Dealing with Put Downs
Goal-Wish Problem Solving
Grief
Human to Human
I Messages
In His Shoes
My Potential
Personal Space
Values Clarification

Self-esteem
Acknowledgment Process
Assertiveness
Body Imaging
Carefronting
Contract with Self for Future
Dealing with Put Downs
Dots
Goal-Wish Problem Solving
Grief
Guided Meditation
Human to Human
I Messages
Injunctions of Childhood and Life
Lifelines
Magic Carpet
Perceptions Based on Partial Knowledge
Personal Space
Projection
Three Questions on Oppression
Whispered Affirmations/ Forgiveness Circle
Who Says I Am?

EXERCISE APPROXIMATE TIMES - Alphabetically

Exercise	Minutes
Acknowledgment Process	30-40
Active Listening	30-40
Addiction to Grudges	30
Aliens	30
All Aboard	30-45
Anatomy of an Apology	30
Assertiveness	40
The Bag	15
Bargaining with Values	15-20
Body Imaging	15
Brainstorming and Web Charts	15-20
Brainstorms Suggestions for Topics	15-30
Brainstorming–the Eruption of Violence	20-30
Break Through	30-45
Bumper Stickers	30
Buttons	30-40
Carefronting	135
Choices	30
Choosing Focus Topic-Goals & Priorities	20
Choosing a Focus Topic with Gathering	15
Choosing a Focus Topic – by Consensus	30-45
Concentric Circles	30-40
Concentric Circles/ Listening/Reflecting	35
Consensus Bean Jar	40
Consensus: Five Exercise Process	180
Consensus Perfect Day	30
Consensus Picture Sharing	30
Consensus Short Exercises	15
Consensus Triangles	30
Consensus Using Transforming Power	90
Consensus You Have to Have a Heart	45
Contract with Self for Future	60
Crossover	30
Dealing with Put-Downs	30-60
Definitions	30
Dissolving Anger	30
Dots	30
Empathy	60
Escalator	20-30
Escalator Variation – Anger	45
Escalator Variation – Fear	30
Exploring the Roots of Anger	60-180
Facilitated Conflict Resolution	40
Facts/feelings Person	30
Fairy Tale Theater	30-40
Fishbowl	30
Forgiveness	30
Forgiveness Quadrants	40
Four Part Listening	45-60
From Another Point of View	30
Getting in Touch	60
Goal-wish Problem Solving	30
Grief	45
Group DaVinci	45-60
Guided Meditation	5
Guided Reflection - AVP	30
Guided Reflection - Forgiveness	15
Hidden Agenda	10
How Do You Feel When ...	15
Human to Human	30-40
I Messages - Don't Give Up!	30
Impediments to Communication	30-40
In Common	15-20
In His Shoes	30-40
Inclusion	60-90
Injunctions of Childhood and Life	30
I Want / I Want	30-60
Labels	30
Let's Go Swimming	60-90
Letter to Myself	10-30
Life Beliefs	20
Life "Bios"	60
Lifelines	30
Listening/I-Statement Combination	120
Principles-Reflective Listening Handout.	30-45
Magic Carpet	30-45
Masks	60-90
May I Share Something With You	30-45
My Potential	20-30
Parallel Construction	20-30
Perceptions Based Partial Knowledge	40
Personal Space	10
A Picture Paints a Thousand Words	40
Picture Perfect	30
Picture Sharing	20-40
Power Game	30-45
Power Grab	10
Power Inversion	90
Processing Anger	30
Projection	60
Query Writing	45-60
Relationship Reflection	30-40
Sculpting	60-90
Speakout	60
Symbols of Power	40-60
Tangram Dog	40
Territory	15
Think and Listen	20-40
Three Question Interview	30
Three Questions on Oppression	40-60
Tinkertoy Dog	40-50
Transforming Ourselves	30
Transforming Power Mandala Expr.	30-45
Transforming Power Quartets	30-45
Transforming Power Reverse Mandala	30
Values Clarification	60
What's in My Circle	30
Whispered Affirm.-Forgiveness Circle.	30
Who Says I Am?	20
You Said / I Said	60-70

EXERCISE APPROXIMATE TIMES - By Minutes

Minutes	Exercise
5	Guided Meditation
10	Hidden Agenda
10	Personal Space
10	Power Grab
10-30	Letter to Myself
15	Body Imaging
15	Choosing a Focus Topic with Gathering
15	Consensus Short Exercises
15	Guided Reflection - Forgiveness
15	How Do You Feel When ...
15	Territory
15	The Bag
15-20	Bargaining with Values
15-20	Brainstorming and Web Charts
15-20	In Common
20	Choosing Focus Topic-Goals & Priorities
20	Life Beliefs
20	Who Says I Am?
20-30	Brainstorming–the Eruption of Violence
20-30	Escalator
20-30	My Potential
20-30	Parallel Construction
20-40	Picture Sharing
20-40	Think and Listen
30	Addiction to Grudges
30	Aliens
30	Anatomy of an Apology
30	Bumper Stickers
30	Choices
30	Consensus Perfect Day
30	Consensus Picture Sharing
30	Consensus Triangles
30	Crossover
30	Definitions
30	Dissolving Anger
30	Dots
30	Escalator Variation – Fear
30	Facts/feelings Person
30	Fishbowl
30	Forgiveness
30	From Another Point of View
30	Goal-wish Problem Solving
30	Guided Reflection - AVP
30	I Messages - Don't Give Up!
30	Injunctions of Childhood and Life
30	Labels
30	Lifelines
30	Picture Perfect
30	Processing Anger
30	Three Question Interview
30	Transforming Ourselves
30	Transforming Power Reverse Mandala
30	What's in My Circle
30	Whispered Affirm.-Forgiveness Circle.

Minutes	Exercise
30-40	Acknowledgment Process
30-40	Active Listening
30-40	Buttons
30-40	Fairy Tale Theater
30-40	Human to Human
30-40	Impediments to Communication
30-40	In His Shoes
30-40	Relationship Reflection
30-45	All Aboard
30-45	Break Through
30-45	Choosing a Focus Topic – by Consensus
30-45	Magic Carpet
30-45	May I Share Something With You
30-45	Power Game
30-45	Principles-Reflective Listening Handout.
30-45	Transforming Power Mandala Expr.
30-45	Transforming Power Quartets
30-60	Dealing with Put-Downs
30-60	I Want / I Want
35	Concentric Circles/ Listening/Reflecting
40	A Picture Paints a Thousand Words
40	Assertiveness
40	Consensus Bean Jar
40	Facilitated Conflict Resolution
40	Forgiveness Quadrants
40	Perceptions Based Partial Knowledge
40	Tangram Dog
40-50	Tinkertoy Dog
40-60	Symbols of Power
40-60	Three Questions on Oppression
45	Consensus You Have to Have a Heart
45	Escalator Variation – Anger
45	Grief
45-60	Four Part Listening
45-60	Group DaVinci
45-60	Query Writing
60	Values Clarification
60	Contract with Self for Future
60	Empathy
60	Getting in Touch
60	Life "Bios"
60	Projection
60	Speakout
60-70	You Said / I Said
60-90	Inclusion
60-90	Let's Go Swimming
60-90	Masks
60-90	Sculpting
60-180	Exploring the Roots of Anger
90	Consensus Using Transforming Power
90	Power Inversion
120	Listening/I-Statement Combination
135	Carefronting
180	Consensus: Five Exercise Process

SECTION C

Transforming Power in this Workshop

Transforming Power: On Violence

Transforming Power Talk

Transforming Power Short Talk

**Transforming Power—
What Makes it Work**

Transforming Power Mandala

**Transforming Power Guidelines
Related to the Mandala**

**Transforming Power Talk
Using the Mandala**

Transforming Power Indicators

**Guides for Being Open to
Transforming Power**

TRANSFORMING POWER
In This Workshop

The concept of Transforming Power was introduced in the Basic Workshop. It is important to keep building on that concept. No two people perceive it in quite the same way. The team needs to allow for everyone's developing understanding, and not try to impose uniformity, yet not allow the concept to be distorted (a delicate, difficult balance to maintain). *Keep the concept alive during the workshop.* Possible methods:

Ahead of time:

Prepare posters with a definition of Transforming Power and the TP guides on newsprint so they can be easily read. Post these in the room, so they can be referred to as the workshop progresses.

Gather quotations relating to Transforming Power and post them and/or use them in other ways.

Assemble a set of posters or pictures that deal with Transforming Power. Put them on walls or tables or pass them around.

Assemble *stories* that deal with Transforming Power, and use them.

During the Workshop:

Early in the workshop, do one major exercise that focuses on Transforming Power. (Examples might be: **Transforming Ourselves, Transforming Power Mandala Experiences, Transforming Power Reverse Mandala, Transforming Power Quartets**)

The Transforming Power section has suggestions of TP talks. Keep them brief.

Gatherings:
    My understanding of Transforming Power is ...
    The way I would explain Transforming Power to a child is...

Listening Exercise or Sharing in Pairs:
    The easiest TP Guide for me is, and why ...
    The most difficult TP Guide for me is... , and why ...

Pass out TP cards or guideline sheets. Refer to them during role plays and other suitable exercises.

At the end of each exercise, ask the question:
    Which TP Guide(s) did this exercise illustrate? Or
    Which TP Guide might help (whatever challenge the exercise brought out)?

Have a Claremont Dialogue or Fishbowl on the subject (particularly valuable if a problem or dissension has arisen).

Use Picture Sharing with a focus on Transforming Power.

Have group write queries on Transforming Power, or hand out prepared Queries.

Consider having TP as a focus topic.

TRANSFORMING POWER: ON VIOLENCE

Since we are seeking an alternative to violence, it is helpful if we first have some understanding of the dynamics of violence. Most violence erupts as a spontaneous reaction rather than a planned action.

I would like your cooperation in a little demonstration. First, I would like you to introduce yourself to your neighbors on both sides. Now I would like each of you to put your right hand on the left shoulder of the person sitting to your right.

How did the hand on the shoulder feel? You probably decided in an instant how to react to the hand on your shoulder. You may have felt a shudder of fear or a touch of kindness.

There were probably two factors in your reaction to the hand on your shoulder:
1. How much do you trust your neighbor?
2. How do you feel about yourself?

AVP focuses on developing trust and self-esteem.

If your neighbor has built some trust with you by the way he or she introduced him or herself, you will probably interpret the hand on your shoulder as a sign of friendship rather than a threat.

The second factor is how you feel about yourself. If your inner attitude is one of fear and powerlessness and low self-esteem, you may interpret any hand on your shoulder as a threat. We all feel powerless at times. We especially feel powerless when we are in prison. Even the hand of a dear friend could lead to violence.

AVP provides alternatives to powerlessness.

Much violence stems from this inner feeling of powerlessness. We all need some sense of power. People find many ways to overcome this feeling of powerlessness.
(Ask the group to suggest positive and negative ways that people can become powerful.)

There are many positive ways to become powerful. Some make themselves powerful through the development of their physical strength: they work out; they pump iron. They also improve their self-esteem at the same time.

Education is another way to become more powerful. Developing leadership skills is also a way to become more powerful. Becoming an AVP facilitator is a way to develop a sense of power and self esteem. Others make themselves powerful through language and communication. They develop their intellectual skills.

Others choose negative ways to make themselves more powerful. This may be by putting others down. Or it may be by getting a gun or a weapon. Weapons are just another way of dealing with a sense of powerlessness.

AVP offers another alternative to becoming powerful. AVP seeks to replace that inner feeling of powerlessness we all have at times with a sense of inner power which is available to everyone. We call this Transforming Power. This is our spiritual power and our power of moral strength. This is a key concept in all AVP workshops and we will discuss this in greater detail in the workshop.

The AVP program is about personal growth and personal change and getting in touch with our Transforming Power.

TRANSFORMING POWER TALK

Here is one way to understand Transforming Power.

At the core of every human being is a jewel, a blazing spark of the divine.

This is the true core of every person, the foundation, the center.

And when that brilliant core shines in its full glory, it reaches out beyond the person to shed its light on everything around it, to connect with everything and everyone.

Unfortunately, in every human being, that jewel of light is covered in many layers of crud. Our fears and insecurities, our pain, and our defensive walls cover the jewel and dim its brilliance.

Our prejudices and our pride will not let the light shine forth.

Our narrow egos tell us that the crud, rather than the jewel, is who we are.

But it is important to remember that however many layers of crud cover the jewel, the jewel itself is never dimmed. Inside the shell of darkness, it still shines as brightly as ever, and every now and then it blazes through a crack.

The crud can hide the light, but can never extinguish it.

Transforming Power ...

...is that force in the universe which can burn away the crud. And it always begins within. I cannot burn away the crud that hides your jewel. What I can do is allow Transforming Power to do its work within me, to burn away the layers of fear and prejudice and pain which hide my shining core, and then let my light shine forth as an invitation for you to do the same.

When I can free my soul of the layers of crud which cover it (which I must continually do, day after day — for the business of living in this world has a tendency to lay down new layers by the hour), and I let the light shine forth, that light stretches out to those around me and reaches for its mirror in their soul: reaches — and with that reaching the jewel in the soul of the other person answers, through all the crud, and reaches back.

Being connected ...

...is the true state of being human. **Transforming Power** is that force in the universe which shows us how to do that.

TRANSFORMING POWER SHORT TALK

There is a power that works though us and between us — a transformative power — that can change a destructive situation into a cooperative one. We call it Transforming Power. It's the heart of AVP. To be open to this inner and outer power, our purpose must be morally right. Every person has an inner wisdom that knows what's right and wants to do what's right, and it can be called forth, as Dr. Martin Luther King, Jr. once said. There are laws of harmony at work in the, world. As we act, think and speak in harmony with them, we bring about harmony in our world of interrelationships with other people.

Transforming Power has four basic principles:
1. Everyone has an inward goodness. Realize that people's actions and words are sometimes mistaken, wrong or violent. People themselves are good. In your understanding, separate the person from the behavior. There is goodness within. Look for it. Find it. Judaism, Christianity, Islam and other religions all teach this.
2. We can start out realizing a violent reaction is only **one way** of responding in a conflict. Somewhere in every conflict situation there is the possibility for a nonviolent solution. Maybe it's hidden. We all know people with negative attitudes who often have negative experiences, and we know people with positive attitudes who have more positive experiences. Attitude and expectation set the stage. We say, "Expect the best." Then it's more likely to happen.
3. To change situations in positive ways, start with ourselves, our attitudes, beliefs, manners of speaking, tone of voice and behavior. Someone in a workshop said he had to go to the adoption agency and adopt a new attitude. When we do, the universal law, "like begets like," will kick in.
4. Non-violent conflict resolution is a skill. It improves with practice and optimistic persistence. It takes courage and may even be risky, but not more risky than violence. It recognizes both your rights and the rights of others. Look for where rights and values of opponents and yourself overlap, and find common ground. There can be a win/win outcome — no one the loser.

Nonviolence is not being submissive and passive. It is an active course of action which involves risk. With violence, you know there will be pain and suffering, while with nonviolence there is the chance there will be no pain and suffering, or if there is, it may be greatly reduced. It is also an assertive course of action; it is not letting someone take advantage of you. Your rights are worthy of respect and you are entitled to assert them.

Examples:
- *A caring attitude about others:* Think positive thoughts about others. We are all affected by negative/positive vibrations, (e.g. when you meet someone for the first time and feel good or uncomfortable about them.) For example, Jerry Jampolsky was offered the last seats on an over-booked flight and the ticket agent said it was because he had been so nice to him. What Jerry had done was to sit in a corner without making any contact with the agent, who at the time was being harassed by over 50 would-be passengers. All Jerry did was to think positive thoughts about the ticket agent.
- *Risk Taking:* A couple in a nearby apartment was fighting. Ann simply knocked on the door and asked if everything was all right. The man said yes. Later he met Ann in the hallway and said he was going to treat his wife better from now on.

- *Surprise:* Becoming aware of footsteps following her in Central Park at night and of a man following her closely, Marge Swann turned and said, "I'm so glad you came along; my arms are aching from carrying these books. Won't you carry them for me?" she said as she swung the load into his arms. He took them with a surprised look on his face. At the other end of the park, she took them back and said, "Thank you so much for helping me." He responded, "Lady, that wasn't what I had in mind." (Surprise and appealing to his better side.)

TRANSFORMING POWER — WHAT MAKES IT WORK?

- Reasoning with others, and listening as they reason with me.
- Caring for the other person.
- Thinking – of the possible results of my actions.
- Knowing myself – my values, my strengths and my weaknesses.
- Having good feelings about myself.
- Communicating clearly – after looking inside myself for the truth of my position.
- Having faith and trust in TP to work for me.
- Understanding that there may be other ways to solve problems.
- Being flexible in working out solutions.
- Bringing moral power into play.
- Being willing to seek a win/win solution.
- Seeing a situation from a higher level of consciousness.
- Using my gut reaction – letting TP use me.

To "transform" is to "change the shape of."

**"Transforming Power" is the power
to change the shape of a situation or a relationship,
to move it in a positive direction toward resolution of conflict.**

TRANSFORMING POWER MANDALA

Outer ring: Expect the Best / Think Before Reacting / Caring for Others / Ask For A Non-Violent Path
Inner ring: Respect for Self / (continued around)
Center: TRANSFORMING POWER

QUERIES:

1. Do I try to understand the concern of the other person?
2. Do I ask questions to broaden perspective?
3. Do I say how I feel and try to resolve a concept when it arises?
4. Do I let the other person talk out their anger before seeking reconciliation?
5. Do I reach out to the other person and appeal to his/her reason?
6. Do I admit when I am wrong?
7. Do I forgive myself and others?
8. Do I give what I can give naturally, and accept others as they are?
9. Do I accept responsibility for my own life?
10. Do I work for constructive change when there is injustice?
11. Do I follow my gut reaction on whether to withdraw, or stand my ground and resist non-violently?
12. Do I expect the best?

SPECIAL HELPS

1. Think before reacting.
2. Imagine a variety of solutions.
3. Tell the other person when you see that s/he is are right.
4. Say or do the unexpected to change the mood.
5. Stay calm.
6. Be patient.

TRANSFORMING POWER GUIDELINES
RELATED TO THE MANDALA

Expect the best:
- Look the other person on the eye and appeal to his/her reason.
- Reach for something in others that seeks to do good.
- Know there are some things I am willing to suffer for and thus win allies.

Respect for self:
- Risk changing myself.
- Stand my ground. Hold onto the concept of "my best self."
- Trust my inner sense of what is needed.
- When I am clear about **my** position, expect great inward power to act.

Caring for others:
- Put myself in the other person's shoes.
- Help build a community based on honesty, respect and caring.
- Forget about not liking a person.
- Apply the concept of "my best self" to my opponent.

Think before reacting:
- Surprise and humor might help to transform.
- Put myself in the other person's shoes.
- Step down from my ego.
- Pause, give myself time to think.
- Refuse to let words upset me.
- Follow my gut reaction on how to resist nonviolently.

Ask for a nonviolent path:
- Realize that I am never licked until I give up.
- Admit if I am partly wrong; don't let pride hold me back from admitting I am wrong.
- Talk myself into a nonviolent path.
- If I find my opponent is right, quickly tell him/her so

Transforming Power:
- Be ready to practice TP day after day until it becomes a way of life for me.

TRANSFORMING POWER TALK USING THE MANDALA

Purpose: To have a personal experience of the TP talk

Time: 30 minutes

Materials: A mandala in pieces

Sequence:
1. In this method, the TP talk takes place later in the workshop, after doing exercises on Affirmation, Communication, Cooperation and Trust.

2. Divide into five groups. Give each group one segment of the mandala.

3. Ask them to think of the experiences they have had in the workshop so far and the conflicts they resolved in the activities of the workshop (give some examples). Tell them to ask themselves and discuss among themselves the topic, "In life if we choose to adopt this attitude (as represented by the mandala piece), how will it help in resolving conflicts nonviolently and build a peaceful community?"

4. After 5 to 8 minutes bring them back to the big circle and share the conclusions of each group with the big group.

5. Once this is done, talk about why we, in AVP, call this collective concept Transforming Power.

TRANSFORMING POWER INDICATORS

I know transforming power is present and working when:

1. I am in control of my power.

2. I am learning something positive about or from my opponent.

3. I believe in change, and am actively searching for alternatives.

4. My mind is open to all possibilities.

5. I am accepting responsibility. I am acknowledging that I, too, am a cause in the matter.

6. I am "actively" listening to my opponent.

7. I am approaching my opponent from a position of mutual respect and caring — of love.

8. I have a sense of compassion and empathy for my opponent.

9. My "voices" of pride and ego are calm.

10. I am consciously working toward a "win-win" solution.

11. I am facing risk and suffering without retaliating.

12. I am openly and honestly sharing of myself.

13. I can see common ground or common goals, and through them I can see compromise.

14. I feel very "centered" and in touch with my better self.

15. I am looking for, and speaking to, the better nature of my opponent. I am acknowledging and affirming his/her humanity.

16. I am weighing options and looking to the future.

17. I am freely accepting positive criticism, and not retaliating against negative criticism.

Developed by prisoners during an advanced workshop at the MacDougall Correctional Institution, Suffield, Connecticut, June 1995.

GUIDES FOR BEING OPEN TO TRANSFORMING POWER

We can't use Transforming Power, but it can use us IF we're open to it. How can we open ourselves to this inner wisdom? These important states of mind allow this energy to work through us in challenging situations.

- Respect and care about yourself and your adversary
- Pause—quiet your mind—give yourself time before responding
- Trust you inner sense about what's needed
- Expect the best

CONFLICT RESOLUTION TOOLS

1. I seek to resolve conflicts by reaching common ground.
2. I reach for that something in others that seeks to do good for self and others.
3. I listen. Everyone has made a journey. I try to understand where the other person is coming from before I make up my mind.
4. I base my position on truth. Since people tend to seek truth, no position based on falsehood can long prevail.
5. I am ready to revise my position if I discover it is not fair.
6. When I am clear about my position, I expect to experience great inward power to act on it. A response that relies on this power will be courageous and without hostility.
7. I do not expect that this response will automatically ward off danger. If I cannot avoid risk, I risk being creative rather than violent.
8. Surprise and humor may help transformation.
9. I learn to trust my inner sense of when to act and when to withdraw.
10. I work towards new ways of overcoming injustice. I am willing to suffer suspicion, hostility, rejection, even persecution, if necessary.
11. I am patient and persistent in the continuing search for justice.
12. I help build a community based on honesty, respect and caring.

HELP ALONG THE WAY

- I build my own self-respect.
- I respect and care about others.
- I expect the best.
- I ask myself for a nonviolent way. There may be one inside me.
- I pause – give myself time – before reacting. It may open me to transforming power.
- I trust my inner sense of what's needed.
- I don't rely on weapons, drugs or alcohol. They weaken me.
- When I have done wrong, I admit it, I make amends if I can, so that I can forgive myself; then I let it go.
- I don't threaten or put anyone down.
- I make friends who will support me and I support the best in them.
- I risk changing myself.

WHAT IT FEELS LIKE

The transforming power experience feels like:
- AHA!!!!!
- There is a spirit of caring.
- There is a letting go of something. (Patterns? Grudges?)
- There is a sharing of something.
- I feel right about it.
- I lose my fear.
- I feel a great internal power to act.
- My responses are courageous and without hostility.

SECTION D

Exercises & Techniques
Exercises & Techniques
Exercises & Techniques
Exercises & Techniques
Exercises & Techniques
Exercises & Techniques
Exercises & Techniques
Exercises & Techniques
Exercises & Techniques
Exercises & Techniques
Exercises & Techniques
Exercises & Techniques
Exercises & Techniques
Exercises & Techniques
Exercises & Techniques
Exercises & Techniques
Exercises & Techniques
Exercises & Techniques
Exercises & Techniques
Exercises & Techniques
Exercises & Techniques
Exercises & Techniques
Exercises & Techniques
Exercises & Techniques
Exercises & Techniques

Exercises/Techniques in alphabetical order

LIST OF EXERCISES/TECHNIQUES

Acknowledgment Process	D-3
Active Listening	D-4
Addiction to Grudges	D-5
Aliens	D-7
All Aboard	D-8
Anatomy of an Apology	D-9
Assertiveness	D-11
The Bag	D-14
Bargaining with Values	D-15
Body Imaging	D-16
Brainstorming	D-17
Brainstorming and Web Charts	D-18
Brainstorms Suggestions for Topics	D-19
Brainstorming–the Eruption of Violence	D-22
Break Through	D-23
Bumper Stickers	D-24
Buttons	D-25
Carefronting	D-27
Choices	D-31
Choosing Focus Topic-Goals & Priorities	D-32
Choosing a Focus Topic with Gathering	D-34
Choosing a Focus Topic – by Consensus	D-34
Claremont Dialogue	D-37
Concentric Circles	D-38
Concentric Circles/ Listening/Reflecting	D-41
Consensus Bean Jar	D-42
Consensus: Five Exercise Process	D-44
Consensus Perfect Day	D-47
Consensus Picture Sharing	D-48
Consensus Short Exercises	D-49
Consensus Triangles	D-51
Consensus Using Transforming Power	D-52
Consensus You Have to Have a Heart	D-53
Contract with Self for Future	D-55
Crossover	D-56
Dealing with Put-Downs	D-58
Definitions	D-60
Dissolving Anger	D-61
Dots	D-62
Empathy	D-63
Escalator	D-64
Escalator Variation – Anger	D-67
Escalator Variation – Fear	D-69
Exploring the Roots of Anger	D-71
Facilitated Conflict Resolution	D-73
Facts/feelings Person	D-74
Fairy Tale Theater	D-76
Fishbowl	D-78
Forgiveness	D-80
Forgiveness Quadrants	D-81
Four Part Listening	D-83
From Another Point of View	D-84
Getting in Touch	D-85
Goal-wish Problem Solving	D-87
Grief	D-88
Group DaVinci	D-90
Guided Meditation	D-91
Guided Reflection–AVP	D-92
Guided Reflection – Forgiveness	D-93
Hidden Agenda	D-95
How Do You Feel When …	D-96
Human to Human	D-97
I Messages Another Approach	D-99
I Messages – Don't Give Up!	D-101
Impediments to Communication	D-103
In Common	D-104
In His Shoes	D-105
Inclusion	D-107
Injunctions of Childhood and Life	D-108
I Want / I Want	D-109
Journal Writing	D-110
Labels	D-111
Let's Go Swimming	D-112
Letter to Myself	D-114
Life Beliefs	D-115
Life "Bios"	D-116
Lifelines	D-117
Listening/I-Statement Combination	D-119
Principles-Reflective Listening Handout	D-122
Magic Carpet	D-123
Masks	D-124
May I Share Something With You	D-128
My Potential	D-130
Parallel Construction	D-131
Perceptions Based Partial Knowledge	D-132
Personal Space	D-134
A Picture Paints a Thousand Words	D-135
Picture Perfect	D-136
Picture Sharing	D-137
Power Game	D-138
Power Grab	D-140
Power Inversion	D-141
Processing Anger	D-143
Projection	D-145
Query Writing	D-146
Relationship Reflection	D-147
Sculpting	D-148
Speakout	D-149
Symbols of Power	D-150
Tangram Dog	D-152
Territory	D-154
Think and Listen	D-155
Three Question Interview	D-156
Three Questions on Oppression	D-157
Tinkertoy Dog	D-158
Transforming Ourselves	D-160
Transforming Power Mandala Expr.	D-162
Transforming Power Quartets	D-163
Transforming Power Reverse Mandala	D-164
Values Clarification	D-165
What's in My Circle	D-167
Whispered Affirm.–Forgiveness Circle	D-171
Who Says I Am?	D-173
You Said / I Said	D-174

ACKNOWLEDGMENT PROCESS

Reach for that something in others that seeks to do good for oneself and others.
Guides to Transforming Power

Purpose: To improve self-esteem and build community.

Time: 30 to 40 minutes.

Materials: None.

Sequence:
  Introductory talk:
  We all love to be given strokes, or acknowledged. This is essential to building self-esteem and trust. In daily life, acknowledgments sometimes come unsought and make us feel great. But often we are not acknowledged for the things that are most important to us. Sometimes we are acknowledged for things that seem minor to us. This exercise is a chance to choose what is really important to us and to receive acknowledgment for it. Making this choice may not be easy.

  1. Ask people to think of something about themselves that they really feel good about and that they would like to have acknowledged. Give participants a silent moment to think.

  2. Allow each person in the group to choose someone to acknowledge him/her. The chosen acknowledger can reply as him/herself, or as someone else (e.g., father, mother, wife) who is important in the acknowledgee's life.

     The acknowledgee takes two or three minutes to tell about the quality or accomplishment that s/he wants acknowledged. The acknowledger listens carefully, feeds back what the person has said and, if s/he wishes, expands on it. People may read between the lines and use information from other sources about the acknowledgee. It is also helpful if the acknowledger checks back to see if anything has been left out.

  3. Two of the leaders demonstrate the process for the participants.

  4. All members of each group ask for and receive acknowledgments.

  Note:
  Although this process seems extremely simple, it has great power and depth. It is best done at a point in the workshop when the participants have come to know each other. It is a good tool to use in close friendships and primary relationships. It also works well as an intervention when a primary relationship hits a snag. The problem may be one of self-esteem rather than personal interaction.

Processing:
  - What effect does self-esteem have on a person's ability to resolve conflicts without using violence?
  - Which Transforming Power Guides help to build self-esteem, either in one's self or in others?

ACTIVE LISTENING

Purpose: To give participants the skill of helping others to solve their own problems, by listening for and reflecting back what was said and felt.

Time: 30 to 40 minutes.

Materials: Newsprint poster of "Listening Is..."

Sequence:
1. Explain what active listening is and what it is not as follows:

Listening is:
- Focus – An active listener focuses on the other person rather than him/herself.
- Concentration – An active listener concentrates completely on the other person's words, feelings, emotions and actions rather than on his/her own thoughts.
- Empathy – An active listener seeks to identify with and feel the emotions of the person s/he is listening to and seeks to step into the other person's shoes.
- Feedback – An active listener provides feedback by paraphrasing what the other person has said so that the speaker knows that s/he has been understood.

Ways of not listening:
- Mimicking –
    A. "I had an accident today but fortunately no one was hurt."
    B. "I hear you had an automobile accident today."
- Advice giving –
    A. "I had an accident today but fortunately no one was hurt."
    B. "Did you get the other person's insurance information?" "I have a good lawyer."
- Judging –
    A. "I had an accident today but fortunately no one was hurt."
    B. "You should really watch where you are going."
- Being a Fixit –
    A. "I had an accident today but fortunately no one was hurt."
    B. "I have a friend at Joe's Body Shop that will really get you a good price."
- Mine is bigger than yours –
    A. "I had an accident today but fortunately no one was hurt."
    B. "Let me tell you about the time an irresponsible teenager ran a stop sign and my car was totaled."

2. Divide the group into threes: a speaker, a listener and an observer.
3. Have speakers talk for three minutes about a problem that upsets them.
4. Have the second person practice active listening and giving feedback to the listener. The observer may offer suggestions and help.
5. Exchange roles until everyone has had a chance to speak.

Processing:
- How did people feel about being listened to?
- Was it hard or easy to be a listener?
- Were you able to suspend your own judgment to hear your partner's problem?
- How does this exercise relate to finding an alternative to violence?
- Which Transforming Power guides does this relate to?

ADDICTION TO GRUDGES
Why We Don't Forgive

Purpose: To explore ways of getting rid of grudges and ending the blocks to forgiveness.

Time: 30 minutes.

Materials: Paper and pencils, handout "Addiction to Grudges."

Sequence:
1. Hand out slips of paper and pencils. Then, ask participants to write down one of their grudges on a slip of paper. "A grudge that I find it difficult to let go of is..." They do not need to share their grudges at this time.
2. Give explanation: "Grudges are certainly a major ingredient of the violence we read about every day — acts of retaliation by terrorists, bombers, victims of bullying. Grudges are an ingredient of most gang violence and drive-by shootings. They are a key issue in family violence and stalking cases. Grudges are a very sensitive area. It seems that it is nearly impossible for people to come through the criminal justice system without developing some grudges: grudges at lawyers, prosecutors, judges, witnesses who testified for the other side, fellow defendants and many more. Many are in prison because of grudges."
3. Brainstorm: "Ways that holding onto grudges hurts us." (This may include everything from "high blood pressure" and "ulcers" to "dumping anger on my family and those whom I love" and "getting more time.")
4. Ask the question, "If grudges create all these negative effects, why do we want to hang onto them rather than forgive?" Lead into the discussion by including such concepts as: We have all been taught to forgive. Our parents taught us to forgive; Martin Luther King Jr. taught us to forgive; Gandhi taught us to forgive; St. Francis of Assisi taught us to forgive; Jesus of Nazareth and Mohamed taught us to forgive. We have all heard this message ten thousand times. We know how good it feels to be forgiven and to give up the guilt and anger. We all want to be forgiven for our mistakes. So why do we find it so hard to forgive? Why don't we want to forgive others?
5. Distribute handout. Either have facilitator read aloud, or have it go around the circle to read. Begin discussion by looking at some of the reasons we hang onto grudges.
6. Divide into small groups. Ask participants to get out their slips of paper and share the grudge they would like to let go of. Then discuss the reasons why people hang onto grudges and what they can do to get rid of their own grudges.

Processing:
- Were you able to let go of your grudges?
- What did you find was blocking you from letting go?
- What are some things that people can do to get rid of their addiction to grudges?
- If grudges create all these negative effects, why do we want to hang onto them rather than forgive?
- How does this relate to Transforming Power?

Note:
This exercise may be used as an important introduction to the subject of forgiveness. In addition to Anatomy of an Apology, there are many exercises on forgiveness that might follow this exercise such as Whispered Affirmations/Forgiveness Circle, Forgiveness Quadrants and Forgiveness which focus on forgiving yourself. Magic Carpet can provide a powerful experience in being forgiven, and Carefronting Exercise deals with differences and the difficult task of forgiving others.

HANDOUT
ADDICTION TO GRUDGES
Why we don't forgive

Why we hang onto grudges – Let's look at some of the reasons we hang onto grudges:

1. We believe that letting go of grudges and forgiving someone is a sign of weakness. We might have to give up our tough, macho attitude and tell the truth. In fact, forgiving someone is really a sign of strength. It is usually the strongest and most mature individuals that are the first to forgive.

2. Letting go of grudges and forgiving someone means that we have to give up being a victim. Sometimes we like to feel sorry for ourselves. This is a very human reaction. We may also want people to sympathize with us because we have been hurt or oppressed. Children often feel like victims when dealing with the adult world. But we are adults now and need to give up our childish ways. Taking responsibility for ourselves and forgiving others is the path to personal strength.

3. Letting go of grudges and forgiving someone means we have to give up our anger. Anger can be addictive. Anger may help us to feel powerful. Our anger may intimidate others. But we all know anger is not good for our emotional and physical health. Forgiveness is the step to inner health.

4. Letting go of grudges and forgiving someone means we have to give up our desire for revenge. When we have been hurt, we often feel put down and disrespected. It is a natural urge to want to get back at the person who hurt us in an effort to put ourselves "one up." However, we all know that instead of correcting the balance, we may initiate a cycle of revenge which can escalate. Forgiveness is the tool to break the cycle of revenge.

5. Letting go of grudges and forgiving someone means we have to give up our attitude of self-righteousness. For many of us it is important to be "good" and "righteous" and to oppose anything we see as "wrong" or "evil." In some ways, it may be hard for us to maintain our position as being a "righteous" person unless there are "bad" people out there that we can oppose. In fact, we may need to hang on to the "bad" people out there as a way to maintain our feelings as being "righteous" Forgiving someone may mean that we need to give up our self-righteousness and start being honest and real. Then the people we are in conflict with can become honest and real also.

Learning forgiveness in our personal lives will make us stronger people. We can then share our ideas to help those in our workshop lead more peaceful lives also.

ALIENS

Purpose: To get a deeper understanding of the focus topic(s); to see how our cultural assumptions influence our understandings.

Time: 30 minutes.

Materials: Paper and pencils.

Sequence:
1. Explain that the group will do an exercise to get a greater understanding of the focus topic. ("Anger" is used in the example given below, but this can work for many focus topics: power, forgiveness, stereotyping, fear, self-esteem, etc.)

2. Tell the following story: "It is a very windy day and the wind is howling around the building. The wind has brought in a space ship from another galaxy. Some aliens have come out of the space ship, and they are now with us. In the galaxy that they came from there is no such thing as anger and the task of our group is now to explain in detail everything about anger so that these aliens will get a good understanding of anger."

3. Divide the large group into three or four groups. In each group, have one facilitator who is an "alien." Participants will attempt to explain to the "alien" the nature of anger as it exists here on Earth.

4. The "aliens" will take notes. After about 10 minutes of explanations each "alien" will report back to the large group what they have learned.

Processing:
- Were there descriptions or explanations or definitions that were common to all groups? (You might want to write these on newsprint and post.)
- Were they mostly negative or were there some positive descriptions?
- Where does a person's idea of anger come from? (The same idea can be used for any second level focus topic.)

ALL ABOARD

Purpose: To teach participants to listen for the underlying "essence" in a conversation. This is to help people learn listening on a deeper level than surface conversation.

Time: 30 to 45 minutes.

Materials: One slip of paper marked "Ticket" for each team.

Sequence:
1. Divide into teams of four or five.
2. Give the "Ticket" to one member of each team.
3. The person holding the ticket is asked to tell "a story about a positive experience from childhood" to other members of the group.
4. The person to the right is then asked to express the "essence" of the story. This feedback should focus on the feelings and meaning of the story, rather than just the "facts" of the story.
5. If the person expresses the essence to the satisfaction of the story teller, he or she says "All Aboard" and then passes the ticket to the person on the right. The person with the ticket then tells his or her childhood story.
6. If the story teller does not feel that the "essence" has been expressed, the next person in the circle seeks to express the "essence." The exercise continues until each participant tells a story and the other members of the group understand the essence of the story.

Processing:
Gather in the large circle and explore questions such as:
- How did it feel to have others understand the "essence" of your story?
- Did you feel the other members of the group were "All Aboard" and understood your story?
- Did you find it difficult to express the essence of another person's story?
- Do you find that you are able to listen on a deeper level?

ANATOMY OF AN APOLOGY

Purpose: To develop an understanding of apologies.

Time: 30 minutes.

Materials: Pencils or pens, writing paper and envelopes for all. Handout: The Anatomy of an Apology.

Sequence:
1. Ask participants to write down the name of a person that they need to apologize to and put the paper in their pocket. They may or may not choose to share it later.

2. Distribute the Handout and have a go-around to read it. Discuss the steps and content of a genuine apology. An apology is called for when a person values a relationship. The purpose of an apology is to repair or restore a relationship with an individual, a group or even a nation.

   Some real life examples might be helpful as follows:
   - A US president apologized for his behavior with a White House intern. Was he telling the truth to the American people? Did he regret his mistakes? Did his apology give evidence that he was sincerely sorry and would change his behavior?

   - A US Senator gave the following apology after he was accused sexually harassing at least a dozen women: "I am apologizing for the conduct that it was alleged that I did." Did this "apology" specify what he had done that was wrong? Did it show that he took responsibility for his own actions nor the harm that he caused to more than a dozen women who were his dedicated employees?

   - Former Counter-terrorism Advisor Richard A. Clarke testified before the commission investigating the possible errors in intelligence prior to the 9/11 terrorist attacks on the World Trade Center and Pentagon. Witness after witness had made excuses or otherwise avoided admitting responsibility. Richard Clarke turned his back on the committee and faced the audience, which included many of the victims of the 9-11 tragedy. He then looked them in the eye and said, "I failed you; we all failed you!" He then went on to state in what ways he thought the intelligence community had failed, and what steps it should take in the future. Was he sincere? Did his apology show that he was taking responsibility for his actions?

3. Divide into groups of three and ask participants to write a letter of apology to the person that they listed on their slip of paper. Participants may share their letters with members of their group and ask for help if they wish.

Processing:
- Was this a difficult exercise?
- Was the exercise helpful?
- How do you feel after the exercise?
- How does this relate to Transforming Power?

Note:
This is a good exercise to follow Addiction to Grudges.

HANDOUT

THE ANATOMY OF AN APOLOGY

Some of the elements of a genuine apology are:

1. The apology must acknowledge responsibility.
    The person making the apology needs to take responsibility for having done something wrong. It is an effort to right the balance between the offender and the offended. For example, saying, "I'm sorry that you're upset by what I said," is not taking responsibility for your actions and blames the other person for the upset.

2. The apology must be specific.
    It names the mistake that caused the harm. It is more than saying, "I'm sorry for what I did." It identifies the error that you've made. Generalities will not do.

3. The apology must express how the mistake hurt the other person.
    It should let the other person know that you understand his/her feelings. It should express some empathy for the other person. "I understand you were really worried that something might have happened to me when I was an hour late for dinner."

4. The apology may involve regret and guilt.
    The apology needs to express remorse. A real apology involves pain, suffering and soul-searching regret. It may express your concern that your mistake may have jeopardized your relationship and that you value the relationship.

5. The apology must express a willingness to change behavior.
    It lets others know that the mistake will not occur again. Sometimes some sort of restitution is called for. One way of handling this would be to say, "Let me know if there is anything I can do." Or if you broke something of value, you can offer to replace it.

6. If the offense was made publicly the apology should be public also.
    It is not fair to offend somebody publicly and then make an apology in private.

    Most of all, an apology is a willingness to let go of the ego and treat another person with respect. It is an expression of honesty. It is a sign of strength rather than a sign of weakness.

ASSERTIVENESS

Purpose: To develop the concept of assertive behavior.
Note: It is important to review I-Messages in the workshop before doing this exercise.

Time: 40 minutes.

Materials: Newsprint, markers, handouts: Principles of Assertiveness and Basic Human Rights

Sequence:
1. Post three sheets of newsprint titled
    I'm being assertive when I ...
    I'm being aggressive when I ...
    I'm being manipulative when I ...

2. Brainstorm each one until the group has a clear definition of the differences among them.

3. Pass out the "Basic Human Rights" handout, and have participants read it aloud.

4. Say: "Having heard these basic human rights, let's come up with some scenerios of situations where someone might believe his/her rights have been violated." Write these on another newsprint.

5. Choose one of the following processes to have the participants do in small groups:
    a) Choose one scenario and discuss what would be an assertive response, what would be an aggressive response and what would be a manipulative response. Record your responses on newsprint for reporting to the large group.
    b) Prepare three skits of the scenario in which you act out the assertive response, the aggressive response and the manipulative response.
    c) Prepare one skit of the scenario in which you act out an assertive response.

6) Have the groups return to the large circle and report or act out the skits. After each report or skit, ask the group to respond as to whether they agree or disagree with the response, and why.

7) You may have the groups take a second scenario if there is time; otherwise, move on to the next step.

8) Ask participants to read the handout Principles of Assertiveness. Then, ask each participant to choose and respond to:
   - The easiest for me would be .... and why
   - The most difficult for me would be ... and why.

Processing:
- Where is assertiveness appropriate and where is it not?
- How do the relative degrees of power in a relationship affect the use of assertiveness?
- Which Transforming Power guides relate to being assertiveness, and how?

HANDOUT

PRINCIPLES OF ASSERTIVENESS

- By standing on our rights we respect ourselves and get others' respect.

- Not letting others know how we feel is a form of controlling them.

- If we don't tell others how their behavior affects us, we are denying them an opportunity to change.

- When we do what is right for us, we feel better about ourselves and have more authentic and satisfying relationships with others.

- Everyone has the right to courtesy and respect.

- We have the right to express ourselves as long as we don't violate the rights of others.

- Much is to be gained from life by being free and able to stand up for ourselves, and also from honoring the same rights in others.

- When we are assertive, everyone involved can benefit.

To think about:
- What is the difference between "assertiveness" and "aggressiveness?"

- What is the difference between "rights" and "power?"

- Where is assertiveness appropriate and where is it not?

HANDOUT

BASIC HUMAN RIGHTS

Assertiveness begins with the belief that you and others have basic human rights, including the right to:

1. Be treated with respect and consideration.

2. Say NO without feeling guilty or selfish.

3. Have and express directly one's own opinions and feelings, including anger.

4. Express one's talents and interests through any ethical channel.

5. Make mistakes.

6. Set one's own priorities as to needs.

7. Be treated as a capable adult and not be patronized.

8. Be listened to and taken seriously.

9. Be independent.

10. Ask others to change behavior that continues to violate one's rights.

Every right has a corresponding responsibility
to respect the rights of others.

Role rights (vested authority) and legal rights
differ from human rights.

THE BAG
(variation of "Hidden Agenda")

Purpose: To help remove the blocks to community in the beginning of the workshop.

Time: 15 minutes.

Materials: Newsprint and markers.

Sequence:
1. Participants are asked to brainstorm things that might block the sense of community in the group. This would include items such as fear, put-downs, ego, jealousy, etc. All the items are written down on newsprint.

2. Then the sheet is placed in a transparent trash bag to symbolize that this is the trash which needs to be avoided in the workshop. The bag is then taped to the wall for the remainder of the workshop.

3. If problems arise during the workshop, the participants are then referred to the Trash Bag to see if this problem is listed. This can lead to a discussion of how to keep the problem in the trash bag rather than in the workshop.

BARGAINING WITH VALUES

"When you are clear about your position, expect to experience great inward power to act on it. A response that relies on this power will be courageous and with out hostility".

                 Guides to Transforming Power

Purpose: To aid participants in getting in touch with their deeply held values and to test the strength of these values.

Time: 15 to 20 minutes.

Materials: Pencils, 5 slips of paper for each participant.

Sequence:
1. Divide group into pairs and distribute materials
2. Read the Guides For Being Open to Transforming Power (page C-13). Explain the purpose of the exercise and lead the group into a guided reflection as follows:
   "Get in a comfortable position ... put both feet on the floor ... relax your body ... close your eyes ... and relax your mind ... breathe easily and deeply ... count your breaths.
   "You are sitting in a room by yourself ... as you relax in your chair, you notice in front of you a large blank television screen ... this screen can show any picture you wish ... you begin ... to see a face on the screen ... it is the face of someone your admire and respect ... it may be a political leader you admire, or a sports figure you respect or an important person from history.
   "Think about the values this person represents to you ... this might be courage, honesty, loyalty, whatever ... Take a moment to write down that value on slip of paper ... then close you're eyes again ... now think about another person you respect and admire, someone you know ... a grandmother, uncle teacher or friend ... think about the value this person represents to you also ... take a moment to open your eyes and write that value on a slip of paper ... then close your eyes again.
   "Continue the process until you have a value written on each slip of paper. Then raise your finger to show you are finished."
3. Now that participants are aware of their important values, have them read their five values to their partners. Say "One way of testing our values is asking 'What would I do to defend this value?' For example, some people are willing to defend their values with their lives; some are willing to go to jail to defend their values. I am sure you can think of many people through history who have done these things."
4. Have each participant chose one of their partners values and ask for it. The response to the question "May I have this value" may either be "Yes, you can have that value" or "No, you cannot have that value. I am willing to go to jail for it."
5. Have each partner go through this process with each of the values. When all have completed, return to the large circle.

Processing:
- Were you surprised at some of your responses?
- What did you learn about yourself and your values from this exercise?
- How can you apply this learning to your life?

BODY IMAGING
Can Be Used To Image Anger Or Fear

Purpose: To experience in one's own body the physical characteristics of an emotion. To increase awareness of the relationship between one's body and one's feelings. To suggest possibilities of making use of this awareness.

Time: 15 minutes.

Materials: None.

Sequence:
1. Sit in circle, relax, become comfortable. The facilitator leading the exercise should give a few relaxing instructions (tense parts of body, relax them, let hands drop, feel all tension run out of body).

2. When people are relaxed, the facilitator instructs group as follows: "Each person, fantasize your anger (or fear); image it, feel it in your body, let your muscles tense, feel it more ... hold it. Open your eyes, feel and look how your body is now. Then relax. Be aware of which muscles relax."

3. Ask for one volunteer to be the image for an experience of anger or fear. Sculpt that image, call for people to say what muscles should tense, how body should be positioned, etc.

4. Then, using the same person as image, sculpt the body taking a stance — a body empowered to deal with that fear or anger — again calling for suggestions from all. If someone wishes to come up and help sculpt, fine.

Processing:
Ask the image person:
- how it felt to be put into a physical state of anger (or fear).
- how did the empowerment position (the stance) feel?

Then ask other people.

Note:
A similar purpose may be achieved in a slightly different format; that is, hassle lines. Give relaxing instructions, have partners push against each other, imagining that the other is a person they are angry at, feel fear of, whatever.

BRAINSTORMING

Brainstorming is a basic and indispensable technique in all our workshops. It has specific purposes: To get the whole group freely contributing ideas; to get out as many ideas as possible; and to help people to expand their ideas and build on the ideas of others. It also gives facilitators the opportunity to introduce ideas.

What is presented here is a general description of brainstorming as a technique. Many groups are very accustomed to brainstorming so use your judgment about how much of an introduction you want to give. Participants in most Second Level Workshops will have experienced brainstorming in the Basic Workshop and will already be familiar with the concept. For such groups, a brief reminder of the rules is enough. Sometimes, however, workshops given in the community blend elements from both the Basic and the Second Level programs, and may also include participants unfamiliar with brainstorming. For them, a complete introduction, suitable for use in the first brainstorm in a Basic Workshop, follows.

Describe the process:
Everyone should throw out ideas on the subject of the exercise (e.g. Violence/Nonviolence, appropriate subjects for role plays, whatever). These ideas will be written down, without censorship or judgment, whether other people in the group agree with them or not. If anyone disagrees with an idea, that person may call out a contradictory idea, and both should be written on the newsprint, without comment.

Start the brainstorm:
It is often helpful if two facilitators work together, one writing and the other eliciting ideas. The writer should try to put the ideas in as few words as possible, and keep going until everyone feels satisfied that all of the group's ideas are listed.

This has been found useful to remember:
Put acronym on board: IDEAS

   I - Ideas listed
    D - Delay judgment
     E - Expand on others' ideas
      A - Abbreviate
       S - Strive for quantity

Important:
The facilitators may and should make contributions. An important part of our task is to make sure that all essential ideas get listed. If the group does not bring them up, the facilitators must do it. For example, in a brainstorm on "What is Violence," the facilitator needs to be sure that institutional, psychological, and societal violence are included.

Many brainstorms are followed by a summary by the facilitators and then a discussion by the whole group. During the summary, the facilitator should note some of the contradictions and say something of what seems important to us in AVP.

Other brainstorms are used as a first step in making a choice.

Materials: For all brainstorms, newsprint, markers and masking tape are needed.

Time: Most brainstorms are about 30 minutes. Give everyone a chance to speak, but do not let them drag on.

BRAINSTORMING AND WEB CHARTS

Purpose: A web chart can be used to explore many subjects, and can bring out and focus on the multitude of factors and influences that are a part of or affect any particular problem.

Time: 15 to 20 minutes.

Materials: Blackboard or large piece of newsprint and chalk or marker (more than one color of the latter is useful).

Sequence:
1. Draw a circle in the middle of the blackboard or newsprint and within it write the name of the problem or focus topic (e.g., "communications problem") to be explored.

2. Invite the group to throw out, brainstorm-fashion, things that contribute to the problem (e.g. fear, racism, stereotyping, hidden agendas, institutional distortion of truth.) Write all these things outside of and all around the circle.

3. Now invite the group to suggest lines that should be drawn to connect those factors which are related to each other (e.g., between racism and stereotyping). Any factor may be connected to any other factor. You end up with quite a spider-web.

4. (Optional): Carry the exercise one step further by asking each person to make a private web chart of the factors that may bear on a problem that concerns him/her. This is to be done for the person's own benefit and is not necessarily to be shared with anyone. Allow a brief time for the group to work on this.

5. When people seem finished with the web charts, they might be used as a basis for an exercise in Goal/Wish Problem Solving.

BRAINSTORMS: SUGGESTIONS FOR TOPICS

BRAINSTORM: WAYS TO PREVENT OR DECREASE VIOLENCE
After the "What is Violence?" brainstorm, focus on ways to decrease violence.

BRAINSTORM: WAYS OUR SOCIETY TEACHES OR PROMOTES VIOLENCE
Following the "What is Violence?" brainstorm, explore the way that culture contributes to violence.

BRAINSTORM: WAYS I WANT TO CHANGE
1. After completing the "What is Violence?" and "What is Non-Violence?" brainstorms, participants can gain ownership of the workshop by considering what they would like to work on changing in their lives.

2. Ask participants to volunteer in circling items on the violence side of the brainstorm that they would like to change in themselves and then circle items on the non-violence side that they would like to improve in themselves. It is important to do this portion of the exercise in a silent and meditative atmosphere.

BRAINSTORM: TYPES OF FEAR
Follow this by circling "inborn fears" and "fears that are learned."

BRAINSTORM: CREATIVE SOLUTIONS
Purpose:
To explore a wide variety of solutions to a conflict situation. To enable the entire creativity of the group to be focused on a situation where one person may feel stuck or blocked in a role play.

Sequence:
1. The leader reads a scenario to the group such as the following:
   You have been released from prison and you are visiting your girlfriend's family for the first time. Those present are your girlfriend, her father and mother and her uncle and aunt. Her father comes to the door and escorts you into the living room. He introduces you with "I'd like you to meet my daughter's boyfriend, Henry the Jailbird." How do you respond?

   or:

   You are on a job interview and the job specifications have been presented and discussed. You have shown how you meet the requirements. In fact, you are overqualified to some degree. The employer seems to like you and seems ready to offer you the job. He then discovers that you have been in jail. He backs off and says, "I'd like to interview some other candidates before I make the decision." How do you respond?

2. Place several sheets of newsprint on the wall and brainstorm creative responses. Generally many creative and humorous solutions will be suggested. The group will also have fun in the process. Discuss briefly which options will have the greatest chance of success.

BRAINSTORM: VIOLENCE/NONVIOLENCE

Purpose: To help people identify the patterns of violence that are a problem for them and that they most need to work on, as well as the patterns of nonviolence they most need to acquire.

Sequence:
1. Do violence brainstorm, What Is Violence?
2. Pass out markers or flare pens, in as many colors as possible. Each participant is to pick out and circle on the newsprint the three causes of violence they feel they personally most need to work on. They should also make their own listings of these.
3. Do nonviolence brainstorm, What Is Nonviolence?
4. Have participants circle the three items they feel they personally need to work on, and again make their own list.
5. Ask for comments.

Note:
If many have circled the same items, use these as a list of issues for future sessions.

BRAINSTORM: WHAT IS A MAN

Purpose:
To use toward the beginning of a workshop to stimulate thinking about how our attitudes change as we are affected by people and events in our lives.

Sequence:
On three sheets of newsprint, write the following titles:
- When I was a child, I thought being a man meant ...
- Now that I am an adult, I think being a man means ...
- Events/People who caused the change

or, variation questions:
- What is a man?
- What kind of a man would you like your son to be?
- What kind of a man would you like to marry your daughter, sister, mother or other woman you care about?

If you can, hang them so that participants see only the first sheet at the beginning. Then, when that one gets filled up, hang it to the side and begin the brainstorming of the next. At the end, you should have the three brainstorms hanging in a row.

Processing:
Invite participants to "speak to" or explain anything that is on any of the sheets. Announce that these will hang throughout the workshop and if anyone wishes to add anything to them, they are welcome to do so.

D-20   Brainstorms: Suggestions for Topics

BRAINSTORM: WHAT'S IN A WORD?

Purpose: To make people think about the importance of language in communication; to use as an introduction to reviewing I-Messages.
Make sure participants have Transforming Power guides.

Materials: Post a separate sheet of newsprint for each of the following pairs:
"Need" vs "Want", "Assertive" vs "Aggressive", "Right" vs "Power",
"Self-esteem" vs "Ego", "I need…" vs "I want…"
"I am assertive when…" vs "I am aggressive when…"
"I have the right to…" vs "I have the power to …"
"My self-esteem causes me to…" vs "My ego causes me to…"

Sequence:
1. Introduce the brainstorm by explaining the following:
    Language comes out of our experience; that experience which is shaped by our generations, our cultures, our genders — many things. Words can have different meanings for different people, and a word that suggests something positive for one person can have a negative effect on another person. It is particularly important that we have a common understanding of some pairs of words that we use in dealing with conflict situations. THE WORDS IN EACH OF THESE PAIRS DO NOT MEAN THE SAME THING. Let's see if we can help one another define the differences. They are (and you will have them posted so you can point to them.)

NOTES:
a. In this brainstorm, there should be discussion. You have already explained that the words in each pair do NOT mean the same thing. Therefore, all answers are not right, and the leader/facilitator should be prepared to ask leading questions in order to get people to question and analyze. Other facilitators sitting in the group should be prepared to offer examples (" I need love … I want you to love me") rather than definitions or explanations. You are trying to guide the participants to definitions by illustration, rather than lecture.

b. It is important to write the words in parallel order as they are above (the "positive" word in each pair comes first — they are positive in the sense that if you are operating on the basis of need, being assertive, protecting your rights, and dealing from pride, you are more ready to work on resolving a conflict than you are if you are operating from the second column. HOWEVER, IT MAY BE EASIER TO LIST WHAT WE HAVE THE POWER TO DO BEFORE LISTING WHAT WE HAVE THE RIGHT TO DO. Simply put them in the right columns, i.e., I have the power to kill but do I have the right?

c. One way of getting everyone started on the right track is to ask people for our basic needs in order to live (air, water, food, shelter, clothing). Then, give one example: "I need air and water … I want to be on permanent vacation on a beach in Hawaii."

Processing:
- What connection is there among these? (point to "want," "power," "aggressive," and "ego"). What connection is there among these? (point to "need," right," "assertive," and "self-esteem").
- How could it help us in communicating with someone with whom we are in conflict if we could make certain that we are operating on this level (point to "need," "right," "assertive," and "self-esteem") rather than on this level (point to "want," "power," "aggressive," and "ego").
- Which of the Transforming Power guidelines relate to the need for operating on the basis of needs, rights, self-esteem, and being assertive?

BRAINSTORMING — THE ERUPTION OF VIOLENCE
(Variation on "What is Violence")

Purpose: To understand how a buildup of "pressure" can lead to violence. To brainstorm ways to relieve "pressure."

Time: 20 to 30 minutes.

Materials: Newsprint and markers or blackboard and chalk.

Sequence:
1. Draw a shell of a volcano with lava bed and steam vents. Make large enough to write on the insides of the volcano and lava bed.

2. Give a brief explanation of why a volcano erupts, emphasizing that a build up of pressure in the lava bed leads to eruption of lava from the volcano.

3. Brainstorm "What is Violence?" and write responses where lava is spewing from the top of the volcano.

4. Brainstorm "Roots of Violence" and write these responses inside the lava bed.

5. Brainstorm "What is Nonviolence?" and write these responses inside of the volcano.

Processing:
- What are the similarities of an active volcano and a person acting violently? (A buildup of pressure causes violent eruptions.)
- What are the similarities of an inactive volcano and a person acting non-violently? (Using "venting" to reduce pressure can prevent the eruptions.)

Note:
The use of different colored markers will visually enhance the effectiveness of the chart. Example: Blue --- non-violence, Black --- roots of violence, Red --- violence.

BREAK THROUGH

Purpose: To have an experience of what stops us from effecting change in our lives and what inner resources (or allies) we can call on to aid us in moving beyond our perceived limitations.

Time: 30 to 45 minutes.

Materials: A chair for each participant, two sheets of newsprint, felt pens. One newsprint should be labeled "Barriers to Change," and one labeled "Allies to Change."

Sequence:
1. Participants sit in their chairs on one side of the room, facing the other side.
2. Ask participants to take a moment to tune into an aspect of themselves that they are wanting to change — something in their life where there is violence or stress, perhaps.
3. Stand in the empty area across the room, and say: "This is where you will be when you have made this change. Imagine what it will be like. (allow time to think) What are some of the words for how it will seem? Feel? (Invite responses.) Now, between you and this place is what blocks you. Our chairs will represent the blocks. These blocks have voices. As you see one of your "blocks" or hear its voice, one at a time, come out and sit with your chair here and express that block's voice back at yourself as if you were still standing there. Let the block name itself." At this point the facilitator should model the process, shifting his/her chair to the middle and saying, for example: "I am your fear of failure, (name). What a waste of energy if you fail!"
4. When all are in the barrier position, have the voices expressed one at a time. Invite people to write the name of their block(s) on the sheet of newsprint headed "Barriers to Change."
5. After all have expressed their blocks, say something like "Here are the blocks that are holding you back from change. Luckily, we all have inner resources to overcome these blocks. What we can call our "Allies to Change." As you identify an ally, come out, face your block and express the voice of your ally, who you are, and how you can help." At this point the facilitator should move his/her chair to the other side of the room and say, for example, "I am (name) sense of adventure and I help by saying 'you never know until you try'."
6. When all are in the area of change, have participants call out their ally's name one by one. Invite them to write their ally's name on the newsprint "Allies to Change."
7. Move to a large circle to process.

Processing:
- How does it feel to be in the change-achieved position?
- Is it as you expected?
- Which Transforming Power Guide(s) can help us recognize our allies?

BUMPER STICKERS

Purpose: Useful to reach and convey insights on any subject. This example centers on Transforming Power. The exercise provides an opportunity to focus on a subject, cooperate, create, and laugh together. It is an affirming experience.

Time: 30 minutes.

Materials: Copies of Guides to Transforming Power, or Transforming Power Indicators, (Section C) enough to give one to each member of the group.

Sequence:
Ask participants to study the Guides or Indicators for a few minutes and select those that particularly speak to them. Ask participants to group in pairs and to agree on one advice important to both and to write a bumper sticker for it. Go around group after enough time has passed and share bumper stickers.

Examples of some bumper stickers suggested in the past:
- Reach for your real self. Think before you act
- Love Thine Enemies: That'll Keep You Busy
- We take out our opponents with the left hook of understanding and the right cross of patience
- Change enemies to friends by sharing
- Think and remember: 15 will get you 20

Alternative:
Ask participants to create bumper stickers based on the theme of the workshop. This is a good way to have participants explore their feelings about the topic in the third or fourth session of the workshop.

Note:
This exercise may be used to reintroduce the concept of Transforming Power.

BUTTONS

Purpose: To become more aware of why certain situations "push our buttons" so that sometimes we "lose our cool." To consider how we might calm ourselves in such situations and to practice doing just that.

Time: 30 - 40 minutes.
(This exercise can be split: first, steps #1–#5; later steps #6 and #7.)

Materials: Button Circle Poster (next page.)

Sequence:
1. Explain that sometimes certain situations "push our buttons" so that we may "lose our cool." In trios, we're going to consider why this might be so.

2. Form trios, in or near the circle. Ask participants to share a situation that often "pushes their buttons." Allow about 5 to 10 minutes for this.

3. Point out the Button Circle poster. Mention that probably most people mentioned a situation and a feeling connected with it. For example, "If people start to tell me what a great time they had getting drunk, I get angry."

4. But why? What lies between the situation and my anger? It's my "point of view." I value not getting wasted myself. Also, my brother's an alcoholic and I hate it when he tells supposedly funny "war stories." It's my old experiences. Underneath my anger, I'm sure there's hurt and fear.

5. Back in trios, have people consider what in their "point of view" comes between their situation and their feelings. Allow about 10 minutes.

6. In the big circle brainstorm possible ways to calm or cool our "buttons." If "self-talk" isn't mentioned, ask if anyone has ever tried it.

Processing:
- What insights did you gain?
- Might you be able to use your calming method(s) in real life?
- How does this relate to Transforming Power?

Note:
Having co-facilitators participating or observing is helpful. This exercise is particularly useful before or after any Feeling exercise.

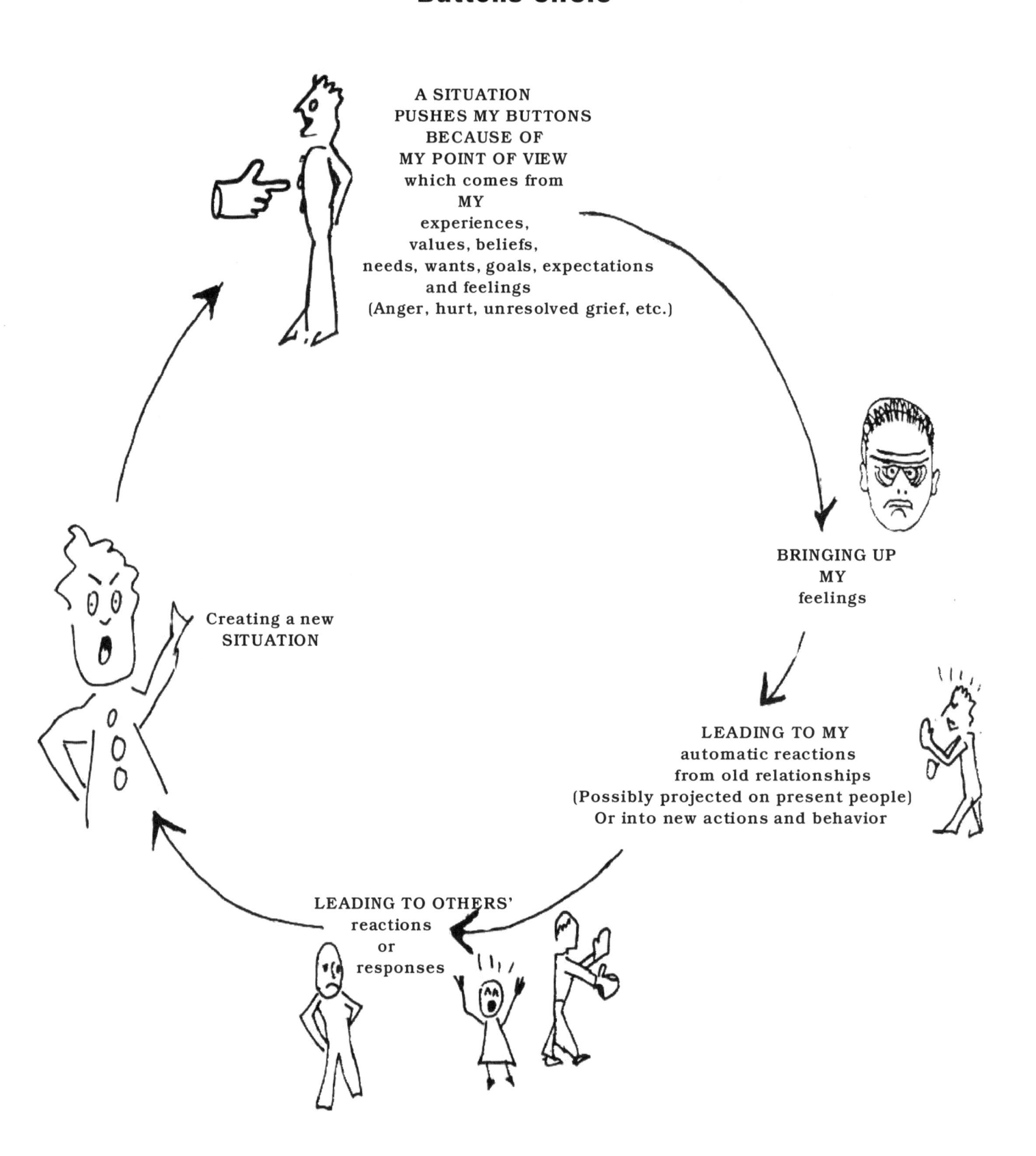

Buttons Circle

A SITUATION PUSHES MY BUTTONS BECAUSE OF MY POINT OF VIEW which comes from **MY** experiences, values, beliefs, needs, wants, goals, expectations and feelings (Anger, hurt, unresolved grief, etc.)

BRINGING UP MY feelings

LEADING TO MY automatic reactions from old relationships (Possibly projected on present people) Or into new actions and behavior

LEADING TO OTHERS' reactions or responses

Creating a new **SITUATION**

D-26   **Buttons Circle**

CAREFRONTING

Purpose: To be in right relationship with others. To speak truth in love. To learn to be open and honest in difficult matters without using your openness as a weapon.

Time: About 2 hours 15 minutes (total). Estimated times of completion, based on groups of 20 participants, are given below for the Introduction and Parts 1 through 7 of this exercise.

Note:
Used in its entirety, this is a very long exercise. Efforts to condense it, however, have led only to the conclusion that no part of it can be omitted if the objectives are to be fulfilled. Therefore the only solution appears to be to keep it moving right along. A fast pace is the only way to avoid being bogged down and drowned in it. (The guide reflection, however, must not be rushed.)

It is possible to use only the first three parts of this exercise, or parts 1 and 3, as an assertiveness exercise.

Introductory Talk (5 minutes)

Materials: Newsprint on which the diagrams are copied.

Truth and love are intrinsically related. The Latin word for the unity of truth and love is "agape" (ah-gah-pay). Christianity and Islam both teach that truth/knowledge is for the sake of bringing everyone to the experience of oneness in love. Buddhism teaches that compassion/love is for the sake of bringing everyone to the experience of wisdom, called "gnosis," (no-sis) (or the knowledge of spiritual mysteries). The difference is one of emphasis.

Carefronting is a way of being in relationship, of speaking the truth in love, of combining caring and confronting. CONfronting is putting your heads together; CAREfronting is doing so with a loving attitude.

The opposite of carefronting is conning: neither caring nor confronting.

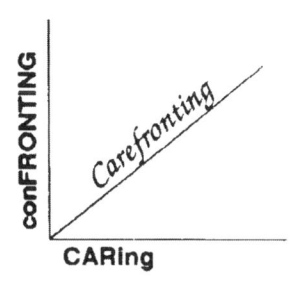

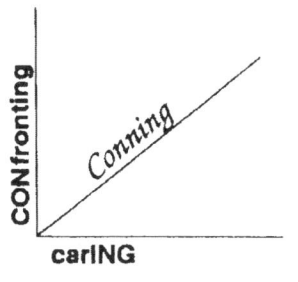

Part 1: Meaning of "Confront (15-20 minutes)

Introduction:
One sure sign of caring is listening, not giving advice, nor telling people not to feel the way they do or that they are silly, nor trying to solve their problems, nor doing something for them. Ugo Betti said it well: "Nothing matters half so much ... to reassure one another, to answer each other ... perhaps only you can listen to me and not laugh."

Process:
1. Say: "Close eyes, become aware of breathing, think of the word confront, let ideas and associations come. Remember the first three words you just thought of."

2. They are to call out, popcorn-style, their three words.

3. Note that Confront usually conveys an image of fighting. However, it does not mean fight. Confront means to come face to face with, from the Latin "confrontare," (con-fron-tah-re) to have a common border — con = together, and frons = forehead; in other words, to put our heads together — an intimate act.

4. Put people in pairs. They are to find a topic that is controversial between them (examples: abortion, child rearing, prison abolition, women's liberation, what TV show we watch tonight). They are then to put foreheads together physically and, while holding that position, give their opinions forcefully. Eventually they should seek common ground.

Processing:
What was that like for you?

Part 2. Guided Visualization (15 minutes)
Introduction:
1. Tell group: "find a comfortable position, relaxed, feet on the floor and to try to clear your heads of everything but the awareness of your own body. Close your eyes, be comfortable, be aware of breathing, breathe deeply to slow count of 4-2-4 (inhale, hold, exhale)."

    Say (slowly): "You are walking by yourself, there is no one else around, it is a warm, sunny day, you are feeling good. In the far distance, you see someone approaching whom you care about and with whom you have unfinished business or an unresolved conflict ... What are your thoughts, assumptions? ... How do you feel? ... As you come face to face, what do you say or do? (Pause for at least 10 seconds) ... How does the other person respond? ... (Again pause for 10 seconds) You each continue on your way. Be aware of how you feel ... When you are ready, return to the room."

2. Put people in groups of three. For two minutes, each may share as s/he chooses:
    - what happened? and
    - how satisfied did you feel as you continued on your way?

    (Write these questions on newsprint for guidance of the group in sharing.)

Part 3. Rights and Equity (30 minutes)
Introduction:
In this exercise we are going to look at why carefronting is often difficult and what keeps us from carefronting in our relationships with others.

1. Put group in pairs by counting off one, two, one, two, etc. Put them into two lines, and try to separate the pairs from one another as far apart as possible.

2. Have the Ones stand with arms folded, expressionless. The Twos stand facing the Ones, keeping eye contact. The Twos are to shake their fists at their partners, saying, "I have a right" over and over, until the sentence finishes itself. Tell them: Do not program yourself ahead of time. Let the "right" you are claiming come out of your depths and surprise you. And then demand the "right" with authority. It may be an irrational "right." That's OK. It need not be logical nor make sense.

3. Reverse roles.

4. While facing each other, have the partners take turns finishing the observation : "What that was like for me ..."

5. Ask the Ones: "Now think of the 'right' that you just expressed. Imagine that your partner is someone who stands in the way of that 'right.' Find a way to say with authority, 'I have a right to ... and you are standing in the way of my right by...' "

6. Reverse roles.

7. Return the pairs to a large group circle. Process with the following questions:
   - Is my "right" (discovered in the exercise) a universal right, or individual to me?
   - What keeps us from expressing our rights assertively rather than aggressively?
   - Unfinished "business" or issues in our past often make us bring anger to the table when we try to express what we believe to be our "rights." What other emotions or conditions does anger mask?
   - How can we free ourselves to be who we are? To do what we aspire to? To be free to love without fear?
   - What Transforming Power guide(s) might help us to take this path?

   Additional questions if you want to get into a general discussion (these could be used if you want to use parts 1-3 in one session and follow up in another session):
   - What is the difference between saying "I have the right to" and "I have the power to"?
   - What is the difference between assertiveness and aggressiveness?
   - What is the difference between what I need and what I want?

Principles of Assertiveness and the Basic Human Rights handouts (see D-12 & D-13) would be helpful at this point. A simple way of using them is to have people take turns reading them out loud and then asking each person to share which statement seems most challenging.

Part 4 Differences (35-40 minutes)

Introduction:
   We have said that anger often masks another emotion, very often fear. When we experience fear for too long, it is like "stewing in our own juice." So we channel that fear into anger, because anger has direction; it can be aimed at someone else. It is often hostility, produced by unresolved anger from our past, that keeps us from carefronting others with whom we have issues. Where hostility is worked through, we get to honest differences: of opinions, perceptions, needs, or whatever. Any two people always have some degree of opposition to each other's point of view or approach to issues. Acceptance of another person is recognizing and accepting both similarities and differences.

Post the "Three Ways of Dealing With Differences" on newsprint.

Confluence: denial of differences
   - as two rivers flow together
   - as infant-on-mother's breast is one with mother
   - as one falling in love sees only similarities
   - as white and non-white meet and deny differences of culture, of experience, etc.

Conflict: rejection of differences
   - Why don't you see things the way I do?
   - Why don't you want what I want?
   - Why don't you feel the way I do?
   - I certainly would not want, see, or feel as you do.

Contact: appreciation and exploration of differences
   - I have never looked at it that way
   - Contact is the willingness to become more deeply aware of differences, to explore without trying to change the person. Then there is no need to falsify ourselves, manipulate others, overpower, push away, destroy, fight, ignore, reject, or at best tolerate.
   - Our strengths and weaknesses balance one another

Process:
a) Have newsprint ready. You will be writing, for the group's reference, some of the phrases they are to say.
b) Ask group to form pairs, This time each participant is to pick a partner who is most different from him/herself. (It may be necessary to negotiate to get a partner as different as possible.)
c) Instruct the pairs to take turns saying, "You are the same as I... " or "There is no difference in the way we ... " (Write these phrases on newsprint.) Imagine similarities if you know of none. The other person responds only "agree" or "disagree," (no conversation). Then alternate. Try to cover all four areas: physical, emotional, cognitive, spiritual.
d) Now have group form new pairs, this time picking partners who are very similar to each other. Again negotiate. Take turns saying, "Something I see in you that I don't like in me is ... " or "Something I don't like in me that may also be in you is ... " The other responds, "That is true," or, "That is not true." (Be aware of the possibility of projection! It takes one to know one; people are most critical of their own worst faults in others .)
e) Ask people to choose new partners, this time choosing one who thinks or believes differently. Say: "I think you are different than I ... Tell me more about that. How did you come to see things that way?" Then alternate.
f) Large group: Debrief by asking if anyone wants to share something about the experience.

Part 5 Guided Visualization (15 minutes)

Have the group sit in a circle, and ask them to find a comfortable position. Then say: "Close your eyes if that is comfortable for you. Be aware of your breathing, breathe deeply by counting to four as you inhale, then hold it for two, and then exhale for four. Repeat."

Begin the guided visualization: "Walking alone, on a warm sunny day, you see in the distance the same person of your previous fantasy. Be aware of how the other person perceives, feels or wants differently from you ... (pause for 10 seconds) Be aware of a fear you have of the other and how that affects your behavior (Pause) ... Realize that there is something you want from that person ... As you come face-to-face, say, "I have a right." Be specific ... The other person responds ... Imagine the dialogue (pause for at least 10 seconds) Take leave of one another. Continue on. Be aware of how you feel... When ready, return to this room.

Have them get into groups of 3 and share as before:
- What happened differently this time (or did it?)
- How did you feel as you passed on? Were you satisfied?

Part 6 Process whole exercise in large group (10 minutes)

Processing should avoid exploring content and concentrate on what was experienced:
- How did you feel, and what did you learn?
- What helped?
- What did not help?

CHOICES

Purpose: To explore the idea that no matter where we are and how helpless we may feel we still can make choices; to consider which choices will enhance (increase) and which will diminish our freedom to live our lives the way we want to live.

Time: 30 minutes or more.

Materials: Newsprint and markers enough for 4 or 5 groups; a poster as follows:

CHOICES	
Some Diminish Freedom	**Some Enhance Freedom**
and can lead to	and can lead to
prison, death, addiction,	health, good jobs, long-life
illness, loss of options.	family ties, peace of mind.

Sequence:
1. Explain the purpose as stated above. Read the different sides. Show the poster and ask for volunteers to read the different sides.

2. Say that in small groups people will brainstorm choices that might diminish their freedom and choices that will enhance their freedom. Encourage them to think of choices that they can make in the present — right now! You might ask for one example of a choice that would diminish freedom, (e.g. trying drugs), and one that would enhance freedom, (e.g. getting an education).

3. If there are no questions, form groups, assign work places, distribute materials and have them begin. Let them know that they'll have about 10 minutes.

4. When each group has some things on both lists, have people return to the circle, staying with their groups. Post the lists and have volunteers read them.

Processing:
- What do people think about the choices listed?
- Are some of the choices difficult to follow? Which ones? Why?
- Do we always have choices? What about the "I didn't have a choice" line?
- Might difficult situations arise because of unwise choices made in the past?
- What can we do to help us stick to wise choices?

Note:
The idea that we have choices is a key concept of AVP. Freedom is an integral part of the picture because freedom of choice is what it's all about.

Before Step 1 above, you may wish to brainstorm how people would like to be living in four or five years. Then you can proceed as above.

CHOOSING A FOCUS TOPIC

GOALS AND PRIORITIES
Part One

Purpose: To help participants set personal goals and understand the things that keep them from those goals. Part One should be done at the beginning of the workshop. Part Two could be used as a follow-up at the end of the workshop.

Time: 20 minutes.

Materials: A piece of newsprint and a marker for each small group.

Sequence:
1. Divide the group into small groups of from three to six people. Each group should appoint a recorder.

2. Each participant will share with his/her group (allow three minutes for each person to talk on each subject):
   a) an experience I had applying what I learned in the Basic Workshop.
   b) a goal I am working on that I hope this workshop will help me with.

   After a person is finished, the recorder should ask how this goal could be described briefly on the newsprint and record it in that way.

3. Return to the larger group. Post newsprint lists on the wall (fairly close together in a row) and invite people to ask questions or comment on any.

4. Post the following list next to the row of group reports:
   Things that keep us from achieving our goals
   a) fear
   b) anger
   c) issues of power, powerlessness
   d) stereotyping
   e) lack of self-esteem
   f) need for forgiveness
   g) poor communication

5. Read the lists that the participants in the groups made. Ask the group to suggest for each one, which of the things that keep us from achieving goals might be a problem. Write the numbers of the suggestions next to the goal.

6. After you have gone through the lists, explain that in this workshop we will be working on those things that keep us from achieving our goals. Ask that participants help prioritize what things we should concentrate on, by circling one or more on the posted list of "things." Offer the marker, and explain that if someone has circled a choice that someone else also wants to work on, he should put a check next to it. At the end, we will be able to see what most people have checked. Everything circled or checked will be a part of this workshop. (At this point, give time for people to think, mark what they want and pass the marker along.)

CHOOSING A FOCUS TOPIC

GOALS AND PRIORITIES
Part Two
(For the Closing)

Purpose: To bring closure to the workshop with a personal reflection of what went on during the workshop and what changes each individual wants to work on in his/her life.

Time: 20 minutes.

Materials: Pencils or pens and paper for each participant.
Have written on newsprint (but don't post it yet):
- a) some of the things I'm going to do to help myself.
- b) some of the things I'm going to need help with.
- c) some places (people) where I'm going to look for help.

Sequence:

This will be most effective if facilitators have put some order into the many papers which hang on the walls. Hanging the agendas for the sessions in a sequential order helps participants remember what they have done throughout the weekend. If you have taken them down, or covered them, rehang the original group lists of goals created by the participants along with what might prevent their achievement."

1. Draw attention to the posted lists of goals that we began with in this workshop.

2. Explain that this is going to be a silent reflection time for people to think about the goals that they had at the beginning of the workshop and what thoughts and feelings they might have about them now. Participants will not be asked to share with the group what they have written or thought about.

3. If you think there are people who have trouble reading, read through the lists aloud. Ask participants to think about the goals listed at the beginning of the workshop and list on their paper the goals they want for themselves. Remind them that they may have changed their goals or added to them.

4. Now post the three statements you prepared above.

5. Read the three things aloud, and ask the participants to think about each one and write a response on their sheet of paper. Remind them that this is for themselves alone to take with them. Ask that people who finish earlier than others respect the need for silence.

Note:
By this time, you should know if there is someone who needs help with writing, and a facilitator should be with that person to help.

CHOOSING A FOCUS TOPIC
With a Gathering

Purpose: A simple method of establishing a focus topic.

Time: 15 minutes.

Materials: Newsprint.

Sequence:

1. In the second session have the gathering "The issue I would really like to work on this weekend."

2. During the gathering, a facilitator takes down notes and then picks out common themes expressed and posts these themes on newsprint.

3. The facilitating team works with these broad topics to be woven into a series of agendas without formally establishing a weekend topic. This gives the them more freedom to choose and adapt the weekend to the needs of the group.

CHOOSING A FOCUS TOPIC
By Consensus — 1

Purpose: To have participants choose a focus topic using consensus; to have a physical demonstration of consensus.

Time: 30 - 45 minutes.

Materials: Marker and about 15 sheets of 8 ½ x 11 paper torn in half lengthwise to form thirty (30) 4 ¼ x 11 strips.
Poster or sheets with consensus guidelines. (see D-43)

Sequence:

1. One facilitator asks members of the group to brainstorm topics for the theme of the workshop. A second facilitator quickly prints the same topics on separate strips of paper and places the strips on the floor. Twenty or thirty topics may be suggested.

2. Discuss the topics and point out similarities. You may want to group similar topics together. Stress that this exercise is about consensus and making choices.

3. Ask all the participants to get up and stand next to the topic they prefer for the workshop. Several people may select the same topic. The facilitators then pick up any sheets at which no one is standing.

4. Ask the participants to look at the topics that have been selected and discuss similarities. Then ask them if they would like to reconsider their choice and join another group. Or they may decide to combine their topic with another group. Remind the group that this exercise is about consensus and making choices.

5. Continue this process until you have narrowed down the theme to two or three topics.

6. Post the final topics on the wall and begin to build the workshop around these themes.

CHOOSING A FOCUS TOPIC
By Consensus — 2

Purpose: To arrive at a group consensus on a statement of purpose and a focus topic for the workshop.

Time: As long as it takes

Materials: Newsprint

Sequence:

Part I: Statement of Purpose

Place a large sheet of newsprint on the wall, on which you have written a statement of purpose, and leaving plenty of room for revisions. You may wish to have a blank newsprint sheet on either side, as you add input from participants. The following is a sample:

"We have gathered for this workshop to create a space in which we each feel safe, to share our personal wisdom and experience in order to understand our own contribution to the violence in our lives and our power to resolve conflict in ways that maximize the benefits to all involved."

Part II: Presentation by the facilitator:

1. Make a statement similar to the following:

    "One of the things that distinguishes AVP from other groups is our commitment to using the consensus process in making decisions. We believe that any other process, however democratic, ends up imposing the will of some on others.

    "Through the consensus process, we appreciate conflict as an opportunity for growth. Our goal in establishing the consensus process is to create a space in which objections are not heard as attempts to defeat a proposal, but as concerns which, when resolved, will make the proposal stronger. An essential element of consensus is each participant's contribution. So, our first step is to decide where we are now.

    "The Statement of Purpose posted on the wall might describe our common purpose and define our principles and values. Once we decide on its final form, the statement will determine the make up and direction of the rest of the workshop, and help resolve concerns if conflicts arise. Our goal now is to refine the Statement of Purpose so that it not only describes our purpose in being here and the values we all share, but that it reflects the needs and expectations of every member of the group."

2. Go around, like a gathering, having each person answer:

    "Does this statement completely describe my purpose in being here? If not, how can it be changed so that it does?" (Note: You can begin a session with this exercise rather than doing a gathering.)

    If a participant's change or addition is expressed at length, ask him/her when finished to tell you how to put it in a few words and then write it into the statement or to the side for inclusion later. You may need to put participants' changes on the blank sheets to the sides of the statement, and then insert and/or edit them when the gathering has been completed.

3. The facilitator tries to include each person's contribution in a way that doesn't just generate a list of purposes. (One of the goals of this exercise is to recognize our common needs and desires.) Ask each participant: "Does this say what you wanted to express?"

4. At the end of the circle, the facilitator asks, "Does anyone have any reservations about this statement? Is there anything missing?" Make whatever changes are necessary to establish the group's consensus.

Part III: Choosing the Focus Topic:
1. Make a statement similar to the following:
   "The major difference between Basic and Second Level Workshops is that we choose the focus topic(s). At the second level, we like the group to come to consensus on a focus topic or topics that will best meet the needs of the group. Now that we have established our Statement of Purpose, we can decide what we want to focus on."

2. Look at the statement of purpose for the words that express what was agreed upon re "the power that we have for resolving conflicts non-violently." Ask the group to consider what keeps them from using that power, and ask if anyone has a particular personal concern they would like the workshop to focus on. Ask their reasons for choosing this topic as it may strike a chord with other participants. (Generally we have found that having had the experience of coming to consensus on the Statement of Purpose for this particular workshop, finding consensus on the focus topic goes fairly quickly).

3. Be sure to check for consensus after closing this exercise: "Does anyone have any reservations about the focus for the workshop?"
   Note:
   Don't start with a list of topics in the manual, because choosing from such a list of options is sometimes one of the hardest things to reach consensus on. If you wish to use this method, try suggesting that the group make its choice by eliminating the topics individuals don't want to explore.

4. If you run into trouble reaching consensus: Be very cautious about NOT singling out individuals or groups for the lack of consensus. Always turn to the group for creative solutions to the impasse. Remember to hold conflict in a positive perspective. If there is an impasse, there is without a doubt another solution that hasn't been proposed yet, upon which people will find they can agree.

CLAREMONT DIALOGUE

Purpose: A method for people to get to know one another in a deeper way; a way to have the group discuss some serious issue in depth, or to resolve a conflict that has arisen in the group; to provide an opportunity for everyone in a group a chance to speak out of some depth, and to give everyone a chance to be moved by the contributions of others.

Time: Allow enough time for everyone to be heard.

Materials: None.

Sequence:
1. Participants sit in a circle. The person leading poses a question, then asks for silence for people to get their thoughts together. Everyone gets an opportunity to speak for awhile, sometimes timed (perhaps 3 to 5 minutes), sometimes not. People may either speak in turn, around the circle, or speak when they feel ready.

2. When the discussion seems to be winding down, the leader needs to ask if anyone who has not spoken wishes to speak now. There should be no pressure to do so. People have a right to be silent if they wish. There should be a short interval of silence after each speaker.

3. After everyone has had a chance to speak, the leader may take things in whatever direction seems appropriate. During the dialogue, no one is to dispute or put down anything that has been said.

Possible Uses of the Claremont Dialogue:
1. To get to know one another. The leader will have prepared a question to start off. This might be a question that asks people to speak in some depth, such as "What was your life like when you were seven years old." The next question should have some real bearing on what the group sees as its reason for being together.

2. To deal with a serious problem that has arisen in the workshop. The leader calls for silence. After a short interval to allow people to settle into their feelings and to become clear about what is important to them. The leader then asks each one to say what is important to him/her. Afterwards, it may be possible to find a fruitful direction in which to move.

3. To elicit material for focus unit, For instance, when the focus unit is on anger, the dialogue might be "How anger was handled in my family."

CONCENTRIC CIRCLES

Over the years this exercise has evolved from a simple communications skills exercise into one that can be used to focus on the topic of a second-level workshop, or any other topic that seems important for any given workshop, and to show people the positive attitudes and coping skills that they have as well as the areas and skills that they need to work on.

1. Divide the participants into two groups, one in a circle facing in; the other in an inner circle facing out. It can also be done in parallel lines.

2. Have people begin pairing by shaking hands and giving their adjective names. This requires them to be close enough to one another to hear. Make certain that both people get a chance to speak on the same topic before moving them to the next partner.

Enhancing Self-esteem
1. A person I really respect, and why.
2. Some ways I show respect for myself.
3. A time I did the right thing even though I felt some fear.
4. A way that I take care of myself or am good to myself when I feel the need.
5. Something I've learned in my life that has been important to me.
6. Something I've done that I'm proud of.
7. Something I'd like to do this year that I can be proud of.
8. A goal I have and some things I'm doing to accomplish it.
9. Some things I like about myself and how I am growing.
10. A peak moment in my life was...

Anger
1. A time I was not in control of my anger and it hurt me and/or others.
2. A time I was in control of my anger and managed to channel it into constructive action.
3. A way I react when another person expresses anger at me.
4. I find it hard to handle another person's anger when ...
5. It is easy for me to handle another person's anger when ...
6. A time I used humor or some other positive technique to transform someone else's anger.
7. A way I have of expressing anger without hurting myself or others.
8. A time when Transforming Power helped me to deal with my anger.

Power
1. An incident that's part of the reason I'm in this Power workshop.
2. A time I felt powerless.
3. A time someone used power against me, and I felt crushed.
4. A time I discovered I had more power than I realized.
5. A time I used power destructively.
6. A time I used power constructively.
7. A time I shared power in a group to achieve something that would have been hard to achieve alone.
8. A time I needed power and it seemed to come to me from outside myself. (If nothing comes to mind now, it may come later. For now, just say whatever the question brings to mind.)
9. Some things I'd like to understand about power.
10. A time I put somebody down was....
11. A time I felt most hurt by someone I trusted was when ....

Man Woman Relationships
1. A man/woman relationship that I respect as a role model, and why.
2. The man or woman I wanted to grow up to be when I was a child.
3. The thing about being grown up that I most feared as a child.
4. A time that I have been victimized — exploited, manipulated, coerced — because of my gender.
5. A time I have used exploitative, manipulative or aggressive behavior to get what I wanted from a member of the opposite gender.
6. The attitude or kind of treatment that I most dislike or resent from people of the opposite gender.
7. The attitude or kind of treatment that I most appreciate from people of the opposite gender.
8. A problem with someone of the opposite gender that I have never managed to resolve and that has become an ongoing frustration.
9. A problem with someone of the opposite gender that I have resolved in a way that I am proud of.
10. A time when Transforming Power played a part in resolving a problem or healing a relationship of mine with someone of the opposite gender.
11. Qualities I would want in the woman/man that I would want my child to marry.

Forgiveness
1. A time I felt most hurt by someone I trusted.
2. A way I have of dealing with personal hurts.
3. An experience from my childhood when I felt forgiven.
4. Something for which I have a hard time forgiving myself or others.
5. Something I am most afraid of in myself or another.
6. Something I have been able to let go of.
7. Something I become defensive about.
8. Something for which I have forgiven myself.
9. When I feel guilty about something, I ...
10. The difference between accepting a wrong and forgiving someone is ...
11. For me, the thing(s) that have to happen before I can forgive is (are) ...
12. When I need to forgive, I can be open to Transforming Power by ...

Identity – My Self
1. A time I did something I needed to do for myself even though I felt some fear.
2. A time I needed someone to take care of me.
3. A time I took care of someone else.
4. A time I lost someone I cared about.
5. When I think about dying, I feel ...
6. If I thought I had a short time to live, the most important thing to me would be ...
7. I have a secret wish that is.
8. One thing I have done I am most proud of.
9. My greatest regret is.
10. As a child, I most enjoyed doing.
11. Now, I most enjoy doing by myself.
12. Think of a person or object that is important in your life and ask the following question(s): What do I receive from _____? What do I give to _____?

Fear
1. A time I was scared or afraid.
2. A time someone was afraid of me.
3. Something I am most afraid of in myself or others.
4. Something I was scared of before I grew up.
5. A time someone helped me with fear.
6. A way I react when I feel threatened by another person.
7. A time I did the right thing even though I felt some fear.
8. A way I am able to take care of myself when I am frightened.
9. Something I do to build up my self-confidence.
10. A time when I discovered my fear was truly a "paper tiger."
11. A time when my fear led me along an inappropriate path—what I did to resolve it.
12. A fear that has saved me.

Transforming Power
1. A time I resolved what might have become a violent situation with a non-violent solution.
2. What are the most important things for me to keep in mind if I want to avoid violence.
3. One thing I do to focus on the humanity in my opponent is... .
4. Ways I can help others to avoid violence.
5. I know Transforming Power is present and working in me when... .

Note:
See Gatherings for many more topics.

CONCENTRIC CIRCLES AS A LISTENING/REFLECTING EXERCISE
A Variation

Purpose: To use the Concentric Circle process to enhance listening skills and build community.
For a second level workshop, this exercise could be used to have participants gain insights from one another on the focus topic(s) for the workshop.

Time: 35 minutes (approximately 7-8 minutes for each pairing.)

Materials: None
See "Concentric Circles Topics" for topics.

Sequence:
1. Divide the participants into two groups: either two facing lines or an outer circle facing in, and an inner circle facing out.
2. The 3,2,1 process is the same as the one outlined in Active Listening in the Basic Manual:

   - The speaker gets 3 minutes to speak;
   - the listener has 2 minutes to reflect back what s/he heard;
   - the speaker gets 1 minute to clarify or correct what s/he said.

   The partners then switch roles, and the listener speaks on the same topic. At the conclusion, and before changing partners, the partners get one minute to share something they found in common (or not) and acknowledge, affirm or thank each other.
   Note:
   It adds to the experience if you have partners shake hands and give their adjective names before they begin speaking.

3. The inner circle moves to the right (several places, perhaps) and to new partners for a new topic.
4 Bring the participants back to a large circle for processing.

Processing:
What have you heard or learned which may have given you a different perspective on something?

CONSENSUS: BEAN JAR

Purpose: To show that group resources together are usually superior to those of an individual. To use consensus as a process to reach group decisions.

Time: 40 minutes.

Materials:
- A transparent plastic jar of beans or hard candy, previously counted (at least several hundred or more) and the correct count taped to the bottom of the jar.
- A newsprint comparative chart on which to record answers at different stages of the exercise.
- Paper and pencils for all participants.
- Enough copies of the handout to this exercise to give one copy to each pair.

Sequence:
1. Distribute paper and pencils. Instruct the participants that they are to determine the number of beans in the jar. Jar is placed on a table in the center of the circle of participants. They may come up close to the table, but they may not touch the jar. This is to be done independently and in silence. Each person is to record an answer on his/her sheet of paper.
2. When all have written answers, the facilitator will record them on newsprint. Call attention to the lowest and highest numbers.
3. Put participants in pairs. "Now you and your partner are to use consensus in reaching a decision on how many beans are in the jar. Consensus is not easy to reach. Here are some guidelines." Distribute Handout: Consensus (Definition and Guidelines). Discuss them. Ask if there are any questions.
4. When pairs have reached decision, facilitator records answers. (Comment on range of answers.)
5. Form pairs into groups of four and proceed as before. Facilitator records.
6. Form groups of eight and proceed as before. Facilitator records.
7. Facilitator records final answers, comments on differences in lists, range. etc. Facilitator gives actual number of beans.
   Note:
   If time is limited, do individuals, then groups of three. then groups of eight.

Processing:

- Did the groups work together? What (who) helped? What (who) hindered?
- How were decisions made? Were they made by consensus? (Refer to Guidelines if needed).
- Were there feelings of satisfaction when the groups worked together?
- At what point were decisions easier to reach by consensus? (Groups of two, four. six. eight, etc.) Explore answers in which the group was closer to the correct answer than were individuals. How was the answer reached?
- Explore answers in which an individual was closer to the correct answer than the group. Why? Did the individual fail to convince the group?

HANDOUT

CONSENSUS
(Definition and Guidelines)

CONSENSUS: DEFINITION

What It Is **Not**

- It is not agreement by vote, coin-flip, or bargaining
- It is not a fast procedure
- It is not arguing for your ranking or changing your mind to avoid conflict
- It is not a win/lose

What It **Is**

- It is agreement by discussions, with everyone's views taken into account
- It is slow and time-consuming
- It is listening, responding, being open and seeking out differences
- It is a new way of thinking

The final product is potentially more complete than individual knowledge.

GUIDELINES FOR CONSENSUS

1. Avoid arguing for your own judgment. Approach the task on the basis of logic, and be willing to change your mind if other group members have persuasive reasons for change.

2. Avoid changing your mind only in order to reach agreement and avoid conflict. Support only answers with which you are able to agree somewhat, at least.

3. Avoid techniques such as majority vote, averaging, or trading in reaching a decision.

4. Understand that differences in opinion are helpful rather than hindrances in decision-making. New and better ideas for solving a common problem will arise from a discussion of the differences.

CONSENSUS: FIVE EXERCISE PROCESS

Purpose: This is an ordered group of five exercises, to prepare participants in a Second Level Workshop to come to consensus smoothly.
Note:
Do not use the word "consensus" until after the completion of the work in the Consensus Flower exercise.

Time: About three hours for the entire sequence.

Materials: Flip chart or newsprint & thick markers of different colors for the group to write down their own guidelines, letter-size paper and pens for use in "in common," a sealed clear jar of beans of any sort, enough colorful pictures (at least three per participant) preferably laminated and covering a wide variety of images, Consensus Flower.

Sequence:

1) **Guidelines:** are formed and agreed upon by the Participants. The facilitators leave the area and wait until the group calls them back in. Facilitators can then discuss the phrasing in the guidelines to clarify what the group means by certain guideline. This is so the facilitator also can adhere to the agreed Guidelines — if needed these can be reviewed anytime during the workshop, by the facilitators or group as a whole.

2) **In Common:** done as usual. The final list is best written down on a newsprint and displayed as part of the sheets that are put up during the workshop. Facilitators can encourage and contribute additions as the workshop progresses and when something that is in common is noticed — for instance, if everyone breaks into a laugh, a facilitator might say "we all enjoy a good laugh, maybe we can add this to our list!"

3) **Consensus Bean Jar:** done as usual — except it is worthwhile that even the facilitation team DOES NOT know the number of beans in the jar.

4) **Picture selection:** Spread out the pictures usually used for Picture Sharing in the center of the circle with two or three times as many pictures as there are Participants.

    Follow the Bean Jar process with the pictures. Start with each participant choosing one (or possibly two) from the floor. Then, put them into pairs; the pairs are to choose one of the ones selected by them as individuals. Put the pairs into groups of four. after the four have selected one picture, join the fours into 8's (or as close to 8's as the group size will allow) to again choose one picture. Finally, combine the 8's into the whole group, and ask them to come to agreement on one of the pictures to become the choice of the entire group.

    Emphasize that this is not to be a voting contest. It is intended to be a process that will allow each person to freely have his/her say as an equal among peers, without "strong-arming," electioneering or pressure from others (or self) to "go along for the group's sake."

When the group has made its selection of one picture, commend them for their work and for the way they carried on that work. Part of that might be to have the group stand in a circle, face right and pat each in front of them on the shoulder, saying, "Good work! Good work, mate!" Then face full around to the left and give that new partner, now in front and not behind, the same comment.

5) ***Consensus Flower:*** Divide the group in whatever way works into eleven subgroups. 1 or 2 in a group is OK, as is a combination of 1's and 2's. Ask each pair to consider how the concept or word that is written on its "flower petal" contributed to the group coming to an agreement on everything that had occurred since they started with the forming of the Guidelines. Ask them to share with the entire group the conclusions they reached.

   After giving the group about five minutes for their deliberations have volunteers come forward, lay their "petal" down in the center of the circle, share with the group what that "petal" says, and continue on with results of their thinking. As the "petal" supply grows, the facilitator can start to arrange them in the circle around the open center, until the circle is closed with all eleven petals in place.

   Add the center piece, to complete the Flower.

   At this point introduce the word consensus, saying that consensus is the heart of the AVP method of coming to decisions, that it brings into the process everyone "as an equal among peers." With consensus there is no opportunity for a disgruntled minority, who had been outvoted, nor for a person to feel that they had been "strong-armed" by someone who was louder, bigger or more dominant — that it takes all of the concepts and attributes displayed in the "petals" for the consensus process to fully work. It is important that the participants recognize that each member of the group was actively adhering to the concepts represented by the Consensus Flower.

   Note:
   > This method is a different approach from traditional AVP workshops, developed by very experienced facilitators. It may be interesting to observe that this is the way AVP does its own decision-making, on facilitation teams and at every other level - it is at the heart of the AVP process. Going through these sequential steps can lead participants to the point where they may smoothly come to consensus on the focus topic for the workshop.
   >
   > This process works best when there is some break time space (such as lunch or overnight) between ending the "Flower" portion of the sequence and starting to look directly at the focus topic for the workshop.

Handout

CONSENSUS FLOWER

Consensus Flower Template

Draw a circle with a radius of 10". Inside that circle, trace another with a radius of 3.5"

Cut out the center circle and label with the words: **CONSENSUS PROCESS**

Use the template to divide the remaining ring into **11 FLOWER PETALS**.

Color petals as desired.

Label each petal with one of the following:

RESPECT	**SELF-EMPOWERMENT**	**UNITY OF PURPOSE**
COOPERATION	**ACTIVE PARTICIPATION**	**COMMITMENT TO THE**
NONVIOLENCE	**CONFLICT RESOLUTION**	**GROUP**
TRUST	**EQUAL ACCESS TO POWER**	
PATIENCE		

D-46 Flower Petal Template

CONSENSUS: PERFECT DAY

Purpose: To develop an appreciation of the consensus process.

Time: 30 minutes.

Materials: None.

Sequence:
1. Ask participants to think of what they would consider a perfect day.
   - What would they do?
   - Who would be with them?
   - Where would they go?

2. Then get in pairs and share their "perfect day" with their partner. After listening, each pair will, by consensus, come up with what feels to both of them to be a description of a "perfect day."

3. Then pairs will join with another pair to form groups of four, and each group will share and come up with a "perfect day" for their group.

4. Continue to get into larger groups as time allows, eventually coming up with one "perfect day" for the entire group.

CONSENSUS: PICTURE SHARING

Purpose: To experience consensus.

Time: 30 minutes.

Materials: Pictures, mounted in plastic jackets for handing around.
The facilitators should prepare a selection of pictures, protected and mounted for passing around. Some of these pictures will be very specifically related to certain themes; others will relate to several possible themes.

(Anger and fear can be shown by photos of angry or fearful people and animals; power can be evoked by photos of people working together, people grown old and strong through struggle and pain. Some nature pictures should always be included — natural phenomena such as mountains, rivers and their canyons, trees clinging to barren cliffs, whatever. Use your imagination.)

The preparation and selection of the pictures is a part of the preparation that each person and facilitator may find useful in getting ready for the workshop. A large core group of suitable pictures may be found in many places. Good sources are Natural History magazine, Smithsonian magazine, and National Geographic magazine. A CD with 190 suitable pictures is available from the AVP Distribution Service.

Sequence:
1. Have each participant choose a picture, and then ask participants to sit in pairs. Have the partners describe the feelings and meanings of the picture to each other. After both have discussed the pictures, each pair to is select and agree on only one picture.

2. Then join the pairs in groups of four and have them select one picture for their group of four. Repeat the process in groups of eight, and then repeat the process with the whole group, selecting only one picture for the workshop. (This picture might be posted during the workshop.)

Processing:
- How did you feel about giving up your picture?
- What did you learn about communication?
- What did you learn about group decision-making?
- What did you learn about conflict resolution?
- How does this exercise apply to your life?

CONSENSUS: SHORT EXERCISES

All of these are exercises in silent cooperation. They allow us to practice coming to consensus in a group, without talking, so that all can agree without any coercion from others. (Transforming Power confers the ability to enter in this way into a consensus with others.)

CONSENSUS OCTOPUS
Time: 15 minutes.

Materials: None.

Sequence:
1. Get people into small groups. Have each put out one hand into center and pile the hands one on top of another.
2. In silence, at the signal, the pile of hands is to move wherever the group wants and in any rhythm it wants: up, down, around. No one may coerce the others or lose contact. When the group feels ready, the movement will come to an end.

Processing:
Ask how it felt. Suggest analogies between this experience and other silent agreements. Ask how the power was experienced in the group. Did everyone have moments of giving a lead to the group? Were they aware of other people giving the lead? How did it feel?

FLAGPOLE (a.k.a. Broomstick)
Materials: Some kind of a pole or handle (broomstick, mop, plain pole) about four feet long.

Sequence:
1. Ask for six volunteers to work on the task in the center of the circle.
2. Give this group the pole or handle. Explain that this pole is a flagpole, and the group's task is to reach consensus on where to plant the flag, but without speaking at all. Each person in the group must keep both hands on the pole until s/he is satisfied with its location; when satisfied, s/he is to raise the right hand as evidence of this. The group may move around throughout the circle area, putting the pole down in different locations. Participants have five minutes to make their decision, which will be signaled when all right hands are raised. Ask if everyone understands, and answer any questions.
3. When ready, say "Go!" Stop the action when all have their right hands in the air, or at the end of five minutes, whichever comes first.
4. Have the participants sit in the center of the circle and share with everyone what they experienced. Ask what roles different participants took, what the process was, and how they felt during it and at the end of the task. If appropriate, point out the relationship between the exercise and the working of Transforming Power.
5. If time permits, repeat with another six volunteers so that more people can experience the silent consensus.

SECRET SPOT

Time: 15 minutes.

Materials: None.

Sequence:
No preliminary explanation of the exercise is necessary before proceeding to do it.
1. Form groups of four. The members of each group are to join hands in a circle. There is to be no talking.
2. Each member of the group has 30 seconds to silently pick out a secret spot in the room to which s/he would like to take the other members of the group.
3. At the signal, each member of the group silently influences the whole group to go to his/her secret spot.
4. Allow five minutes to do the exercise. Instruct participants not to break hands until the exercise is over.
5. Process the exercise: How did it feel? Did any group go to all four "Secret Spots"? How was this idea communicated?

CONSENSUS TRIANGLES

Purpose: To experience the consensus process while making a design.

Time: 30 minutes.

Materials: 3"x3"x3" posterboard triangles of six colors — enough for each person to have one set with each of the six colors (perhaps held together with a paper clip).

Sequence:
1. Explain that this exercise has two parts. In the first part, each person will work as an individual without talking. In the second part, people will work in small groups, and talking is allowed.

2. Form groups of 5 or 6. The groups needn't have the same number. Assign each group a workspace.

3. Explain that each person will receive a set of six different colored triangles. Without talking each person will use the triangles to make some kind of a design, in whatever fashion s/he wishes. If there are no questions, have them begin, reminding them to work in silence.

4. After two or three minutes, call time. Ask each group to have a "go-around" among its members. Each person will explain why s/he made the design that s/he did.

5. Next, the task of each group is this: Use all the triangles and come up with one design that represents the whole group.

6. Before coming back to the circle for processing, have everyone walk around to see all the designs. Ask them to return to the circle, staying with their group.

Processing:
- How did each group come up with the one design?
- Was it easy to reach your decision?
- Would anyone have liked to have more of a say?
- Did anyone say, "Well it's not what I want, but I can live with it?"
- How might we use consensus with family and friends? in work? other settings?

Note:
There may be a variety of results: one group may like one person's design and have each person copy it; a second group may take parts of each person's design and incorporate into a whole in some fashion; a third may create something entirely new. All are fine. The result is not as critical as the process.

CONSENSUS: USING TRANSFORMING POWER

Purpose: To practice using consensus in a practical, down-to-earth way. The facilitator of this exercise must be familiar with the consensus process and committed to it. Do not start this exercise when there is a high level of conflict or tension in the group, or, when the energy level is low.

Time: 90 minutes.

Materials: Newsprint and markers.

Sequence:
1. Begin by explaining that consensus is a nonviolent decision-making process, because underlying it is the assumption that every person participating in the process is of value, and together will come up with a better decision than we would if swayed by the apparent majority. (See Handout: Consensus — Definition and Guidelines, page D-43).
2. Explain the process: In consensus process, we may propose an idea, but we listen to all proposals without being attached to "our idea." The group usually combines elements of proposals in order to get the best outcome.
   Note: The facilitator may ask the group to focus on one idea at a time, listening carefully to the discussion and stating from time to time the agreement that s/he hears is forming, checking with the group to confirm that s/he hears correctly. If no agreement emerges, s/he asks those people who disagree with the majority to speak to their reasons for objecting. The idea is not to try persuade them that the majority proposal is better, but to give them additional information if they need it, or to modify the major proposal to address their concerns if possible. In this way the group moves to unanimous agreement — consensus.
   The introduction up to this point should take no more than ten minutes.
3. Ask for suggestions of ways that this workshop group could take some kind of practical action to promote Transforming Power in the prison or the community where they live. (You don't need very many of these as long as they are do-able and worth doing).
4. Ask the group to use the consensus process to reach agreement on one idea to discuss. At this point the group may very rapidly agree upon the idea they wish to discuss, in which case most of the exercise will focus on that discussion. However, in some groups they will spend most of their time discussing which idea to focus on. If this happens, don't try to rush them. Just help the process and respond to those who are concerned about time, or frustrated with failure to reach agreement, by stating "we are practicing consensus right now. This is learning."

   If the group is pulled among several different ideas, ask the proposer of each idea to speak to why this is the attractive idea to pursue. After each has spoken, ask those who have not spoken to speak about preferences. If most of the group seems to agree on one idea, ask those who represent a minority point of view what will be lost if the other idea is not pursued. Be open and attentive to the group combining ideas.
5. After they select an idea, ask them to discuss how they might carry it out. They may brainstorm or just discuss. And they may wish to have you record agreed-upon steps. They may just list possibilities or they may need to discuss potential steps to the point of consensus.

Note: Depending upon the idea chosen by the group, you may need to have them discuss the possible risks of their actions and how to minimize or avoid them. In prisons, they need to consider how they can do this within the confines of prison rules, or how not to run afoul of the prison administration, and the possible consequences of their proposed actions, both to them and to AVP. There have been many wonderful, creative, powerful projects taken on by prisoners promoting AVP and Transforming Power as a result of this exercise.

CONSENSUS: YOU HAVE TO HAVE A HEART
(Can also be used as a Values Exercise)

Purpose: To have an experience of consensus; to clarify values.

Time: 45 minutes.

Materials: Paper and pencils; sheets with the patient's names and descriptions, or newsprint posting of descriptions.

Sequence:
1. Pass out paper and pencils and sheets with descriptions of the patients to the participants (or, post the descriptions).

2. Give instructions: "You are one of the members of the City Hospital's Judicial Board and must make a crucial decision as to which of five patients on a waiting list will receive the first artificial heart. Each has a serious heart disease. Individually, you must assign priority numbers to the five patients: 1 = first in line to 5 = last in line. Then, after each person has made a priority list, the Judicial Board will meet."

3. Have participants make their individual rankings.

4. Get participants into groups or four or five and explain: "Your group represents a Judicial Board of the hospital. You must work together to come to consensus and finalize the priority ranking of 1 to 5. The rule is, before you can express your opinion, you must validate the thoughts and feelings of another member, even if they are different from yours."

5. After each group has come to consensus, have them report back to the larger group.

Processing:
- What was this process like?
- Did you find yourself agreeing to very different rankings after you heard the reasoning of other people?
- How does this apply to nonviolence?
- Which Transforming Power Guide(s) relate to this experience?

HANDOUT

YOU HAVE TO HAVE A HEART

The Patients:

George Mutti	Age 61. Occupation: suspected Mafia involvement. Married, 7 children, extremely wealthy, will donate a very large sum to the hospital after the operation.
Peter Santos	Age 23. Occupation: "B" average student Single, studies hard, helps support poor family, aspires to be a policeman when he graduates.
Ann Doyle	Age 45. Occupation: housewife Widow, supports 3 children, small income, no savings.
Johnny Jaberg	Age 35. Occupation: famous actor Divorced, wife has custody of 2 children, donates to create shelters for the homeless.
Howard Wilkinson	Age 55. Occupation: state senator married, one child, recently elected, financially well off.

GUIDELINES FOR CONSENSUS:

- Avoid arguing for your own judgment. Approach the task on the basis of logic, and be willing to change your mind if the other group members have persuasive reasons for change.

- Avoid changing your mind only in order to reach agreement and avoid conflict. Support only answers with which you are able to agree somewhat, at least.

- Avoid techniques such as majority vote, averaging, or trading in reaching a decision.

- Understand that the differences in opinion are helpful rather than a hindrance in decision-making. From discussion of the differences will arise new and better ideas for solving a common problem.

CONTRACT WITH SELF FOR FUTURE

Purpose: To crystallize values of participants and what they intend to act on; to help them define their personal goals for future guidance.

Time: 60 minutes.

Materials: Paper and pencil for all.

Sequence:
1. Explain to participants that whatever they write is for their own information only, to be kept for their frequent reference and use. If they want to share anything, that's completely voluntary.

2. Ask them to write on paper:

   a) The things in life which they value most and are determined to act upon.

   b) Under the following categories, list the goals and the strategy or steps they plan to follow to achieve their goals:
      - Spiritual growth
      - Money management
      - Education
      - Health and fitness
      - Vocation or work
      - Social commitment:
        - to society
        - to support system (family, friends, etc.)

   c) Go back to a). If there are any values which have not been addressed in b), include them at this point.

Processing:
- Ask how they are feeling about what they wrote.
- Discuss the purpose of selecting a partner for periodic evaluation. If it seems feasible, have them choose such partners.
- Discuss what use might be made of their contract.

CROSSOVER

Purpose: To look at similarities and differences in our life experiences and at the prejudices/stereotypes we may have about the categories mentioned. (Can be a community builder, but watch out for emotional reactions to sensitive questions.)

Time: 30 minutes (take less time for reflection for a young group.)

Materials: A list of 10 - 12 descriptions that are appropriate for your group. (suggestions below)

Sequence:
1. Ask the group to stand in a row across one wall. Have enough space for some to cross to the other side of the room and feel separated from the initial group.
2. Say: " I will read a number of descriptions. If the description is true for you as you define it, please cross over to the other side of the room. Even though the description is true, you may, at any time, choose not to move. Simply stay where you are, but think about that decision and what it means to you. Please keep a respectful silence during the exercise."
3. Start describing: Please cross over if you were ... After people have crossed say, "Look carefully at who is in your group, those who share this experience with you. Consider quietly, any surprises?"
4. Say to those who did not move. " Observe who crossed over and who is left on your side. While keeping a respectful silence, consider how it feels to be on your side with these particular people."
5. To those who moved , " Look across the room at those who did not cross over. Who is still there? Where are most of the people? Just think about it."
6. Say, "Take a moment to get a good sense of what this (description) or (group) means to you in your life. Would you change things if you could?"
7. Is anyone alone? What is it like to be the only one of your group?
8. Ask the first group to please cross back over.
9. Continue to consider categories as above, working from easy to difficult.

Processing:
- What happened? What feelings came up?
- Any particular reactions about either moving or staying?
- Did you learn something new about anyone? Were you surprised (without pinpointing any individual)?
- Did you choose not to move any time? Can you say what feelings came up about that decision?
- Did you notice anything about the categories, a common thread?

Note:
Be sensitive to the group. Remind everyone of the importance of confidentiality.

When using many of the categories relating to fights and weapons, it is wise to end with some of the positive categories involving nonviolence. This is particularly true for younger participants.

It is possible that some participants may wish to respond to some of the questions asked in the course of doing the exercise. Try to go with the flow and do what you think best meets the needs of the participants. If you have people respond, you may have to remind others to be mindful of keeping a respectful silence when someone is responding.

Possible General Descriptions:
Please cross over if you...

- were an only/oldest/youngest/middle child.
- had 5, 6, or more children in your family.
- had no siblings of the same sex as you.
- were born/raised in the South.
- were born outside the United States.
- were raised in a rural area.
- were raised on a farm.
- were raised in a working class environment.
- were raised in a family with ample economic resources.
- were raised in a family where money caused you stress.
- were raised as Polish, or other Eastern European.
- were raised as African, African-American, or Caribbean.
- were raised as European (Italian/French/German/Irish/English.)
- were raised as Latino/Latina.
- were raised as Asian.
- were raised as Jewish.
- were raised as indigenous/native person/Native-American.
- were raised as WASP (White Anglo-Saxon Protestant).
- were raised as a minority of any kind
- were raised by one parent.
- were raised by a family member other than a parent, e.g. a grandparent.
- are or have been a single parent.
- lived in a home where there was a problem with alcohol or drugs.
- lived in a home where there was physical, verbal or sexual harassment.
- lived in a foster home.
- at one time had or now have a physical, emotional or psychological disability.
- are a person who ran away from home.
- are not or have not been on speaking terms with a family member.
- were ever labeled or assumed to be gay.

Possible Description Pertaining to Fights and Weapons
("seen" means "seen with your own two eyes" [no hype])
Please cross over if you...

- have seen a fight.
- have seen a fight where blood was drawn or someone was stabbed/shot.
- have been in a fight.
- have started a fight.
- have been goaded (persuaded) to fight by someone else.
- have stabbed someone.
- have shot someone.
- have had a friend or family member hurt by physical violence.
- have been hurt by physical violence.
- have hurt someone else physically.

Possible Descriptions Pertaining to Nonviolence
Please cross over if you...

- have been tempted to fight but didn't.
- have talked someone else out of fighting.
- have been talked out of fighting.
- wish someone had talked you out of fighting.

DEALING WITH PUT-DOWNS

Purpose: To get in touch with past experiences of devaluation and hurt. This exercise, using the Sculpting format, is a powerful exercise, which can reach a deep emotional level in the group. Do not be use this exercise just for variety, because it does focus on buried negative experiences. Even seemingly detached groups have experienced a breakthrough. Never use it in a Basic Workshop.

Time: 30 to 60 minutes.

Materials:
1. Index cards and pens/pencils.
2. Four cards, with one each of the following phrases in large print:
   - I am stupid.
   - I can't succeed.
   - No one loves me.
   - I don't exist.

Sequence:
1. Have the group sit in a circle and explain the following:
   "This is called a sculpture exercise. We will do this in complete silence. I will hand a card to each of the two persons on my left and on my right. The four participants will read to themselves the phrase on their cards, and think of a pose to demonstrate that phrase, to show us what it looks/feels like. After a few seconds, I will ask them to strike their poses and hold up their cards so the whole group can read them. We will observe their sculptures for a short time (not longer than 30 seconds). Then I will move on to the next four persons and go around the circle until we have all had the opportunity to share a pose. After the whole group has posed, we'll have an opportunity to talk about what we have experienced."
2. Follow the pattern described above, in silence.

Processing:
Getting feelings out and forgiveness should be discussed first.
- What feelings did this exercise bring up for you?
- How did you feel being that character?
- What did you learn about put-downs?
- Here in the safety of this group, what can you say to the people who might have put you down?
- How did it feel to tell your feelings to these people?
- Does this help you to forgive anyone who has put you down?
- How does understanding our feelings relate to Transforming Power?

Note:
This exercise should be carefully and thoroughly debriefed because of the emotions that may have been stirred up. Some might mention that this has focused on the negative instead of the positive. Empathy is built up within the group.

3. Closing Counterpose.
   The position of our bodies affects our emotions. Have participants stand with faces to the sky and arms out to the side with an upward orientation and say the phrase from the cards all together as a group. Direct the group to come up with and say the opposite of their phrase, e.g., "No one loves me," to "EVERYBODY LOVES ME!!!"

Variations:
1. "When My Family Expressed Anger,"
   - Who would care if I am hurt?
   - It's all my fault.
   - I did something wrong again.
   - Nobody cares if I'm here.
   - I'm all alone.

2. Another variation is to have each participant write on a card one statement which was a put-down. Gather them together, shuffle and hand them out. Everyone goes round the circle and demonstrates their pose, in silence. The cards are then passed along the circle, say five places, and the process repeated with a different statement.

Note:
Follow this exercise with an Affirmation Pyramid or some other healing exercise.

DEFINITIONS

Purpose: To help participants focus on their own sense of dignity, self-respect and self-esteem; to empower and clarify how to make choices.

Time: 30 minutes.

Materials: Paper and pencils.

Sequence:
1. Pass out paper and pencils. Tell participants that they will be asked to write down their own best short definition of the following:
    the word DIGNITY, the term SELF-RESPECT, the term SELF-ESTEEM, the word VICTIM, the word CHOICE. (It may help to post these words.)

2. In groups of three or four, have each member share his/her definition of DIGNITY. Have the group discuss the differences in their definitions. (Allow about two minutes for this.) Repeat with SELF-RESPECT and then SELF-ESTEEM.

3. Have the groups discuss similarities and differences among the three terms (allow about 2-4 minutes for this.)

4. Have members share their definitions of the word VICTIM (Allow 2-4 minutes). Repeat with the word CHOICE.

5. Have members of the groups discuss the benefits and disadvantages of being a VICTIM.

6. Have participants discuss the benefits and disadvantages of being able to make CHOICES. (Be sure they include in their discussion the relationship between accepting a "VICTIM" image for oneself, and the capacity to make CHOICES.)

7. Process in the large group.

Processing:
- Did you find yourself thinking differently about these words after the discussion in your small group?
- What is it about yourself that gives you your strongest sense of dignity, self-respect and self-esteem?
- What is it about your sense of dignity, self-respect and self-esteem that can help you not to react violently, especially if you feel disrespected?
- How does the ability to make choices relate to Transforming Power?

DISSOLVING ANGER

Purpose: To demonstrate that when we are having angry thoughts, the awareness of our body sensations can help dissolve the anger. Anger can be described as a combination of thoughts and body sensations. For example when someone yells at us, we might have the thought "I might get hurt", and in our body we have sweaty palms and tense muscles.

Time: 30 minutes.

Materials: None.

Sequence:
1. Divide participants into pairs.
2. Say: "Close your eyes and notice any sensations in your body (e.g. neck, throat, chest, head, leg) and describe the sensations to your partner." After a few seconds, ask them to open their eyes.
3. Say: "Think of a situation or a person that you are angry about. In a moment I will ask one of you to tell your partner about the situation or person for 2-3 minutes. Then I will call 'stop' and ask you to bring your attention back to your body's sensations. Decide who will go first."
4. Say: "Whoever has volunteered to speak, tell your partner about the situation or person with whom you are or were angry. Try to feel the anger as you speak. Use as much emotion as possible." Allow 2-3 minutes for this.
5. Call "stop" and ask: "Would the person who is talking please close your eyes and once again bring your attention to any body sensations. Describe these body sensations to your partner."
6. Instruct the person who was talking to: "Talk to your partner as though s/he were the person you were angry with." Allow 2-3 minutes and repeat step 5 above.
7. Now, ask the person who was listening to talk and repeat the instructions in steps 4-5 above.

Processing:
- What happened and what did you feel as you described the situation to your partner?
- What did you notice about your body's sensations as you talked with your partner as though s/he were the person with whom you were angry? Was there any change?
- What body sensations did you become aware of?
- Did they get more or less intense when you talked about the situations?
- When did you become aware of your body?
- What happened when you talked to your partner as if s/he were the person you were angry with?
- Do you think this awareness of the changes in your body would help in real-life situations?
- How does this relate to Transforming Power?

DOTS

Purpose: To get participants to understand how we silently communicate our identification with the groups to which we belong, while at the same time we reject those who don't belong. (In-Group/Out-Group.)

Time: 30 minutes.

Materials: Approximately 5 sets of round stickers of assorted colors. (These can be bought at stationery and office supply stores, or improvised using newsprint, marking pens and masking tape.)
Note: People who have read or observed this exercise previously should be asked not to participate in it, as their foreknowledge may prevent the intended experience of rejection and isolation from happening.

Sequence:
Preparation: Get stickers ready to place on the foreheads of the participants.
   a) Select one to three individuals (depending on group size) who will each receive a sticker of a different color from that of anyone else in the room.
   b) Excepting these unique individuals, make sure that there are at least two, and up to five, people in the room who share the same colors.

1. Have the group close their eyes. Explain that you are going to walk around the room and place a sticker on the forehead of each participant.

2. Place stickers on the foreheads of participants. Vary the size of color groups (e.g., 2 greens, 4 reds, 5 blues).

3. Have the participants open their eyes and tell them: "Without talking, arrange yourselves as you think best." Explain that they may assist others but they may not speak. When all have found and joined their groups, there should be only the one, two or three individuals with a unique colored dot who are still trying to identify with a group.

4. Once it is clear to those people that they do not belong to any group, have everyone sit back down and begin debriefing. Explore the feelings of whoever did not belong, as well as the feelings of those who did. Point out that it was never stated that you couldn't let others become a part of your group; then ask if it occurred to anyone to invite the "different" person into their group. Or perhaps someone may have wanted to break off from their own group and form a group with the "different" person.

5. Try to relate this experience to how it applies to our everyday interactions with others, both within and outside of our groups

Processing:
- How did you find your group?
- How did you feel when you found your group?
- Of the ones who were unique, how did you feel when you couldn't find your group?
- How did you resolve the issue of where you belonged?
- What does this have to do with real life?
- Did it occur to anyone to invite the different ones into your group? Why? Why not?
- How can the existence of different groups lead to violence?
- When are groups good and when are they harmful?
- What is good about belonging to a group?
- How does this relate to Transforming Power?

EMPATHY

Purpose: To enlarge understanding of the problems of others and to give help in solving them. To experience what one's own problem looks like seen through the eyes of others. To experience the wisdom of the group aiding with each person's problem. To become aware of common threads in all of our experiences.

Time: 60 minutes.

Materials: Index or file cards and writing instruments for each participant.

Sequence:
1. Divide the group into small groups of no more than 5 persons each. Provide each person with a file card or index card and a writing instrument.

2. Ask everyone to write on their card, "A problem I'm working on is ... " and to finish the sentence. The cards are not to be signed. Once written, they are collected, shuffled, and redistributed at random within the small group. (If in the redistribution, a person receives back his/her own card, this is to be exchanged with someone else's so that each participant has someone else's problem to deal with.)

3. Each person then reads to the group the card that s/he has received in the redistribution, reading it as if it were his/her own problem. S/he then explains it to the group, perhaps including ways s/he thinks of to solve it. Others then give their own experience with solving that sort of problem, and their own suggestions. It is crucial for each "solver" to read the problem as if it is his/her own in order to avoid giving advice and focus instead on empathy. For example, "The way I have worked on solving this problem is...."

4. Repeat this process until every problem raised in the small group has been dealt with by the group.

Processing:
- What was it like to put yourself in someone else's shoes and describe the problem as your own?
- What was it like to hear someone talk about your problem?
- Did you start to think differently about your own problem?
- How does this relate to Transforming Power?

Note:
Give plenty of time to this exercise. For many, it becomes the heart of the workshop. It can be a turning point for a person who had been isolated and not understood.

ESCALATOR

Purpose: To practice analyzing conflict situations, looking for the feelings, values, self-image which may be behind a person actions.
To use this understanding to find alternative responses in conflict situations.

Time: 20 to 30 minutes. (If you are using it as a sample, then cut discussion in order to keep it moving, explaining to the participants that you are only having them practice with this story and that they will be using their own stories to work on.)

Materials: Prepare ahead of time:
1. A sample story of no more than 7 or 8 steps in which the conflict between two people steadily increases. (You don't have to give the outcome; in fact, you may want the participants to predict the outcome.)
2. A large sheet (you may tape sheets of newsprint together) on which you have drawn an escalator with at least the number of steps needed for your story. Make the steps shallow and wide so that you have enough room above and below to write. Write the steps in the conflict above the step line.

Sequence:
Suggested Introduction:
Say, "In this exercise we are going to analyze some conflict situations. We will look at the kinds of behavior that escalate, or increase, conflict and the kinds of behavior that de-escalate, or decrease, conflict. We are going to look behind what an individual says or does in order to understand why that individual might be speaking or acting the way s/he is. We tend to judge what we see and hear, yet there are feelings and needs behind what a person says and does, and we need to learn to look for them. The more we understand the why behind a person's behavior, the more options we have for de-escalating a conflict situation."

Using The Sample Story And Chart:
1. Read your story, pointing out the steps in the conflict as written on the sheet.
2. Ask the audience to brainstorm what the participants might be feeling or needing at each step. Write these (in shortened version) underneath each step.
3. Ask at what points a change in behavior could have sent the parties down the escalator. (Make arrows pointing to those times and write the suggestions for alternative behavior someplace underneath the feelings/needs.)

Processing:
Which of the Transforming Power guidelines have been used in the suggestions given for de-escalating that conflict?

A Sample Escalator Story

Dave and Jim are sitting in English class at a time the class is supposed to be reading their assignment silently. Dave is the co-captain of the football team, which has finished with a winning season. Dave is not doing a spring sport, although he works out regularly in the weight training room in preparation for spring football practice. Jim is the co-captain of the baseball team, which so far this spring has a 2 and 8 losing season. Jim is the starting catcher, and sometimes pitches. His hitting has been poor this season, far behind his record last year as a junior.

Dave, who is sitting behind Jim, begins to kick Jim's chair. Jim turns around and says in an irritated tone, "Cut it out!" Dave kicks the chair again, Jim turns around and says, "I said, cut it out, A-hole!" Dave retorts, "F - you, A - hole, you can even hit a baseball!" Jim does not respond, but pretends to read as he notices the teacher get up. Dave mutters, loudly enough for everyone to hear, "Call me an A - hole and I'll kick your butt!" Jim, red-faced and furious, gets up, turns around to face Dave, and says "You got something to say to me you say it to my face!"

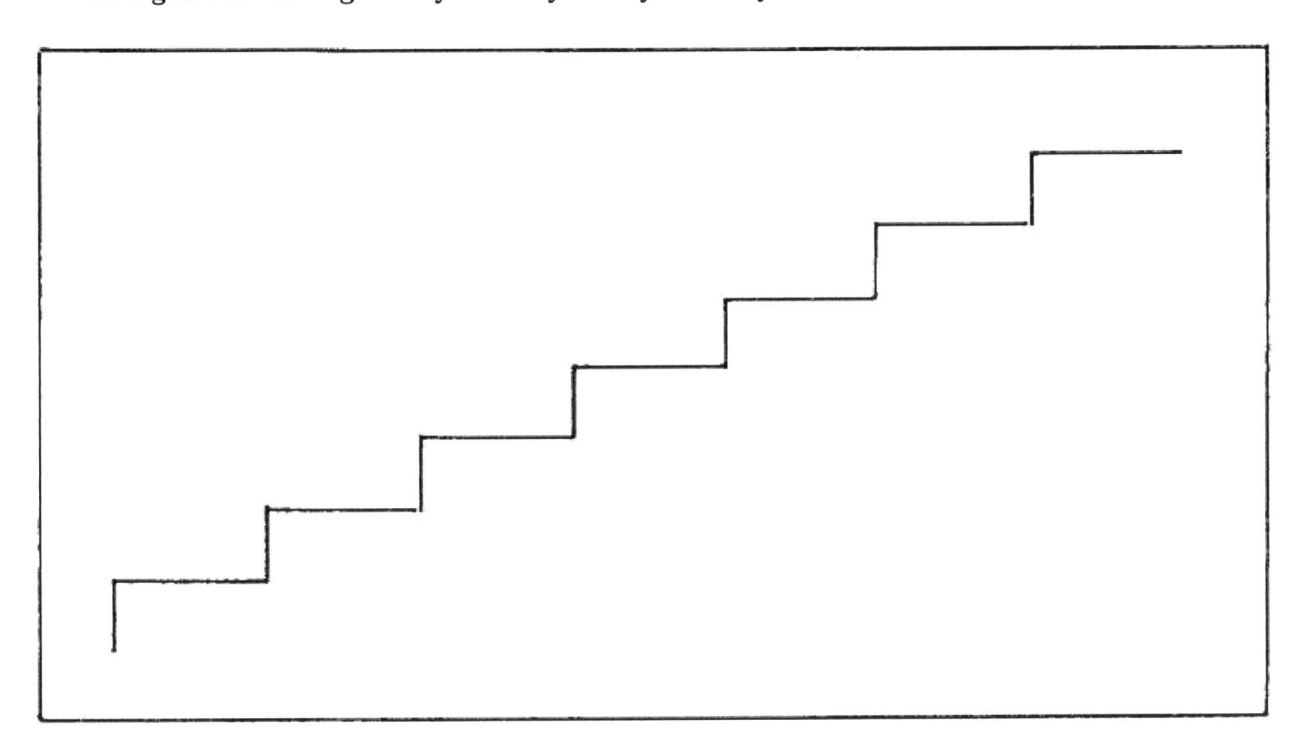

Note: The steps in the escalation are what happened and not the listeners evaluations of what happened. The steps are –
1. Dave kicks the chair.
2. Jim says cut it out (He could have assumed it was a mistake and spoken differently to Dave).
3. Dave kicks again.
4. Jim name-calls.
5. Dave name-calls and insults Jim's skill
6. Dave threatens Jim.
7. Jim confronts Dave with a dare.

Remind the audience that in this case the goal is not to punish the two (you might ask if suspending the two boys would resolve the conflict — most people realize that it would just send the conflict out of the classroom), but rather to resolve the conflict so there is no fight either in the classroom or later.

Using Conflicts Shared In Small Groups For Analysis

If you want to have the participants come up with their own stories, shorten the discussion of your sample. Have the participants suggest the needs or feelings behind each action, and then have them suggest steps where someone might have behaved differently had s/he known what was really going on in the other person's head. But then, organize them into groups of no more than four to share conflict stories for their own escalator exercise.

1. Share stories of conflict situations.
2. Choose one that the group decides would be a helpful one to practice analyzing escalation.
3. Choose someone to write a list of the steps as the group breaks down the conflict into steps.
4. Decide which steps (or behaviors) escalated the conflict and which ones de-escalated the conflict. The recorder should mark all the steps on his/her list.
5. After your group has made these decisions, draw your escalator on the large paper in the shape that will illustrate the escalation/de-escalation, and write the behavior/action above each step.
6. Select someone(s) to present the story to the group and conduct the analysis using the steps in the escalator diagram.

Note:

Once the groups have started, facilitators can create large sheets by taping newsprint sheets together. Give a large sheet and marker to groups only after they have completed steps 1-4.

After the small groups have finished, bring them back into a large group to conduct the analysis.

Facilitators might need to help the participant leading the analysis to move it along so that people don't get bored. At the end of the audience response, you might ask if the person who owned the conflict story would like to respond to the analysis. (But do not require the disclosure of the person's identity.) It is very important to affirm the work of each small group at the end of its report.

ESCALATOR VARIATION — ANGER

Purpose: To develop an understanding of the stages of anger and develop methods of de-escalating.
Time: 45 minutes
Materials: Large flip chart or black/whiteboard, three different colored markers, pencils, Handout: Stages of Anger Worksheet.
Draw the 6-step escalator diagram:

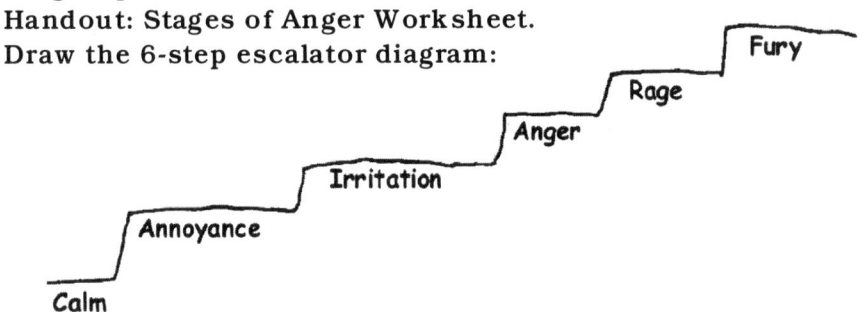

[Diagram: 6-step escalator rising from Calm → Annoyance → Irritation → Anger → Rage → Fury]

Sequence:
1. Ask for other words for each step (for example, "frustrated" "pissed off".)
2. Suggest a story of a conflict which escalates. See Escalator for a suggestion, or, let group brainstorm possible stories, and use "values voting" to quickly choose a story (see below*). Stress that this is not meant to be an actual event anyone has experienced. If the group is prepared for it, and if there's time, they may act it out.
3. Name the two people of the story. (write their names with 2 different colors). What's their relationship (family, boss/employee, friends etc.)? What are they doing at "calm"? Where are they?
4. Then for each step, ask the group:
   - What does one do that annoys the other? Using the color for that person write it under "annoyance."
   - What's the other's response? (If it is an escalation, write it under "irritation.")
5. Go up through all the steps until one or both characters are at "fury." Then, explain how, although sometimes steps may be skipped on the way up or down, we'll look at de-escalating this situation one step at a time.
   - At each step ask what each person could have done to have brought the conflict down instead of up. Write the answer for each one in their color above the diagram.
   - Then, use a third color and ask what an outsider or friend might do at that stage if they came upon the quarreling pair. Work all the way down the stairs.
6. Then, pass out Handout: Stages of Anger to each participant. Ask them to think about a time when they were in a situation where anger escalated. Then, ask them to use the escalator to show what happened to escalate the anger and at what points someone might have de-escalated the anger. Give about ten minutes for them to work on this on their own. When time is called, suggest that they might want to keep these and continue to work on them in their own time. Then ask for any ideas that people came up with for their own stages that were not originally shared in the earlier conflict story.

* Values Voting: After the group brainstorms several possible stories, let the participants vote on the story they wish to use. List each story, asking for votes on whether participants would like to see that story chosen. STRESS THAT PEOPLE MAY VOTE AS OFTEN AS THEY LIKE, choosing several stories they would like to see used. A clear sense of the favorites will probably emerge, with people less likely to feel like their choices were excluded.

Processing:
- What TP guidelines were helpful at each of the different stages of anger?

HANDOUT

STAGES OF ANGER WORKSHEET

For each stage, think of at least 3 things that you regularly experience that trigger that feeling.

Then think of things you can do to resolve or de-escalate each one.

STAGE OF ANGER

RESOLUTION OR DE-ESCALATION

ANNOYANCE

a. _____

b. _____

c. _____

a. _____

b. _____

c. _____

IRRITATION

a. _____

b. _____

c. _____

a. _____

b. _____

c. _____

ANGER

a. _____

b. _____

c. _____

a. _____

b. _____

c. _____

RAGE

a. _____

b. _____

c. _____

a. _____

b. _____

c. _____

FURY

a. _____

b. _____

c. _____

a. _____

b. _____

c. _____

ESCALATOR VARIATION — FEAR

Purpose: To develop an understanding of the stages of fear and develop methods of de-escalating; to give a good overview of the pathway into fear and the possible steps (there could be multiples at any level) that could be used to ease the tensions that otherwise build up.

Time: 30 minutes

Materials: Large flip chart or black/whiteboard, markers, pencils, Handout: Stages of Fear Worksheet.
Draw the 6-step escalator diagram:

```
                                            Terror
                                    Panic
                            Frightened
                    Anxious
           Apprehensive
    Calm
```

Sequence:
1. Brainstorm a story where fear escalates, or use the suggestion given below. Write the incidents on the upper side of each step as the progression goes along, with the corresponding level of emotion written just underneath that step.
2. In large group sharing, ask participants to brainstorm for each step what counter-measure the person might have used to deal more effectively with the different levels of fear.
3. Pass out Handout: Stages of Fear Worksheet and pencils. Give about ten minutes for them to work on this on their own. When time is called, suggest that they might want to keep these and continue to work on them in their own time.
4. Come back to the larger group and ask for sharing of ideas from the handout with the whole group.

Processing:
- Were you surprised to learn new ways to deal with fear?
- What guides to TP could be helpful in dealing with fear?

    Sample Fear Escalator Story: A Single Woman with Young Children
- Sandy" hears little whispers about an employee's performance at the workplace. She moves closer, distracted from her work, and then overhears insulting comments about herself. She becomes embarrassed and apprehensive.
- Over the next few weeks her colleagues openly criticize the way she goes about her job. She becomes anxious, and she sometimes forgets details in her work.
- On the next payday her immediate superior calls her and tells her that she may lose her job unless her work improves, and she becomes frightened. She begins to make mistakes.
- Before the next payday, she is given notice that she is fired. As a single mother with two young teenagers who are not old enough to work but still demand the expensive clothes and other things that their friends have, she panics.
- Weeks go by without her finding a job. She is tired and discouraged from the repeated rejections. The children become sullen and secretive, and she often answers the telephone to hear someone hang up. One day, while putting away clothes in their drawers, she discovers a bag with over $300 dollars in it. A flood of terror washes over her.

HANDOUT

STAGES OF FEAR WORKSHEET

For each stage, think of at least 3 things that you regularly experience that trigger that feeling.

Then think of things you can do to resolve or de-escalate each one.

STAGE OF FEAR

APPREHENSION
- a. _____
- b. _____
- c. _____

ANXIETY
- a. _____
- b. _____
- c. _____

FEAR
- a. _____
- b. _____
- c. _____

PANIC
- a. _____
- b. _____
- c. _____

TERROR
- a. _____
- b. _____
- c. _____

RESOLUTION OR DE-ESCALATION

- a. _____
- b. _____
- c. _____

- a. _____
- b. _____
- c. _____

- a. _____
- b. _____
- c. _____

- a. _____
- b. _____
- c. _____

- a. _____
- b. _____
- c. _____

EXPLORING THE ROOTS OF ANGER

Purpose: To gain insights on anger and its roots; in general, in ourselves, and in others.

Time: This is a focus unit of 3 sessions, each may take up to 60 minutes.

Materials: Newsprint, markers, paper, index cards and pencils or pens.

Sequence:

Session 1:

Brainstorm on Anger in General

1. Divide the participants into small groups. The individuals in the group are asked to state their immediate responses to the word "anger," and these responses are recorded on newsprint.
2. Back in the large group, have people compare these lists to:
   a) look for similarities and differences
   b) classify responses relating to anger in terms of
      - feelings
      - situations
      - actions
3. On the top of a fresh sheet of newsprint, draw a tree trunk and label it "Anger." Ask participants to identify the main roots that feed the "anger." Then draw the root, labeling each root with the words or phrases that were given to describe each root.

Session 2:

What lies at the root of our own anger? Explore this in four stages:

1. Pass out index cards and pencils. Ask participants to think of a particular situation about which they were feeling angry; one from the past will do if no current situation occurs to them. Ask them to record their responses on index cards. (They may write whole sentences, key words, or just quietly reflect on the questions asked.)
2. Share the idea that anger and hurt are often seen as two sides of the same coin.
3. Ask for a further response: Why am I angry about this? (A possible response: "I felt hurt because it seemed nobody valued my opinion.")
4. Now ask everyone to identify an unmet need that lies beneath the hurt they experienced (e.g."I needed to be respected by my colleagues.")
5. Now ask for people to identify a hidden fear alongside their need (e.g."I feared they would never respect me.")
6. Ask participants to share these responses in pairs, with partners helping each other answer any questions they may have found difficult.
7. All together, have people reflect on their experience of the exercise.

Note:

This exercise helps us to discover the hurt, needs and fears underlying a personal experience of anger. We could make a start by expressing those other emotions, rather than sticking with the anger. We thought it was an important step in facing the anger of others to understand what lies beneath our own anger. We could respond to the hurt, needs and fears of the other persons rather than focusing on their anger.

Session 3:

What lies at the root of the anger we receive from others'?
1. Divide into small groups.
2. Ask participants to think of a time when they faced someone else's anger. Then ask them to imagine what the hurt, unmet needs and fears of the other person might have been. Have them share these experiences in the small group.
3. Now have people practice the things they might say in their particular situations to de-escalate the tension and to let the other person know that we want to understand the feelings behind their anger. Ask the groups to support and encourage one another in finding those responses which could communicate with compassion when tempers are running high.

FACILITATED CONFLICT RESOLUTION

Purpose: To give experience of a mediation process in which a third-party mediator is used.

Time: 40 minutes.

Materials: Newsprint and markers.

Sequence:
1. Give a brief explanation of mediation: Mediation is a process in which the parties to a conflict communicate with each other with the help of a third-party mediator, and reach a win/win solution. It differs from arbitration, in which the parties submit their differences to a third party, who then makes a decision for them.

2. Read aloud and post on newsprint the steps to be followed by the mediator in the mediation process. The mediator will:
   a. Explain the mediation process and its rules, and get agreement from the parties in conflict to follow these rules:
      - Each party has a chance to talk.
      - The other party agrees to listen.
      - Either party may call a time out.
   b. Investigate the problem.
   c. Ask for additional ideas and seek agreement.
   d. Remain neutral.

3. Divide the participants into small groups of three. Explain that in each group two of the participants will play the roles of the parties in conflict, and the third will act as the mediator, who will help the two parties to reach agreement.

4. Give a scenario:
   The mediator is to mediate a dispute between a swimming coach and a swimming star. The star has been late to practice four times and has missed it completely several times, although warned. The coach has fired him/her from the team, though probably the star's participation is needed in order to win an important meet. The coach knows this, but as an unpaid volunteer coach, is not afraid of losing his/her job if the meet is lost.

   An alternative scenario:
   The mediator is to mediate a dispute between husband and wife. The husband wants bedroom window left open at night, saying he breathes and sleeps better with fresh air in the room, and that he can't sleep when the room is too warm. His wife wants the window closed. She says it is too drafty and cold when it is open.

5. Begin mediation and continue until either a solution or an impasse is reached.

Processing:
- How did the parties feel in their roles?
- How did the mediator feel in this role?
- Was the mediator able to remain neutral and guide the discussion toward a win-win solution? If not, what were the obstacles?

FACTS/FEELINGS PERSON

Purpose: This is a sensitizing exercise intended to give participants a tool to use and encouragement to use it in private to get in touch with the different layers of their feelings.

Time: 30 minutes.

Materials:
1. Newsprint and marker or blackboard and chalk.
2. Enough copies of the blank Facts/Feelings Person handout to distribute to each participant.

Sequence:
1. Facilitator draws on the board or newsprint a balloon-like human figure large enough to write around and inside of. Above the head, write the word BIRTH.

2. Facilitator explains: "There are hundreds of facts about our lives, things that have influenced us, caused us to react, to feel. This started at the moment of birth (point to the word above the human figure). Each of us can list the many facts — happenings, events & people throughout our childhood, in our teens, as we grew up, on the streets, in relationships, at work, at war ... ." (Begin to add around the outside of the figure common facts or experiences that have affected a person, including, but not limited to, some specifics likely to have been experienced by participants in this group: first day of school, fighting, a spanking, cops, first girl or boyfriend, being busted. After a few samples from facilitators — as few as possible — begin to solicit examples from participants.)

3. When the figure starts to become fairly well surrounded with external facts and experiences, stop and say, "Nothing occurs in our lives that doesn't cause a reaction, whether we show it or even admit it to ourselves. In order to know ourselves, to be honest with ourselves, we have to say "yes" to all our feelings, good and bad.

4. Now solicit reactions/feelings to some of the facts listed around the figure, working towards contradictory reactions to the same facts (e.g. "I was afraid at first ... ," "I hated that brother ... ," "I was hurt ... ," "It felt good to see that cop go down ... ," etc. Write a few of the responses on the inside of the figure with an arrow pointing toward the outside "fact" or experience each response relates to.

5. After a few feelings have been recorded inside the figure, stop and conclude with: "Now we have a hypothetical Facts and Feelings Man (or Woman) started. It is worthwhile for each of you to fill in your own Facts and Feelings. It will take a longer time for you to spell it all out. Be honest in digging it out."

6. Either distribute blank copies of the Fact/Feelings Man/Woman to be worked on privately at this time, or, if time is limited, invite participants to take the sheets with them to work on.

Caution:
Move this exercise along quickly, not permitting discussion or analysis to develop too far. This is a sensitizing exercise to encourage further effort in private. It calls for too much risk of self to permit it to go too far in public.

HANDOUT

FACTS/FEELINGS PERSON

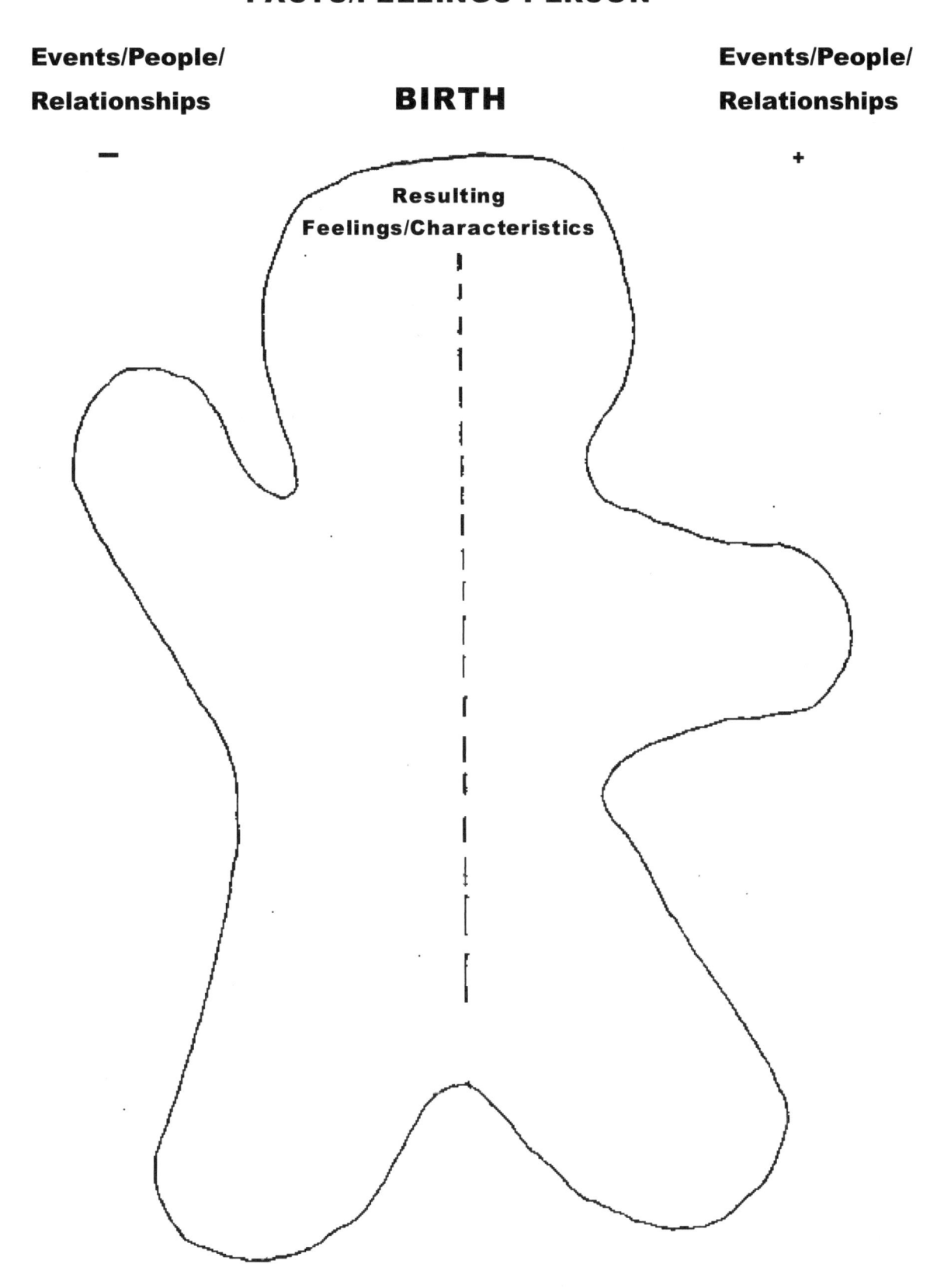

Events/People/Relationships	**BIRTH**	Events/People/Relationships
−		+

Resulting Feelings/Characteristics

FAIRY TALE THEATER

Purpose: Perspective-taking and stereotyping; practice in creative thinking.

Time: 30-40 minutes, depending on size of group.

Materials: Copy of The Old Woman in the Forest (Hansel and Gretel as told by the witch)

Names of very familiar fairy tales or children's rhymes on slips of paper. They must be stories with a "bad guy," a character who could be considered maligned by the way in which the story is told.

Examples:
- Wicked stepmother or stepsisters in Cinderella.
- Troll in Three Billy Goats Gruff.
- Rumplestiltskin.
- Wolf in Little Red Riding Hood.
- Spider in Little Miss Muffet.
- Giant in Jack and the Beanstalk.
- Wolf in Three Little Pigs.

Sequence:
1. Read or tell The Old Woman in the Forest story on page D-77.
   - How did you feel about the witch before you heard this story?
   - Now that you've heard the witch's story, how do you feel about her?
   - How did you feel about Hansel and Gretel before this story?
   - Do you think about Hansel and Gretel any differently now?
   - Have you ever looked at some situation in your own life one way but changed your mind after you listened to another person tell his/her side of the story?

2. Divide into small groups of four or five. Have each group draw a story slip from a hat and rewrite how the maligned character would tell the story from his/her point of view (allow approximately ten minutes).

3. Come together in full circle and have each group share its revised version. They may read it, act it out or even sing it.

Processing:
- Does this relate to real life?
- Is it difficult to change one's image?
- How do I see myself?
- How do I think others see me?
- How would I like others to see me?

Note: The last three questions may be done privately on paper.

The Old Woman in The Forest

The people in the village say that I am a witch. I don't even know what a witch is! Well, there is nothing I can do about people's opinion of me. I came out here to the forest to live alone. I was so tired of everyone laughing at me and little children making fun of me in the street. I guess I do look kind of odd with my big nose and pointy chin, but I didn't choose to look this way; it's just the way I am. No one seems to want to get to know what I am really like.

It is peaceful and quiet here in the forest with no one to bother me most of the time. Sometimes some of the children from the village come all the way out here just to call me names and peek in my windows. I get mad and yell at them to go away. I've heard that they go back with stories about how I said I would kill them. Well, maybe I should control my temper better and not say things like that. I would never do something so awful. I can't understand why anyone would take that seriously.

There were even rumors about me when some children went into the forest and were never heard from again. Personally, I think they must have wanted to leave that little village and go somewhere more interesting. But people said I might have done something to them like cooked them in my big cooking pot. Really! Sometimes people have very creative imaginations.

Then that new pair, Hansel and Gretel, showed up the other day. They certainly weren't too smart about the forest. Imagine leaving a trail of breadcrumbs to find your way back! Don't they realize the woods are full of birds and animals looking for a little extra food?

I felt sorry for them. I guess their new stepmother is pretty mean and kicked them out of the house. They seemed so lost and scared, I had pity on them and invited them in to give them something to eat before I showed them the way home. Well, were they ever rude! They acted scared of me and I even heard Hansel whisper to his sister that I was trying to fatten them up to cook them! And after I gave them my best cookies. Then they ran away while I was getting them some refills on milk. If they do find their way home, I can't imagine what stories they will spread about me now.

FISHBOWL
A technique for exploring many topics or issues

Purpose: A very helpful technique for exploring in depth an issue which is meaningful to a group and about which the group members do not agree. It offers a way to air disagreements and conflicts (real or potential) and provides a mechanism by which conflicting view points and concerns may be expressed, heard, and resolved. It stimulates discussion and makes it possible to share insights, generate new insights from group perceptions, and come to group unity when this is important. It is also useful if a serious conflict arises in the workshop about which people have strong feelings.

Time: About 30 minutes.

Materials: Newsprint.

Sequence:
1. Arranging the Fishbowl:
   Four people at a time are the "fish" in the Fishbowl. They are the people who have volunteered to speak to the issue. The rest of the participants are the observers.

   Place the volunteer "fish" at one end of the room with their backs to a wall, and group the observers in a crescent, (a half "fish" bowl), facing them. In this way no observers will be in back of the "fish," who will thus be spared the discomfort of being watched by people they cannot see, The observers in turn are spared the discomfort of being in back of and unable to hear the people they are supposed to be listening to.

   The Fishbowl dynamic is open-ended, and once set in motion, can be allowed to run until people reach closure on the issue being explored, or until we run out of time. Since it is likely to claim the full attention of the group for a substantial block of time, it should be undertaken only when the issue involved is important enough to the group to warrant this investment of time and attention.

2. Selection of volunteer "fish" can be done in two ways. Before the exercise begins, facilitators must choose either to:
   a) Announce the subject of the exercise and call for volunteer "fish" to enter the Fishbowl without having thought about the subject; or
   b) Pre-select group members who seem to have special concerns or special contributions to make about the subject being discussed, and ask them to volunteer initially for the Fishbowl, so they have some advance warning of their role and can think about what they want to say.

   Whichever way is chosen, three "fish" should be selected initially.

3. Explain the purpose of the exercise and ask the group to arrange the crescent and take their places.

4. Explain the rules:
   a) Three of the four chairs at one end of the room are for volunteer "fish." All volunteers are to talk about one aspect of the subject under discussion (anger, power, stereotyping, etc.) which is meaningful to them, and to state why it is meaningful.
   b) After all volunteers have made an opening statement, they continue to discuss among themselves.

c) Observers sitting in the crescent are to listen and observe, but while sitting in the crescent, are not to interrupt the discussion with comments or questions. However, the observers may get into the Fishbowl and become "fish" in either of two ways:
- An observer may take the fourth (empty) chair in the Fishbowl, and enter the conversation with the three "fish" who are already talking; or
- An observer may cut in on any one of the "fish" by touching the fish on the shoulder as a signal that the observer wishes to replace that fish in the Fishbowl. This should only be done to someone who has already spoken once. The fish who has been replaced then retires and the observer takes that place.

d) Any "fish" in the Fishbowl who has already said all that s/he wants to say, may leave the Fishbowl at any time and join the observer crescent.

e) If there is a time limit for the exercise, announce it now, along with any other rules, (For example: each person can speak for no more than 2 or 3 minutes at a time, and only twice before leaving the bowl, and may choose to come back later if there is more to say).

5. Begin. Let the Fishbowl discussion run its course, or stop it at the end of the time limit set. With people still in place, open the discussion on the Fishbowl topic by inviting the observers to direct questions or comments to any present or former "fish":

6. When the interchange between "fish" and observers has run its course, the facilitator calls all back into circle for general processing and discussion.

Processing:
- Was there anything said that made you think a new way?
- What was said that was helpful to you?
- What was said that may have made you wish you could ask a question, or that you wanted to hear more about?
- Was there any time when you found yourself paying more attention to the person's emotional state rather than to what the person was saying?
- Do you feel different in terms of your thinking and feeling since the beginning of the fishbowl?
- What do we still need to explore and think about?

(It may be helpful to write comments on newsprint in debriefing this exercise.)

FORGIVENESS

Purpose: To identify blocking issues from our past, old guilt trips and overwhelming feelings; to identify and share emotions; to move toward forgiveness for our human errors; to receive validation and affirmation.

Time: About 30 minutes.

Material: 3x5" cards.

Sequence:

1. Distribute 3x5" cards to all participants and ask them to complete the sentence: "What I most need forgiveness for is ... " This will be kept secret.

2. Divide into three-person groups.

3. Each person says whatever they feel about forgiving themselves for the secret they wrote. They do not have to share any more than they are comfortable in sharing.

4. Partners ask questions: (Post them on newsprint.)
    a) What would you have to give up in order to forgive yourself, or what would you lose if you did?
    b) What blocks forgiveness for you?
    c) What could a friend say or give you to help you find forgiveness?

   Using good listening skills, partners encourage the person to work through the questions.

5. Using active listening skills and adapted I-statements, partners validate the speaker's feelings.

6. Continue around the small group, one by one.

Processing:
- In the large group, discuss patterns seen, emotions raised/revealed, things learned.
- If necessary, raise questions about small group process and the feeling of being supported by a small group of friends.

FORGIVENESS QUADRANTS

Purpose: To develop a deeper understanding of the process of forgiveness.

Time: 45 minutes.

Materials: Sheets of 8½" x 11" paper, pencils (Divided sheets with statements already written might be prepared ahead.)

Sequence:
1. Read (or post) the following by Dr. Martin Luther King. "He who is devoid of the power to forgive is devoid of the power to love. Forgiveness does not mean ignoring what has been done or putting a false label on an evil act. It means, rather, that the evil act is no longer a barrier to the relationship."

2. Pass out the papers, and have participants divide the paper in four equal quadrants by drawing a line down the middle vertically and horizontally.

3. Give the instructions: Write responses to statements:
   - Upper Left — **A Time I Was Forgiven**
     How it felt to me. The effect it had on the relationship.

   - Upper Right — **A Time I Forgave Someone**
     How it felt to me. The effect it had on the relationship.

   - Lower Left — **A Time I Would Like to Be Forgiven**
     How it might feel to me. How it might affect the relationship.

   - Lower Right — **A Time I Might Offer Forgiveness,**
     Which would most likely be greatly appreciated. How I might feel if I did it. How it might affect the relationship.

4. In groups of three, have people discuss what they wrote in upper boxes. (For group members who could not fill out any particular box, have them comment on why they felt this was not possible). Then discuss the responses in the lower left box, and anything they believe they could do to make it more likely the forgiveness they wish for could take place. Then discuss responses in the lower right box, and discuss what stands in the way of giving this forgiveness. What would be the best imaginable outcome?

5. Discuss in the whole group general summaries of upper boxes. (Do not take much time with this). Get general overall comments on the lower left box. Write on newsprint any suggestions for actions that might help to overcome the resistance to receiving the forgiveness. Get general comments on the lower right box, and list on newsprint any suggestions for overcoming the resistance to doing the forgiving that could (or should) be done.

Processing:
- What did you feel like when doing this exercise?
- Does it take more courage to forgive, or not to forgive?
- How does this relate to Transforming Power?

A Time I Was Forgiven	**A Time I Forgave Someone**
A Time I Would Like To Be Forgiven	**A Time I Might Offer Forgiveness**

Forgiveness Quadrants

FOUR PART LISTENING

Purpose: To help participants to identify and distinguish among facts, feelings and values, as an introduction to I-Messages.

Time: 45 to 60 minutes.

Materials: Newsprint.

Sequence:
1. Break participants into groups of four. Explain that they are each going to take a turn speaking about a topic. (Example: "A problem I am dealing with in my life.") Ask the group to decide who is A, B, C and D, and to remember their letters throughout the exercise. The speakers will take no more than 5 minutes each to explain their problem, while each of the three listeners will be listening for a different aspect of the story.

2. To minimize confusion, use the newsprint to write which letter is taking which part in each round.

3. The first time around:
   Speaker will be A
   Listener B will listen only for feelings
   Listener C will listen only for facts
   Listener D will listen only for the values and beliefs (e.g. family is the most important thing to me) which seem, to the listener, to be underlying what the speaker is saying.

4. After the speaker is finished, each listener will feed back what s/he heard from the point of view that they were listening to, and the speaker will let them know if there were any misunderstandings or things left out. Give 5 minutes for this, so the total round will be 10 minutes or less, for speaking and feedback.

5. Then switch roles:
   Speaker will be D
       Listener A will listen only for feelings
       Listener B will listen only for facts
       Listener C will listen only for the values and beliefs.

6. Continue two more rounds until each person has had an opportunity to speak, and to take each of the roles.

Processing:
- Was it difficult to separate out the three aspects of listening?
- Were some types of listening easier for you than others?
- How does this relate to Transforming Power?

Note:
   It's suggested that you immediately follow this exercise with an exercise on I-Messages.
      I feel (feelings)
      When (facts)
      Because (values and beliefs)

FROM ANOTHER POINT OF VIEW

Purpose: To practice looking for the good in each person and developing an empathic viewpoint in seeing a situation.

Time: 30 minutes.

Materials: A pad and pencil for the recorder in each group.

Sequence:
Divide participants into groups of four. Have a recorder in each group.
Say to the group: "I will read some scenarios depicting behavior that could easily create anger, annoyance or lead to a fight. However, there might be some understandable reasons that the person is acting that way. See how many good, understandable reasons you can think of, and jot them down." (Allow two or three minutes.) "When I call time, the groups will share their answers."

1. Someone accidentally bumps into a person coming out of a prison hospital visiting room. The person loses it and starts swinging and cussing. Rather than blaming him/her and fighting back, what understandable reasons might s/he have to be feeling and acting this way?

2. A guard is always very stern and frequently denies inmates requests, citing rules and regulations as his reason. What good motives or understandable things could be going on for him/her?

3. A man's wife/woman's husband visits often. Suddenly s/he hears nothing for two weeks, but gets one hastily scrawled postcard saying s/he's busy, sorry, will come soon. What good motives or understandable things could be going on for him/her?

4. A usually cheerful man snaps at his friend when asked an innocent question about what he's been up to. What good or understandable things could be going on for him?

When in groups, read each scenario, giving five or six minutes for them to make a list. After each scenario, have groups report on their lists, adding items not reported by other groups.

After all scenarios have been read and reported on, come back to the large circle for discussion.

Note:
This exercise is similar to "Quick Decisions." It helps to start with a different group after each scenario.

Processing:
- Was this experience hard or easy?
- Do appearances sometimes prevent thinking of these underlying factors?
- Do these factors matter?
- Is the information helpful?

GETTING IN TOUCH

Purpose: To work on some of the eternal questions that confront the peacemaker (and everyone else) about anger and violence. To help members of the group disclose some of their anger safely and creatively.

Time: 60 minutes.

Materials: Four file cards per person (or paper divided into quadrants). A dark marker for each person (so that people can read the cards from afar). Roll of masking tape. (If literacy is a problem, consider using prepared cards, so that persons need only add a single word if they wish.)

Sequence:
1. Distribute the four cards, writing implements, and a strip of tape to participants. Tell participants that you will read four sentences to them. They will be open-ended or unfinished sentences. Participants are to complete them with the first response that occurs to them. They should not censor or modify the response. Caution the participants to print their response clearly — one to each card. This is so others can easily read the answers.
2. Read the following four sentences, one at a time, allowing enough time for the answers to be transcribed. When a card has been completed, the participant should tape it to his or her chest.
3. When everyone has taped all four cards to his/her chest, ask the group to stand up and circulate around the room, reading one another's responses to the questions. This should be done in TOTAL silence! Allow 10-15 minutes.
4. After the silent milling reconvene the group. Suggest to them that you would like to begin the discussion of their feelings about the topic chosen.

Anger:
1. I feel angry when ...
2. I feel that my anger is ...
3. When I experience other people's anger directed at me, I feel ...
4. I feel that other people's anger is usually ...

Power -
1. I feel powerful when ...
2. I feel my power is ...
3. When I experience other people's power I feel ...
4. I feel other people's power is usually ...

Self-control
1. I have self control when...
2. I lose self-control when...
3. When I see a friend who is out of control, I feel...
4. Ways that I help a friend to have more self-control are...

Patience
1. I feel patient when...
2. I feel impatient when...
3. Things that help me to become more patient are...
4. When people are impatient with me, I feel...

Stereotyping
1. When I am labeled or judged I feel...
2. Ways I deal with being stereotyped are...
3. I tend to judge or stereotype others when...
4. Ways I have learned to avoid stereotyping others are...

Potential
1. I think I reach my potential when...
2. When I reach my potential, I feel...
3. When others reach their potential, I feel...
4. One way I help others reach their potential is...

Fear
1. Things that scare me are...
2. When I'm scared or afraid, I tend to...
3. Things that help me deal with my fear are...
4. Ways that I help a friend deal with his or her fear are...

Communication
1. I find it easy to communicate when...
2. I find it hard to communicate when...
3. Ways that other people can communicate with me..
4. Ways other people block communication are...
5. Ways I block communication are...

Processing:
- Why was it easy or difficult to share these feelings in a public way?
- When you look at the responses of people, are they ones you would have predicted? Why? Why not? Were there any surprises?
- In your life, do you usually let people know how you feel: In your family? With people you know well? With people you don't know well or at all?
- Which Transforming Power guidelines can help us?

NOTE:
This is a tricky and complicated area. Go slowly, but be thorough in searching out feelings and socialized attitudes.

Variation: Taking Stock

After completing Getting in Touch, post each person's sheet on the wall with masking tape. Then, at the end of the workshop, hand out another piece of paper/card and give them the same open-ended statements as 'Getting in Touch' and ask them to complete them, assuring them that this is for their eyes only.

After they have completed the four statements, ask participants to go and pick up their statements from the wall and compare the two.

Invite the participants to share thoughts and feelings. Often participants will be surprised to find how much they have moved from their original space when they first did the exercise early in the workshop.

GOAL-WISH PROBLEM SOLVING

Purpose: To share and work on individual problems in a safe setting. To become aware of and benefit from the wisdom of the group and the value of imagination and fantasy in solving problems. To get perspective and affirmation in handling problems. To increase awareness of the role of affirmation, safety, and other factors in communications and problem solving.

Time: 30 minutes.

Materials: Pad and pen for one person in each group, who will act as recorder.

Sequence:
1. Divide into small groups (try to avoid "good friends" in same group).

2. Each person is to pick a problem that feels safe to share. (Give a minute to think about this.)

3. Each in turn briefly lays the problem before the group.

4. The group then takes up each problem in turn, going around twice on each:

    a) On the first round, each person should "make a wish" for the best thing s/he can think of that might happen concerning the problem. (Encourage the participants to let their imaginations go on the wish solution, ("I wish you would grow wings ten feet tall, and fly to Massachusetts, and ... "). It has a freeing effect on the reality insights, influences them, makes them fuller and richer.)

    b) On the second round, each person should contribute whatever reality-oriented insights he has to offer on the problem.

A recorder should take down, for each person, both the wishes and the reality insights. The person who owns the problem then gets to keep the record.

Processing:
- What is the difference between imagination and logic?
- How can imagination help us in solving problems?
- How can logic help us in solving problems?
- Which Transforming Power Guides ask us to use imagination?
- Which Transforming Power Guides ask us to use logic?
- Do any ask us to use both?

GRIEF

Purpose: To learn that it is normal to take time and different steps to deal with traumatic experiences and loss.
- To identify with others who have shared similar experiences.
- To move toward dealing with loss and trauma.
- To receive validation and affirmation.

Time: About 45 minutes.

Materials: Five large newsprint sheets headed: SHOCK, DENIAL, STRUGGLE, DEPRESSION, ACCEPTANCE. Masking tape strips.

Sequence:
1. Tell the group you wish to take some time to get in touch with the shocks life has given them and deal with the losses that come from that. Remind them of their desire to move forward. Ask them to remember how they felt the day they heard their sentence, the loss they felt being separated from family, friends, etc.

    The purpose of this exercise is to try to heal from those traumas and get support from those that have had hard life experiences. As you go through the following steps, try to bring up comparisons between disease (cancer, AIDS), co-dependency, and physical or post-trauma shock. The experiences are in many ways similar; the experience of crime, sentencing and incarceration is also parallel.

2. Put up the first sheet of paper: SHOCK. Say, "When we get bad news, or something traumatic happens to us, the first thing that happens is we go into shock." If someone can talk about physical shock, compare it to psychic shock. Ask people what emotions they've experienced when they were shocked.

    List them on newsprint. Then ask what are the symptoms of someone in shock; how do they act? List whatever comes up.

3. Put up the next sheet: DENIAL. Tell the group that because we cannot (as usually demonstrated in the previous description) function in shock, we have to protect ourselves from reality when it feels too harsh to deal with. Ask those who have been in a 12 step program what the symptoms of denial are. Why does one go into denial? What emotions are experienced in denial? Point out that this can include bargaining with God (Devil, others) to try to improve the situation or eliminate the problem.

    List responses on newsprint. If anyone brings up stories about what moved them through these stages, encourage their sharing.

4. Continue with the third sheet: STRUGGLE. Talk about how sometimes people want to kick a drug habit, or lose weight, or overcome an enemy and they put all their negative energies into combating it. Ask about feelings while in struggle. List symptoms of struggle, be sure to include Anger or Rage (Kubler-Ross's original name for this stage). Remind them that sometimes we do the same thing with grief, loss and trauma. We will suddenly strive extra hard to overcome the problem. Why does this not work? — because loss is part of life, grief is normal, trauma is unchangeable. The more we fight, the more we get stuck on the "Tar Baby" like Br'er Rabbit. So our weight see-saws; we go cold turkey and then fall off the wagon; we try weird remedies; we feel one day we're winning and the next like committing suicide.

5. Next comes the state of DEPRESSION. Put up the newsprint and list the emotions and symptoms of this stage.

6. Finish the last sheet: ACCEPTANCE. Ask anyone who has experienced this stage in any part of their life.

    Remind them that it is possible to be in different stages of this process at the same time about different parts of one's life (e.g. in denial about drugs, in depression about a loved one's death, in struggle about some bad news at work, and in shock about the latest event in one's life.)

    People sometimes make inappropriate comments telling us we should be finished with one step or another. We really can be hard on ourselves if we try to be finished with the process before we've had a chance to mentally let go of what we had in the past. Sometimes we pretend we're in acceptance when in reality we are very skilled at denial. There is a "gray zone" that we must move through after saying goodbye to what was, and finding or moving on to the hello of what will be our new lives.

7. Because of the hurts and unhealed wounds of our childhoods or past events, most of us have a harder time moving out of one stage or another. Put up the five posters in different parts of the room. Ask participants to move to the poster that most closely matches where they are with the issue they are trying to recover from right now in their lives.

    Tell them to sit down in a small group near the poster and take 10 minutes to discuss whatever each person in the group wishes to ask or hear from others.

Processing:
Regroup in a large circle and ask someone to speak for each of the groups and share the most significant issue that was discussed. Ask if anyone has a better insight into where they need to move. It may bring hope to those who are stuck in struggle or depression as they realize that these may be necessary steps for healing.

Note:
This exercise works well on the second day in preparing the group for grief/loss work and after they've had a chance to identify what their losses, traumas and needs for forgiveness are. It provides the language for discussing the emotions that arise as one goes deeper with the Facts/Feelings or other work.

Based on concepts from Dr. Elizabeth Kübler-Ross.

GROUP DaVINCI

Purpose: To engage in a group creation process, to practice cooperation skills and to experience group decision making.

Time: 45 to 60 minutes.

Materials: Markers, crayons, scraps of gift wrapping paper, construction paper and paste.

Sequence:
1. Get everyone into groups of four. Pass out markers and other materials to each group. Announce a theme for the pictures: Power, Love, T.P., Courage, etc.
2. Ask each group to produce a single work of art which abstractly or realistically conveys the theme selected. Give 20 to 30 minutes to complete the project. Assign a facilitator to observe the process in each group,

Note:
Explain that the purpose of the exercise is to use consensus to produce the work, not how "beautiful" the work is.

Processing:
- How were decisions made in the group?
- Did anyone have more influence than others in the outcome?
- Did your efforts combine, compliment or interfere with one another?

GUIDED MEDITATION

Purpose: To impart a sense of self-worth and encourage people to act according to the best in them.

Time. Five minutes, maximum.

Materials: CD or tape cassette player for soft, calming music to be played in background.

Sequence:
Gather the group in a circle and ask them to relax and close their eyes. Begin playing soft music in the background.

Read slowly:
I am me.

In all the world. there is no one else like me.

I have this one life to live.

The way I live can make a difference:

To the people close to me,

To those I live with — play with — work with,

To the community I live in,

And to people I may never see.

I can use the love given to me to help others.

Sharing this love makes me happier and others happier.

When I am unkind to others in words or actions, I destroy something in myself.

Love brings people together and builds.

Let my life be built on love.

Let me find the good in myself and the good in others.

Let me be a part of making this world a better place.

Let me be the REAL ME.

I am me.

I am a valuable person.

There will never be another me.

GUIDED REFLECTION – ALTERNATIVES TO VIOLENCE

Purpose: This is a technique to get in touch with past experiences and feelings on selected subjects related to the purpose of an exercise. It might be a time when you were in conflict and couldn't seem to find your way through. Or perhaps a time when you weren't satisfied with the outcome, didn't feel good about your part in it. It can be used to help participants focus on their personal needs and goals. The process is illustrated here by the following sequence focusing on nonviolence. (In the case of prison workshops, this sequence may put participants in touch with the event that brought them to prison. This may be somewhat uncomfortable, so proceed gently.)

Time: 30 minutes.

Materials: The Processing reflections posted on newsprint.

Sequence:

"We are going to focus on an important memory you have in your life — a time when finding an alternative to violence would have been important.

In a calm, soft and clear tone of voice, the facilitator gives the following directions, pausing at the points indicated by dots, to allow time to focus and recollect.

"Settle yourself in a comfortable position in which your body will not demand your direct awareness for 5 or 10 minutes ... Close your eyes. If your position is uncomfortable, adjust it ... If you have feelings or thoughts that are absorbing you, notice them ... ask them to step aside for the time being and you will return to them ... Focus on your breathing ... If thoughts or feelings still come, notice them and return to awareness of your breathing.

"Remember a time when finding an alternative to violence would have been helpful to you ... where are you ... what is happening ... are you involved, a spectator, or on the fringe of the action ... what has led up to this ... what are you doing ... is anyone with you ... what are you feeling ... what do you say or do, by words ... tone of voice ... actions ... what do you need ... does anyone support you ... did you ask for support ... is communication important ... what is missing for you ... what would you like to learn ... come back to the present ... you are leaving this event in the past ... you cannot change it ... you can learn from it ... open your eyes."

Processing:

In the large group or in groups of three have participants share these reflections which should be posted on newsprint)
- What did you assume?
- What was the escalating point? Possible deescalating point?
- On reflection, how would you have acted differently?
- What Transforming Power guides could have been used?
- What did you learn?

GUIDED REFLECTION - FORGIVENESS

Purpose: To imagine offering forgiveness to someone with whom we have unfinished business.

Time: About 15 minutes.

Materials: The reflection script on the next page; 8x10 paper and crayons or markers for everyone.

Sequence:
1. Explain that this exercise will be done in silence, easiest, with eyes closed. It involves the imagination. Some may find this type of activity unusual. If after starting, some wish to pass, that's fine. Say: "If you choose to pass, please just relax and remain in your seat, keeping a respectful silence so you don't disturb others."

2. If there are no questions, begin reading the attached reflection. Read slowly and thoughtfully. As the reader, try to imagine what the reading suggests yourself, so that you give others enough time to picture what is being suggested.

3. As people are "returning to the room" after the reflection, explain that you and a few facilitators are going to distribute some drawing materials to everyone. Do so as quietly as possible.

4. After most people have opened their eyes, invite everyone, in silence, to make a sketch of what they imagined. The sketches will be shared only if people wish to show them. They don't have to be "great art." Say that they'll have just a couple of minutes for this.

5. After a few minutes ask if anyone would like to talk about the picture s/he has drawn.

Processing:
Would anyone like to share his/her experience? Learnings? Were there any surprises?

Note:
You may wish to dim the lights during the course of the reflection.

Guided Reflection on Forgiveness

All, right. Let's begin. Please relax in your chair and close your eyes. Adjust your body so you feel comfortable. Take several deep breaths. As you inhale picture yourself breathing in the positive, and, as you exhale, feel yourself getting rid of the negative.

Imagine that you are some kind of land animal — see yourself and feel yourself as this animal. Breathe deeply as this animal.

Now imagine that some person, this individual with whom you have some unfinished business, is also a land animal. Try to picture him or her as animal as clearly as possible.

Next, see yourself as animal, at the edge of a beautiful green meadow. It's a lovely day—warm but not too hot — one might call it a soft day. You're enjoying the day and feeling good.

But then, on the other side of the meadow, you suddenly see the animal with whom you have unfinished business. What feelings well up inside of you? Are you angry? Or scared? What other feelings might lie beneath this anger or fear? Maybe there is hurt? Sadness? Pain? Try to breath deeply, even with these difficult feelings.

Now look across the field and see that other animal approaching. That other animal is not yet aware of your presence. Can you look at this animal with new eyes? Can you see any good in this animal? Is he or she also vulnerable? Has he or she any unmet needs? What might these needs be?

Slowly approach this animal with respect — being open to the positive. Suggest that you both rest beneath a shady tree. Ask if you can both talk about how you feel.

Ask this animal to try to tell you where he or she is coming from — what has been going on for them — what his or her point of view is. Listen carefully. Perhaps even if nothing is said, the silence may speak to you.

Now speak about how you feel. Say if you've been angry, or scared, or hurt. Perhaps this other has never fully realized your pain. Perhaps, just perhaps, he or she may ask for forgiveness. But maybe he or she has trouble speaking. Asking for forgiveness is not easy. But at least you've expressed your feelings. Let yourself feel that relief. Perhaps you can offer forgiveness regardless of how the other responded.

Quietly leave the other animal and come back to the edge of the meadow. And, whenever you're ready, come back to the room. Breathe slowly and gently as you notice how you are feeling. When you're ready, slowly open your eyes but remain quiet.

HIDDEN AGENDA

(variation on "The Bag")

Purpose: To let go of other agendas and concentrate on the workshop.

Time: 10 minutes.

Materials: Paper and pencil for each participant.
Waste basket in center of circle.

Sequence:
1. Give each participant a piece of paper and a pencil.

2. Ask everyone to write down two or three things on his/her mind.

3. Popcorn style, have them read one of their concerns and throw the paper away into the center of the circle.

4. Ask them if they are ready to let go of their other agendas and focus on the workshop activities.

HOW DO YOU FEEL WHEN...

Purpose: To get in touch with how we feel in certain situations and how others may have a very different response.

Time: 15 minutes.

Materials: 5x8 cards with names of feelings written on each: Happy, Embarrassed, Frustrated, Angry, Sad, Excited, Proud, Apprehensive, Fearful.

Sequence:
1. Post the feelings cards at intervals around the room. Tell the group you will be making some statements and participants are to stand in front of the card that best describes how they feel in that situation. If there is no word which describes their feeling they can stand in the middle.

2. After participants go to their cards, ask each (or some) why they feel that way. Ask people in the middle what they feel and why.
   How do you feel when:
   a) a good idea you have works out.
   b) you haven't prepared for a test.
   c) everything is under control.
   d) you get compliments.
   e) you don't know what's going to happen.
   f) you see bullies picking on someone.
   g) you get blamed for something you didn't do.
   h) you can't get something to work.
   I) you win a game.
   j) you enter a room full of people you don't know.

Processing
- Do the processing in the large group; ask those who have not shared how they felt about doing it.
- Are you surprised at anything? At your own reactions? At others' reactions?
- Why, do you think, different people can have very different reactions under the same circumstances?

HUMAN TO HUMAN

Purpose: To have an experience of Transforming Power, of our common humanity, and of the goodness within each of us. To experience empathy and trust. To learn to see self and others more clearly, beyond the masks.

Time: 30 to 40 minutes.

Materials: None.

Sequence:
1. Divide into pairs. You may want to have participants choose their own partners and tell them that they may have a more powerful experience if they choose someone they feel is different from them. Have them decide who is A and who is B.
2. Have them close their eyes and listen to the instructions: "The exercise will be done in silence. No talking, no laughing, no touching, no smiling or other facial gestures."
3. Proceed with guided meditation. The following is an outline of a basic talk, but you may alter it according to what feels right for the group in this moment. Be sure to leave suitable pauses for them to get into the experience.

> "A, keep your eyes closed throughout the next part. Your partner will be looking at you. Now B, open your eyes ... Look at this person in front of you, who has the same desire you have to feel good and safe and loved, who has your same will to survive ... the same desire you do to make sense of his or her life ... Take this rare opportunity to look at this person without embarrassment ... Look into his/her face; you may see clues that reveal traces of sadness, hope, fear, loss ... like having loved someone who died, or left ... We've all experienced these things, so find it in your partner's face ... Then realize that it's in your face too ... and it's all right ... See all the common experiences you share ... of being hurt, of being lonely ... of feeling shame, of being scared, of feeling worthless, of praying for help ... of feeling guilty and ashamed, of looking for some kind of relief, some kind of peace ... and yes, of the things that have brought happiness to your heart ... moments of joy, pride, satisfaction, and of the yearning we all have to love and be loved."

> "Keep looking for signs in your partner that help you to realize how similar life has been for both of you ... The details may be different, but the feelings and experiences are so much the same! ... As you see them in your partner, recognize them in yourself too ... Including that foggy feeling we have as we keep guessing our way through life without really understanding what's going on or what went wrong ... See that your partner is like you ... and appreciate that s/he trusts you enough to let you look at him/her while his/her eyes are closed ... What a gift! And realize that s/he can trust you — and you can trust him/her, because you see how much the same life is for both of you ... At a real level you know this person ... s/he's just like you ... So allow your heart to soften and your compassion to grow as you recognize these things in your partner."

"Now B, I want you to give your partner the greatest gift you can give him or her: I want you to keep looking at him or her, with total understanding ... total forgiveness, total compassion for all that s/he's experienced ... for anything s/he could reveal to you ... Whatever stupid, violent, ugly, shameful, crazy thing you could find out about him/her. You understand, don't you? ... Show him or her you understand through the power of that divine love in your eyes ... Allow that compassion to beam from your eyes so that you're bathing him/her in love ... You don't have to "try" to do anything; just relax and get your ego out of the way and let divine love shine through your eyes."

"Now A. what I want you to do now ... before you open your eyes, is to bring to mind those things in your life that you want to let go of ... all your burdens ... your loneliness, pain, shame, fears, hopelessness, weariness, your secrets ... all of it ... Be prepared to let them all go. Because you can do that ... Now. I want you to open your eyes and look straight into the eyes of love across from you ... Receive the compassion, understanding and forgiveness that are there ... You can let go of those burdens now ... all your pain and shame and secrets ... Surrender it all into the eyes of love ... Let it all go. Your partner understands ... S/he really does ... You can allow him/her to see the real you ... maybe more than you've ever allowed yourself to be seen by anyone ... maybe for the first time ... Because it's OK."

"Now, both of you close your eyes. We're going to switch roles."

"B, keep your eyes closed ... [continue to talk]
A. open your eyes. Look at this person ... while I continue"

Repeat the foregoing meditation, but reverse the "A" and "B." When you are complete with this part of the meditation, tell them to do the following:

"Now, for just a minute. sit and just look into each other's eyes, with no games, no pretense, no power trips, no staring competitions, no roles at all ... without your act, your front, your present. Don't smile or make any other facial gestures. You can relax and just be you and just human beings on the path, who have recognized each other.

"Before you close your eyes again, give each other some nonverbal expression in appreciation for what you have just experienced together.

"Now close your eyes. Feel that experience you just had. That deep sense of your common humanity. of the goodness that's there in each one of us ... That is at the heart of Transforming Power."

Note:
Like the trust lift and the trust leap. this exercise calls for a huge amount of trust and community feeling in order to succeed. If the group has not built up that kind of environment, it will be uncomfortable to say the least, even traumatizing perhaps. and probably should not be done.

Since the exercise can be very powerful for people, we often schedule a break right afterward so they can have some silent processing. After the break, re-gather with a sharing about their experience of the exercise.

Based on material from Bo Lazoff.

I MESSAGES: ANOTHER APPROACH

1. The Talk, or Explanation:
   I-Messages are statements we can use to address a conflict situation. The I-Message does three things:

   a) it focuses on the behavior, and not the person who commits the behavior;
   b) it offers the possibility that the person who commits the offense is operating from a very different life experience and does not realize his/her behavior is offensive;
   c) it commits the speaker to "owning" the opportunity to share responsibility for solving the conflict with the person who offended/irritated.

   The I-Message formula is meant to take the offended person on a search for truth BEFORE s/he addresses the offender. It is an internal journey.

   WHEN (Whatever happens)

   I FEEL What feelings does the behavior evoke? Anger often masks another feeling; frustration or fear, for example, let's "stew in our own juice," while anger allows us to direct our emotional energy outward at someone else.

   BECAUSE The speaker has to question where in life experience his/her reaction has come from — to allow that the person who has committed the offense may not share that experience or be offended if the same situation occurred in reverse. Our reactions to others' behaviors are based in our own life experiences — those things which develop our values, our self-esteem or lack of it. What irritates one person doesn't necessarily irritate someone else. We need to own those pieces of our selves which cause us to react in a particular way.

   AND WHAT I LIKE TO SEE HAPPEN IS

   This would be what you see as a next step, and should be something that you also are willing to do. It should offer you and the person you are addressing the opportunity to become partners in the search for justice and fair play.

   If a person uses the I-Message formula for an internal search for truth, the words which come afterward in addressing another person will have lost blame and hostility and will be an affirmation of what is good in all of us.

2. Group Activity
   After explaining I-messages, take a sheet of large paper, and write on it:

   When _____, I get irritated

Ask people to give examples of things people do that irritate them or make them angry. After you have three or four, take each one and ask why the action makes you angry. You now have the first three parts of the I-Message: WHEN (the action), I FEEL (irritated, angry) and BECAUSE (the reasons the participants gave). Now have the group brainstorm what might be in win-win suggestions to give to the person who is doing the irritating action. You then have the WHAT I LIKE TO SEE HAPPEN IS.

I-Messages are based in Transforming Power guidelines 1-6. When talking about and practicing I-Messages, it is helpful to have participants review the first six guidelines. Ask the questions: How do I-Messages use guideline #1? #2 ? #3? #4? # 5? #6?

One inmate gave this example of an I-Message:
> I want to say something about what just happened. We're both in prison, right? The prison system is set up to take away our self-respect. It's set up to make us feel like children instead of men. They take away all our rights and try to make us act like animals. So let's not help the system. Let's give each other respect. What just happened made me feel disrespected, so I'm telling you, man-to-man. And if something I do makes you feel disrespected, tell me, man to man. That's respect, that's telling the prison system we respect ourselves. That's showing them we are men.

The elements of the I-Message are in this:

When: What just happened could be replaced with what actually happened, and it could include the word "You."
I feel: disrespected
Because: I'm in prison where everything is designed to take away my self-respect, and I'm trying to keep my self-respect and my sense of being a man.
And what I like to see happen is:
Let's give each other respect by telling each other when something that's done is disrespectful.

Note:
"Disrespected" is used in prison as a feeling, even though literally it is not. Because the feelings are so complex when one experiences the loss of freedom, personal dignity and even humanness, we can't find a "feeling word" that adequately replaces it.

I MESSAGES – DON'T GIVE UP!
(A Response to Blocked I-Messages)

Purpose: To build on the I-Messages worked on in the Basic Workshop; to develop strategies to deal with blocked I-Messages; to understand the importance of HOW you say something as well as WHAT you say; to offer practical examples of assertive behavior.

Time: 30 minutes, (or 15 minutes the first day, 20 minutes the second day.)

Materials: Handouts.

Sequence:
1. VERY BRIEFLY, go over I-Messages. State that it is a frequent problem that appropriate I-Messages are blocked by the receiver, and we need to find a way to stand up for our rights and be assertive without being violent. Say "Let's look at some examples of what blocking is, and some possible responses, which you will put in your own words." Distribute the Handout.

2. Give, or ask for a simple scenario to work on. Example: A cell-mate who leaves a mess that gets into your space. You have already spoken to him about this.

3. Go over the handout, but don't drag it out or argue about responses. Say "The key thing is to stay assertive. Don't give up! Write your own responses on the handout."
   Note: Some facilitators ask people to bring these back with them overnight so that they have some time to think about it, and report the next day. Assume that some will forget them, and give the handouts to them again.

4. Go around the circle, reading responses. When someone suggests that they might go off on someone after they had tried to be humble and use I-Messages, point out that this is a chance to try a new behavior, and the whole group can help.

Processing:
- What did you learn about what works for you?
- How would you respond to some of the responses given?
- What Transforming Power guide does this relate to?

Note: This exercise is best led by an inside facilitator.

HANDOUT

I MESSAGES – DON'T GIVE UP!
Responses to Blocked "I-Messages"

How a person might block an I-Message
1. Changing the subject.
2. Not paying attention.
3. Refusal to discuss the issue.
4. Increased anger which may be real, or may be fake.
5. Personal accusations ("wimp", "chicken", etc).
6. Laughing it off.

Possible responses to blocked I-Messages
1. "I really need you to deal with (the subject) first."
2. "What do you think... about (this situation) and about what I just said?"
3. "I feel disrespected when I can't discuss this with you without your (laughing it off, changing the subject, etc). When can we talk about it?"
4. "I can see that I am not handling it well. It's not personal. I am sorry you are so angry. I'd like to get along better, but first we need to work something out that is fair to both of us."
5. "I am trying to be respectful of you so that we can work something out. It is obvious that you are mad about my bringing this up, but I would really like to work something out."
6. "Am I right in being concerned about this?"

WRITE HERE YOUR OWN ASSERTIVE, RESPECTFUL LANGUAGE WHEN BEING BLOCKED.

1. _____
   _____
   _____

2. _____
   _____
   _____

IMPEDIMENTS TO COMMUNICATION

Purpose: To develop our awareness to some of the impediments to successful person-to-person communication and various other learnings.

Time: 30 to 40 minutes.

Materials: One blank sheet of paper, pencil, thin felt-tip pen per participant.
Pre-prepared a set of two irregular designs on paper or cardstock.
Keep designs clear, simple, and one that does not tend to resemble a known shape ("tree," "crescent moon," a letter such as "Q," etc.). It can be of several different smaller designs spread on different areas of the paper. Make the two sheets distinctly different from each other. Experience has shown that this exercise can be used to bring out any topic that is chosen in the Second Level Workshop. Hence we say "various" as the purpose of this exercise.

Sequence:
1) Divide the group in half. Arrange seating so that, when seated with chairs back to back, one line of participants will have a clear view of the design to be displayed, and the other line will be facing the opposite direction and can not see the design. It is helpful to leave some space between pairs of neighbors, if space is available. When all participants are seated back-to-back, pass out blank paper and writing devices to the group facing away, and give the following directions:
   "There will be a design posted on the wall The task of those of you facing the design is to describe it to the person sitting directly behind you, so that s/he can make a copy of the design. Those facing away are not to turn so they can see the design. Those facing the design are not to turn so they can see what their partners are drawing. Communication is to be verbal only. Questions between partners may be freely asked as often as is felt necessary."
2) When it is clear that the people doing the drawings are satisfied they have followed all the instructions their partners have given them, have the partners share the work with each other. (In most cases this will produce gales of laughter.)
3) Instruct the partners to switch seats and pass out paper to the new set of "artists." Repeat with the second (different) design poster displayed for the new set of "artists."

Processing:
- Bring the group back into a circle. Look for signs of blaming, accusations. Point out that everyone did the best they could.
- Why did the made-up drawings only vaguely resemble the original? (Experience with this exercise indicates that when the drawing does resemble the original, the "artist" has peeked.)
- What does that show us about what we need in order to communicate effectively?
- Look for comments centering on "wrongness" and "rightness." How can there be "right" and "wrong" when everyone is doing their best? Or, what went wrong while both were giving it their best.
- What happens to the message as the image is seen by the person's eyes, is processed through the brain, out the mouth? What happens as the message goes in the ears, gets processed by the brain and is made visible by the efforts of the hand?
- Our language — our vocabulary and the way we use words — comes out of our experience, our family and our environment. How does coming from different environments affect communication?
- What can we learn from this exercise?

IN COMMON

Purpose: To get used to talking to people we may not know well. To begin building a sense of community.

Time: 15 - 20 minutes.

Materials: Paper and pencils for each pair; newsprint or poster paper and markers for each group of 4 (or 6).

Procedure:
1. Explain that this exercise will be done in 2 parts, first in pairs and then in groups of 4 (or 6). The task is to find as many things as possible that they have in common. Encourage people to find deeper things in common than facts that are fairly obvious, (e.g. "We are both in prison. We both are males.") Suggest such things as likes, dislikes, where you'd like to live, favorite foods, music, children ...

2. Divide the group into pairs by counting off by ½ the number of the group. One facilitator may have to sit out to have the number come out even. Partners are people who have numbers "in common" (i.e. the same).

3. Give the pairs paper and a pencil and ask them to make a list of things they have in common. Tell them they'll have about 3 or 4 minutes.

4. Next move the pairs into groups of 4 (or 6). Give them newsprint or poster paper and a couple of bright markers. Ask them to compare their lists. Put those things that all share in common on the newsprint. Perhaps they'll find things that weren't on their initial lists. Again, give them about 3 or 4 minutes.

5. Ask people to come back to the big circle, staying with their group. Ask each group to read those things which its members have in common.

Processing:
- Were you surprised at the number of things you had in common with others?
- How might it affect the way we approach a person about a conflict if we have things in common with that person?
- What effect does a keen awareness of having things in common with others have on people who are in prison?
- What Transforming Power guide does "In Common" relate to?

IN HIS SHOES

Purpose: This exercise is to sharpen our skills of empathy. It is to see how well we can learn to feel what it would be like to be in another person's shoes.

Time: 30 to 40 minutes.

Materials: Pencils; reproduce handout and cut into 5 slips of paper (one role-play character on each slip.)

Sequence:
1. Get a group of five volunteers to enact the scenario.
2. Give each of them a slip of paper listing the emotions they have visibly and under the surface. (Spend a minute with each to make sure that they can read their slip of paper and understand the emotions involved.)
3. Get five audience members to focus specifically on one of the actors and the remaining ones to focus on all of the players.

Scenario:
A man and a woman are riding in a car. The woman is driving. A young man plows into them from behind at a stop-light; he was going 30 miles per hour at the time he hit. A fourth motorist is a witness. A fifth person is the cop who arrives toward the end. No one is hurt, but both cars are smashed-in. This is all the audience is to be told.

The Group Performs:
The five actors roleplay the auto collision.

Observers Report:
Call on each observer and ask them to say how they think the person they observed:
1. felt
2. what his or her concerns were
3. what were his or her motives during the scenario

Ask the general observers if they noticed a different feeling or disagreed with the observers. Then ask each actor to read his or her slip and say what feelings they were acting or having (they might have changed the role somewhat).

HANDOUT

IN HIS SHOES

Woman Driver:
    This is your one-year-old car. You are really angry that it is badly damaged. You can't believe this young jerk is so careless. Your passenger is a married man you are having an affair with. The affair is casual to you. You know it won't last and are just enjoying it for now. You had a nice afternoon, but now all you can think of is how mad you are.
        Feelings: Anger and shock.
        Concerns: You want total repayment for the damage.
        Motives: To vent your distress. You generally put your needs first.

Male Passenger:
    You are shocked by how stupid this guy is and start off pissed. However, you are a married man having an affair with a single woman, a client. You have spent a pleasant afternoon with her, but you quickly click to the fact that if, as a result of this accident, your wife or company finds out, you are going to be in deep trouble. You would like this settled without a cop, or at least without your name being in any report.
        Feelings: Pissed off at the young guy, afraid of getting in trouble, vaguely sympathetic to the woman.
        Concerns: You must not get found out at all costs.
        Motives: To serve yourself first, the woman second, to hell with anyone else.

Young Driver:
    You were completely preoccupied with other things and didn't realize it was a red light, so you thought the car would keep moving. You are upset about your car, getting a ticket, your insurance going up. You are scared, shaken, feeling terrible, defensive.
        Feelings: Scared, shaken, guilty, defensive.
        Concerns: You are afraid of what these people might do, the cop and the ticket. You don't want even more trouble.
        Motives: To reduce your losses as much as possible or not add to them.

Third Motorist:
    You had a so-so day. You were amazed to watch this accident. You are full of adrenaline. You rush up to make sure everyone is OK and say you will call the police and you bound off before getting a response. You just want to be helpful. You are a very caring person.
        Feelings: Amazement, concern for all the people in the accident.
        Concerns: You would like to see the young guy get a ticket since it was clearly his fault, but you do feel sorry for him. Not thrilled that you might have to testify in court.
        Motives: To be helpful and serve "justice."

Cop:
    You have had a pressured day. This is just one more thing to deal with. People are always upset and angry at accidents. You think accidents are usually the woman's fault and so suspect this woman. You just want to deal with it quickly and not have to argue with anyone.
        Feelings: Irritation at the whole thing.
        Concerns: To deal with it quickly, to assert your authority.
        Motives: You have a bias against women-drivers.

INCLUSION

Purpose: This is an exercise to build community at the beginning of a workshop and to begin to build awareness of problems of communication, stereotyping, etc. In the exercise, one of our key senses, our sense of sight, will be cut off. Since we often make judgments about others by the way they dress and by their body language before we talk to them, we may not be able to truly hear what they are saying. Frequently we stereotype people based on visual cues. This exercise is an opportunity to meet people in an entirely new way.

Time: 60 to 90 minutes, depending on the number of participants. Allow about three minutes per topic per participant, plus one minute to mill around between topics, plus time for introductions of each other by partners in the group, and at least 10 minutes to process.

Materials: None.

Sequence:
1. Participants are asked to stand up and move their chairs against the walls.
2. Explain that you are about to ask them to close their eyes, mill around the room and find a partner to talk to by using their sense of touch alone —no words. Then they will be given a topic. After both partners have spoken on it, all will be asked to open their eyes briefly to acknowledge their partner, and immediately close them to mill around again and find a new partner. This will be repeated with four topics. Check with participants to see that they understand this procedure.
3. Have people close their eyes and mill around to find their first partner, nonverbally.
   Note: Tell people that if it is more comfortable for them, they can cross one arm across their chest and hold out their other hand.
   Topics:
   a) What keeps me from really being here now? Concerns on my mind, left-over feelings, back-home problems?
   b) How I usually react in a new group — my feelings, assumptions, attitudes, behavior.
   c) What I like about myself; what I dislike about myself.
   d) Something I have done recently that I really feel good about.
4. After all questions have been answered, ask the participants to open their eyes. Then ask them to find a person that they would like to get to know better. Give them three minutes to talk to this person and share perceptions of each other. Partners should be sure to get each other's names.
5. After the three minutes are up, ask the participants to sit with their partners. Then ask each person to introduce his/her partner to the group as follows: "My partner's name is ... and his/her essence as I see it is ... "

Processing:
a) How did it feel to talk to a person you didn't know and couldn't see?
b) Did you experience any surprises upon opening your eyes and seeing your partner(s) for the first time?
c) Did your feelings or assumptions about people change? How? Why?
d) Did you find you could concentrate on the person's words better with no sight?
e) Did you feel closer to the person you talked to than you would have if you had been able to see?

Note:
After processing, a possibility for second-level exploration is to get together with another pair and share your expectations of the workshop. Share with the whole community. The leader may want to record some expectations on newsprint.

INJUNCTIONS OF CHILDHOOD AND LIFE

Purpose: To heighten awareness of how the things that were said to us in childhood affect our lives.

Time: 30 minutes for starters.
CAUTION:
People may get deeply and emotionally involved in this exercise, and it is unwise and painful to interrupt them before they are finished. Allow for the possibility of a longer period for the exercise.

Materials: None. (If the floor of workshop site is dirty or in disrepair, and if it is feasible, blankets or plastic drop-cloths to lie on might be desirable.)

Sequence:
1. Explain: This exercise is to help us realize how things that were said to us in childhood, or as we grew in our lives, affect our lives. We call these things "injunctions." Injunctions might be clichés, such as "Big boys don't cry"; or orders, such as "You get yourself pregnant and you're not my daughter"; or admonitions, such as "If you hang out with those guys you're going to get into trouble"; or put downs, such as "You can't do anything right."

2. Have the group lie in a circle like spokes of a wheel, heads pointing inward. If having the group lie on the floor is not convenient, ask them stand in a circle facing outwards or turn their circle of chairs around facing outwards. If possible, dim the lights and ask them to close their eyes. People then randomly call out injunctions (orders or admonitions) they heard as children (or later in life) from their authority figures. Allow at least 10 minutes for this.

3. When people have begun to wind down with injunctions they remember, have them sit up and face inward in a circle. Ask them to call out the responses they have made or fantasized making to those injunctions. (Allow at least 15 minutes for this.)

Processing:
- Did you identify with the responses others had said to the others' injunctions?
- Have any of the ways you behave in your responses today come from those injunctions?
- Have you changed your responses to injunctions or do you respond in the same ways you did when you were younger, are they still a pattern?
- How can Transforming Power help us to affirm ourselves?

I WANT / I WANT

Purpose: To help to clarify the underlying concerns and issues of each person in a conflict situation; to move us to real understanding of "I-Messages," by owning our own fears; to develop empathy; to experience unity beneath our concerns.

Time: 30-60 minutes (2-4 scenarios) Allow about ten minutes for each scenario (2 minutes for each person, 4-6 minutes for processing). Exercise must be done in pairs of scenarios to allow participants to experience different roles.

Materials: None.

Sequence:
1. Divide groups into pairs, with an A and B partner.
2. Read prepared scenarios, (or if time allows, participants may offer suggestions for scenarios) with A and B roles.
3. A begins, completing the sentence, "I want ..." with respect to their position in the conflict. Allow two minutes. This should be a series of simple, quick, top-of-the-head sentences, "I want...I want...I want..." No lengthy explanations. B listens attentively without interrupting. This is not a dialogue. The purpose is not to persuade, but to clarify issues and offer insights into the other person's concerns and needs or feelings.
4. B completes "I want...I want..." sentences, while A listens.
5. Allow participants to share quick discoveries with the group. Save thorough debriefing until the end of the exercise.
6. Read a second scenario, making sure to switch power/authority position of A and B. Repeat exercise and brief sharing/ventilating.
7. Sequence may be repeated with two more scenarios at this point.

Processing:
- Have group form circle, staying seated next to partners.
- What happened in your pairs?
- Were there any surprises/"a ha!" experiences?
- What was it like to have to stick to "I want..." statements?
- What insights did you gain from your partner's sharing?
- What did you learn about the other's issues/position?
- What did you learn about your own issues/position?
- Did you feel more understanding of your partner's position listening to"I wants..."?
- How does Transforming Power apply here?

Sample Scenarios
1. One partner wants to save; the other to spend
2. One partner wants to spend more time together. The other partner has little free time."
3. A friend/partner is concerned about the other's drinking.
4. One cell mate deals drugs; the other is afraid of being incriminated.
5. One cell mate listens to loud music; the other prefers silence.
6. One housemate likes neatness and order; the other likes a "lived in" feeling.
7. Parent wants youth to stay home and do chores; youth wants to go out with friends.
8. Parent concerned about youth's new friend with reputation for drug use.

JOURNAL WRITING

Introduction

Journal writing can put us into contact with patterns in our lives. It helps us to uncover past growth, and can lead to future growth. We are by nature storytellers, but our culture does not encourage this. Journal writing helps uncover the hidden treasures of our lives and explore different paths to the future.

Ideally, time should be made for it at several points in a workshop. However, a start can be made at some point in the workshop, and then participants can be urged to continue their journals after the workshop is over.

Journals are private. Explain that the reflection time is important, and that people can draw pictures or use symbols as well as words to express themselves. Spelling, of course, is unimportant, as you will remember what an incorrectly spelled word stands for, since you wrote it, and ultimately, if you so choose, read it. So let go of your censor/critic, and write freely... first thoughts!!!

Suggestions for a beginning journal writing session:

- Free writing of whatever comes to mind (stream of consciousness). Use all thoughts that you can't admit. Use dashes rather than bothering with proper punctuation. Later go over this and see what comes out.

- Write a letter: dialogue with persons with whom you have a conflict. Dialogue with anything else with which you have a conflict: society, your body, yourself. Bridge the conflict and reach out to the whole world.

- Make a time-line of hopes for the future: where are you now and where you hope to go; in one year, in five, in ten?

- Remember timeless sacred moments in your life. Reach for depth. Go down into the waters of life. Celebrate.

- Imagine a higher power to be your audience (God, Allah, Supreme-being). Share your concerns, your hopes.

- Imagine the journal being a letter to you from a very wise friend, higher power, grandparent or teacher you loved ... what will they say to you about how to move forward?

- Write the answers to the following: What I wonder about ... what I worry about ... what I wish for ... .

- Write the answers to the following: What I would like to hear someone say ... what I wish I could change in my life ... who or what might help me ... .

LABELS

Purpose: To experience being labeled; to see if being labeled influences our attitudes towards ourselves; to develop empathy towards others who are labeled.

Time: 30 minutes or more

Materials: Sets of "stick-on" notes with the following: "Ignore me"; "Tell me I'm right"; "Tell me I'm wrong"; "Encourage me"; "Listen to me." (4 sets for a group of 20); paper and pencils for the recorders; a poster with the task: "Brainstorm a list of oppressed people in our society." (Slips of paper and masking tape should "stick-on" notes not be available.)

Sequence:
1. Explain that people will be working in groups of 5. Each group's task will be to brainstorm a list of oppressed people in our society (point out the poster).
   Each group will need a recorder to write the brainstorm list.
2. The challenge is this: the 5 people in each group will each have a "label" placed on his/her forehead. People won't know what their label says. Everyone will try to treat others according to the instructions on the labels.
3. You may wish to model this, e.g., put a label on another facilitator teammate that says, "I'm a clown." (Explain that this is not one of the labels the groups will be using.) Have your teammate suggest that: "Farmers are an oppressed group." You might reply, "Are you serious? Farmers? You're always joking. Get serious."
4. If there are no questions, form groups of 5, arranged in semi-circles facing away from other groups (so no one sees the labels of other groups). With the help of other facilitators give paper and a pencil to each group and place the "stick-on" notes on people's foreheads. Then have each group choose a recorder and begin.
5. Allow about 10-15 minutes for group dynamics to develop. (You may wish to have facilitators act as observers in each group.) After each group has a few things on its list, have everyone return to the circle, staying with their groups.

Processing:
- How was this challenging?
- What has this got to do with AVP?
- Has anyone ever felt labeled?
- What happens to us if we're ignored (or told we're wrong, etc.) all the time?
- What happens if we are encouraged? Listened to?
- Do we ever respond to others as if they had labels?

Note:
This may stir up some deep emotions. If so, you may wish to have everyone take several deep breaths for a calming effect. Have people slowly breathe in the positive and then have them exhale, getting rid of the negative.

Another option for a task to accomplish: Give each group a set of tinker toys and have them discuss and agree on what to build and how to build it, following their labels. They must come to agreement before they open the box of toys.

Some people choose to do this exercise with all labels being negative. Other options are "Ignore me," "Laugh at everything I say," "Humor me," "Disagree with everything I say," "Don't make eye contact with me."

LET'S GO SWIMMING
Testers, Waders and Plungers

Purpose: To demonstrate stereotyping of others. To increase awareness of self-stereotyping. To help us look at how we build rigidity into our perception of others and how we can dissolve it.

Time: 60-90 minutes.

Materials: One pad and pencil for each group.

Sequence:
Chairs for all and space for three small groups. One pad and pencil for each group.
1. The facilitator explains that people tend to fall into one of three groups in their approaches to life, which can be illustrated by the way each might enter a pond of cold water to go swimming:
    1. People in the first group, called Plungers, go out on the diving board and plunge right in.
    2. Those in the second group, called Waders, walk steadily in from the shore.
    3. Those in the third group, called Testers, feel the water first with their toes and then very gradually ease themselves in.
2. Next, the facilitator designates a different corner of the room for each of the three groups and asks all who consider themselves Plungers to form a group in one corner; all who consider themselves Waders to form a group in another corner; and all who consider themselves Testers to form a third group in a third corner.
3. Give each group a pad of paper and a writing instrument. Explain that they will be asked to make four lists, so they should label each list. (Illustrate what you mean by labeling.) Ask them to list, as in a brainstorm, the responses of members of their group to the following questions:
    a) How does your group describe each of the other groups? (Label the list)
    b) How does your group describe itself? (Label the list)
    c) How does your group think each of the other groups would describe themselves? (Label the list)
    d) How does your group think each of the other groups would describe your group? (Label the list)
4. Ask each group to announce its answers to questions a) and b) and compare their answers.
5. Ask each group to announce its answers to questions c) and d), and compare those answers.
6. Give each group 5 minutes to discuss how accurate or inaccurate their perceptions were and what attitudes on their own parts might account for their stereotypes of the other groups. Ask them to decide whether they wish to reevaluate any of these stereotypes and, if so, how.
7. Have participants join the larger circle and process the exercise. It is important to take people to a deeper level of awareness of themselves and the issues that have arisen. First, help them to ventilate any strong feelings aroused by this exercise. Then, help them process the exercise with the following questions:

Processing:
- What feelings did you experience as you listened to other groups' descriptions of your group?
- When you reevaluated your judgments, did you change your opinions? In what direction? Why?
- How does stereotyping affect self-esteem?
- What kinds of stereotyping goes on in families (or relationships) that block communication?
- What are ways that we can counteract stereotyping in families, in communities, in prison?
- Which Transforming Power guides are helpful in counteracting stereotyping — in ourselves? In others?

WARNING

This exercise is capable of generating much anger. Be very careful, therefore, not to leave people in an angry state. In order to make sure there is closure on this exercise, the first thing is to make sure that we finish it. If there isn't time to finish it, do not begin it! Secondly, if anger is generated, the facilitators should convey to the group that it's good to have some meat to work on. People do change in the final round, and it's a very healing thing to see oneself and others change.

Some facilitators prefer to approach this exercise in a lighter way, inviting people to take the parts of each group. They then bring it back to its serious purpose through the debriefing questions.

LETTER TO MYSELF

Purpose: To focus on the personal changes that take place during a workshop; to help participants chose their personal goals for the workshop.

Time: Part I: 10 minutes, Part II: 30 minutes.

Materials: Sheet of paper and envelope for each participant.

Letter Writing –

Often, in a workshop, the facilitators may wish to increase the dimension of reflection. Among the structures for doing this are the writing of journals and letters. Both, of course, are useful only with fairly literate participants.

Letter writing can provide participants an opportunity to express thoughts they may chose not to share out loud. It also gives them a record of these thoughts to consider at some later time. It is important that participants are given the information that these are not necessarily letters that will actually be mailed, although some might chose to do so.

Suggestions for letter writing:
- A letter to the person you were at a younger time in your life.
- letter to your parent or some other important person.
- A letter to someone with whom you have a grievance.
- A letter to someone from whom you wish forgiveness.

Sequence:

Part I:

1. In the second or third session of the workshop, each participant is given a sheet of paper and an envelope. (Do this earlier if it is used as a tool to develop goals for the workshop). They are asked to write a letter to themselves, answering a question such as:
    - "The way I feel about myself right now is…."

    or
    - "The way I feel about the conflicts and difficulties is my life now is…"

2. Participants are asked to complete the letter on a meal break or on the evening of the first day of the workshop. It should be emphasized that the letter can be short or long, one sentence or ten pages. Letters should be sealed and returned to the facilitators the next session.

Part II:

In the last session, the letters are returned to all participants. They are then asked to share what changes they have experienced as a result of the workshop. They may also wish to share some feelings expressed in the letters. This may the lead to an evaluation of the workshop. Participants may also be encouraged to set further goals for the future, to seal the envelope and open it at some later date of their choosing.

LIFE BELIEFS

Purpose: Community building; to develop self-awareness.

Time: 20 minutes.

Materials: None.

Sequence:
1. Have the group stand and move chairs out of the way. Draw an imaginary line down the middle of the room. Explain that the line is a continuum, and that the ends are extreme positions on each of the questions which will be asked. "For example, if you answer 'yes' to a question you would stand at this end, and if you answer 'no' stand at the other end. If you are in between, place yourself at the spot along the line where you think you are: in the middle, leaning toward 'yes,' or leaning toward 'no.'" (For each question be certain to indicate which end of the line is one extreme and which is the other.")
2. The facilitator will read each question, and ask participants to line themselves up according to how they believe they stand on that question. Participants can be at any place along the line, depending on how strongly they feel about the question. After each question, ask a few volunteers to explain why they answered the question the way they did. Don't drag it on. Move on to the next question.

The Questions:
1. Do you believe humanity is basically good OR evil?
2. Do you believe in a higher power (however you define it)? YES OR NO?
3. Which is more important: "Who you are" OR "What you do"?
4. Is your fate or destiny predetermined (decided in advance without your input) OR are you free to make your own choices?
5. Which is more important: individuals OR the community?
6. Do you believe that society should help its members who are unable to help themselves? YES OR NO?
7. Do you believe that some people are entitled to special consideration under the law? YES OR NO?
8. Do you believe that people should be allowed to make their own choices regardless of harm to themselves? YES OR NO?

Processing:
- Were you surprised at the different positions that people took on the line?
- Were there any of these questions where you were not sure what you believe?
- Do you think you might have answered any of these questions differently at some other time in your life?

Note:

Sometimes we break this exercise into two segments and do four topics early in the workshop and four later on.

Some facilitators prefer to simplify this by making all the questions statements, as in "Here is a statement – 'People are basically good.' If you agree, stand at this end of the line; if you disagree, stand at this end."

LIFE "BIOS"

Purpose: To build community and trust among us. To help us experience empathy and practice looking for the good in each person.

Time: 60 minutes.

Materials: None.

Sequence:
1. Explain that whenever someone does something, they are operating from a good or understandable motive on some level. For instance, let us say a young boy runs away from home a lot. Society labels this "bad"; however, this may have been the only way he could survive, or perhaps he was seeking some place where he would feel wanted or cared about. Or a boy acts out at school basically because it was the only way he got his father's attention; underneath his bad behavior was a very natural desire for love. (These are good or understandable motives.)

2. Get in groups of 3 (try to get with someone you don't know). Each of us will have 10 minutes to briefly share our life story. The other two will listen especially for the good that underlies. The teller can tell whatever s/he feels comfortable with and does not have to stress the good points.

3. At the end of each speaker's 10 minute story, the two listeners will have 4 minutes to reflect back the good things they heard in the story. This is not a time for giving advice or telling your own similar story.

Processing:
- How did it go?
- Did it change how you heard it when you listen for the good points?
- Did you find common points in people's stories? Were the differences interesting?
- How does this relate to Transforming Power?

LIFELINES

Purpose: To affirm accomplishments in life so far, and to define values and set major life goals for the future.

Time: 30 minutes.

Materials: A pencil, 8 ½"x 11" paper, and a long envelope for each participant.
Newsprint with sample lifeline. (see box below.)
Newsprint with values from Step 4.

Sequence:
1. Explain to participants that whatever they write is for their own information only, to be kept for reference and use. What they want to share at the end of the exercise is completely voluntary.

2. Pass out pencils and papers.
    - Ask participants to place the sheet of paper horizontally and to draw a horizontal line on the paper. Demonstrate on newsprint.
    - Ask them to place a 0 on the left of the line and the age to which they expect to live on the other end of the line. (It may be good to explain that you believe that people have a choice about how long they live, and point out that they may have experienced that sometimes people make a choice to die.)
    - Next, ask them to make a mark on the line indicating the age they are now.
    - Finally, ask them to write above the line their major accomplishment(s) in life so far.

Major accomplishment in life so far ...

Birth	Present Age	Age To which you Expect to live
0		X

Major goal to accomplish in the rest of your life ... (to be completed later)

---

3. Guided Fantasy: Tell the group that they are going to take a trip into the future and instruct them as follows:

    Get into a comfortable position ... Put both feet on the floor ... Relax your body ... Close your eyes ... Relax your mind ... Breathe easily and deeply ... Count your breaths ... Think of the innate gifts and talents you were given for which you are grateful ... Remember these ... We are now moving into the future ... It is no longer (name present year) ... We are moving into (name following year) ... It is now (name the next year) ... It is now (name the next year) ... You may move as far into the future as you wish ... If everything goes well, how will things be in 10 years? ... How will you be feeling then? ... Think what you will be doing then ... How will you be using your gifts and talents? ... Think about the things that you will have accomplished ... Take as much time as you need. (Allow a period of silence.) When you are ready, come back to the present ... Indicate that you have come back to the present by opening your eyes.

4. Values: Ask everyone to turn over his/her piece of paper and place it vertically. On the paper they are to write the following: (Post on newsprint)
   - The things in life that you value most and are determined to work on actively.
   - Considering these values, what are your principal goals in life? List three.
   - List at least three steps that you will take to achieve these goals.

5. Ask them to turn the piece of paper over again to the side with the lifeline. Below the lifeline ask them to write the major goal that they plan to accomplish in the rest of their life. Then ask them to put the paper in the envelope, seal it, and put today's date in the upper left corner. In the center of the envelope, write the date when they think they will be ready to open the envelope and take the first step. Ask them to open it again in a month or on whatever date they choose.

Processing:
- How do you feel about what you wrote?
- What helped you to reach for that something good in yourself, maximizing your gifts and talents?
- What will help you to experience that great inward power to act on your steps (an expectation for yourself)?
- How might you use this contract?

LISTENING/I-STATEMENT COMBINATION

Purpose: To practice combining listening and I-Statements to resolve conflicts.

Time: 120 minutes.

Materials: Pencil and paper for each participant. Newsprint with anger level diagram. Handout – Principles of Reflective Listening.

Sequence:

A. LISTENING: (35 minutes)

The facilitator of this section can use the Listening Exercise in the Basic Manual and our handout on Listening. The important thing to remember is that in the Basic Workshop they already did the Listening Exercise, so you are trying to go for a higher level of listening with this practice time. Therefore, it is appropriate to go from uninterrupted listening as is practiced in the Basic with Reflective Listening as it is explained in the handout. Your introduction should not be longer than 10 minutes. Therefore, encourage the listener to periodically interrupt to reflect meaning (not to comment on the content or give opinions or their own stories)

1. Give 5 minutes for each person to be listened to. Call one minute at the end for the listener to summarize, and then another for the speaker to give the listener feedback on their listening before switching. (A good tip: with another facilitator you might model good reflective listening for a minute before the exercise begins.)

2. Crucial for this sequence: You must use only this topic: "A conflict I recently had with another person was ... " If they really can't think of a recent conflict, then any other one they can think of will do; however, recent is more fruitful. It is important that the conflict not be with a group, institution, philosophy, or inner conflict but be with another person.

3. Debrief this sequence (briefly) using the same debriefing questions as listed in the Listening Exercise. Debriefing should only be about 10 minutes.

B. I-STATEMENTS: (35 minutes)

1. Review the three parts of an I-Statement, again remembering that they already did this in the Basic, so it is not a new concept. Ask for questions and put a couple of examples on the board. This whole intro time should be only about 10 minutes.

2. Tell them to go back to their original partner with pencil and paper; give them 5 minutes each to help each other write an I-Statement that could be (or could have been) delivered to the person with whom they had the conflict. The bulk of the time should be for coming up with an I-Statement, not for your explanation. Circulate around to give help to those who are struggling, and assure yourself that they have gotten these statements made. They will need them for the next part.

3. Debrief (should only be a few minutes): Is there an observation anyone would like to make before we continue?

    If a break is needed during this 2-hour exercise, it is best to take it before beginning sequence C below.

C. COMBINING THE PARTS (50 minutes)

The facilitator explains that now we are going to practice combining these two skills, that both are powerful and crucial for good resolution of conflicts, but that they are most effective when combined. The facilitator explains,

"No matter how good an I-Statement we make, sometimes people don't respond well. It is not because the I-Statement is flawed, or that I-Statements do not work. Perhaps the person is already having a bad day and can't take one more thing. Maybe they have been so blamed in their life that they are convinced that you are blaming them even when you are not! Maybe in their heart-of-hearts they really know that their behavior is out of line, and are already feeling guilty and defensive about it. Maybe you remind them of one of their parents. There could be all kinds of reasons for their response.

Similarly, no matter how good a listener we are, no matter how well someone feels that we understand, if we do not also assert our needs or feelings they do not become known and part of the resolution of any conflict. Therefore, it is crucial that we both let the other person know they are heard and understood, and make sure that we are heard and understood, too, by asserting ourselves. Thus combining these two skills becomes the means to do this."

The facilitator reviews the posted diagram and asks if there are any questions (20 minutes):

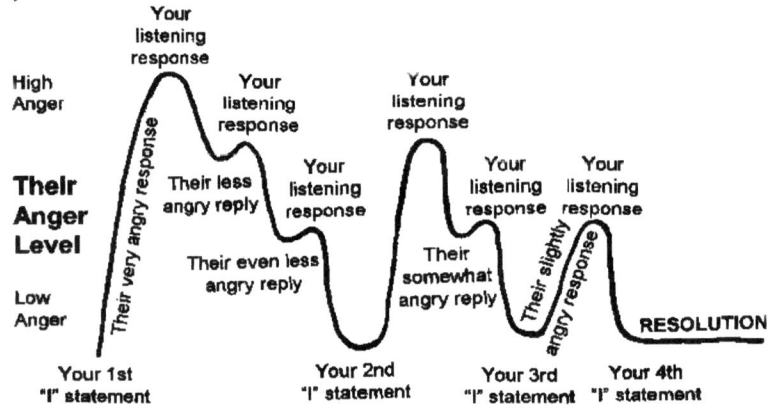

1. Facilitator then explains that we begin the dialogue by asserting what we need to be understood with our I-Statement. We should be prepared for any response, from calm agreement and corporation, to angry, hostile outbursts. But let us say the person responds with anger, name calling, etc., then this is the place to insert listening. So our next line is a listening response: "So you really think I'm a jerk for bringing this up, and that it is an unreasonable response on my part," etc. This will surprise the person who expects an argument. His/her next response, while still aggressive, should be calmer. So again we give a listening response. We may have to give three or four listening responses before the person seems calm.

Then we again assert our I-Statement. The person will probably blow up again, and we will have to use listening again several times. However, after every cycle s/he should be less angry and defensive and increasingly responsive to what we are saying rather than tripping off the person's own stuff. This is because as a person feels heard s/he becomes less angry, and because you are calm and non-argumentative, anger is not escalated. Your reasonableness brings out the reasonableness of the other person. You do these cycles until the two of you are able to come to some understanding, or until you feel it wise to give it a rest for awhile.

2. Now ask participants to get a new partner.
   Explain: Tell your new partner:
   (a) who s/he is (you are John Smith, you work with me);
   (b) give a brief summary of what has already happened (you told me you thought I was doing a bad job, and you hope I lose my job); and
   c)) just a bit of the person's manner and way of reacting to things (you are always very businesslike; you think you are better than everyone else, you are kind of gruff, etc.)
   So you are giving three pieces of information: the relationship/roles between the two people, a brief history of the conflict to date, and something about the person's personality characteristics.

3. Have them each take turns delivering their I-Statement to their partner in conflict, and then using listening and reasserting to try to make progress on resolving the conflict. The person playing the other character should respond in the way s/he thinks a person of that nature would, trying to be realistic. You as facilitator should announce when it is time to switch and should circulate around and help people who are getting stuck. (Usually they are either not using listening or they are not asserting again their I-Statements, but have gone back to arguing. You will need to strongly encourage sticking with those two tasks.)

Processing:
   Debrief how the whole thing went. Acknowledge that using these skills together may be difficult, but keep the group focused on the value of working within these cycles.
   - How did it feel to use this process?
   - Describe any successes with this process.
   - Was there any difficulty not getting hooked by nasty things said?
   - What power is there in not getting swallowed up by people's stuff — which is really their stuff?
   - Is who is right as important as coming to a resolution that will be "right" for both parties?
   - What guidelines of Transforming Power does this relate to?

HANDOUT

PRINCIPLES OF REFLECTIVE LISTENING

A listener can enhance the art of listening through a method known as reflection. In reflection, the listener tries to clarify and restate what the other person is saying.

This can have a threefold advantage:
1. it can increase the listener's understanding of the other person;
2. it can help the other to clarify their thoughts; and
3. it can reassure the other that someone is willing to attend to his or her point of view and wants to help.

Listening carefully and reflecting back what you heard are mutually reinforcing. Empathy, acceptance, congruence, and concreteness contribute to making a reflective response.

Some Principles of Reflective Listening:

- More listening than talking
- Responding to what is personal rather than to what is impersonal, distant, or abstract.
- Restating and clarifying what the other has said, not asking questions or telling what the listener feels, believes, or wants.
- Prefacing our remarks with phrases like "Sounds as though...", "So,...", "In other Words...", "You're saying..."
- Trying to understand the feelings contained in what the other is saying, not just the facts or ideas.
- Reflecting the emotional tone of the message as well as the words. Such as: "Sounds as though you feel _____ because _____".
- Working to develop the best possible sense of the other's point of view while avoiding the temptation to respond from the listener's point of view.
- Responding with acceptance and empathy, not with indifference, cold objectivity, or fake concern.
- Avoiding absolute words such as "always" and "never"

MAGIC CARPET

Purpose: To affirm individuals, build self-esteem and help people deal with or resolve some of the "unfinished business" in their lives.

Time: 30 to 45 minutes depending on the size of the group.

Materials: One blanket for the group, and a paper and pencil for each participant in the workshop. (If a blanket is not available, a few sheets of newsprint taped together and then taped to the floor may used.)

Sequence:
1. Give each participant a pencil and paper and ask them to write down three things that they "really want (or wish) to hear" such as "I really love you son" or "You are forgiven for what you have done" or "You have changed your behavior and you deserve to go home." Explain that "it would be really wonderful to hear these from the actual people, but for some of us that may not be possible. We can, however, hear them for ourselves." Ask them to imagine that the message is coming from someone important in their lives, such as a mother, brother or the parole board.

2. The exercise is done in pairs. Form pairs by counting off by half the number of participants. For example, if there are 18 participants, starting to your right, count off by nines and then, starting from your left, count off by nines. Have them write their numbers on the back of their papers, so that they remember.

3. Place the blanket in the center of the circle and tell the group: "This is the magic carpet which will grant your wish. Each of you (us) will have a chance to sit or lie down or curl up on the "magic carpet." As the words are being read to you, you can imagine the person you want to say the words. When it is your turn to read the words to someone, stand behind him and gently rub his/her shoulder or back and quietly read the three wishes. A quiet and meditative atmosphere is needed during this exercise, so that people can feel comfortable and that they can hear with their imaginations the voices they want to hear."

4. Starting to your right, ask the # "one" to come forward to be on the carpet, and the # "one" to your left to read. When he is on the carpet and ready, have him give his paper to his partner to read. When he has finished, ask the reader to give back the paper and motion to him to come back to his seat, while saying to the recipient, "You may stay on the carpet until you are ready to come back to your seat." After he returns, ask the # "two" on your right to take his place on the carpet and the # "two" on your left to join him as reader. After all the group to your right have been on the "magic carpet," follow the same process with the participants to your left being on the carpet and the people to your right as readers.

Processing:
You may want to have the participants write their responses to some of the debriefing questions and suggest that they take them with them to reread at another time. It is important to acknowledge that when we have unfinished business, sometimes the only way it can be "laid to rest" is within ourselves.

Ask the participants to read silently the words on their papers, and then ask:
- As you heard those words, how did it feel?
- How did you feel to be the person reading another person's wishes?
- Do you feel differently after the exercise?
- What Transforming Power guidelines does this relate to?

Note:
This can be a powerful exercise. Be sure to note any who seem upset after the exercise and seek them out.

MASKS
Exploring In-Group/Out-Group Attitudes and Feelings

Purpose: To help surface the feelings that surround social discrimination of all sorts and to inform a discussion about the roots of violence\conflict that live in that discrimination.

Time: 60-90 minutes.

Materials: Enough masks to cover the faces of half the group. The masks can be the paper "Lone Ranger" style often sold for costumes. They can be of any color. Masks can also be made of construction paper in any design that obscures most of the face. The masks can be attached to the players faces with strips of masking tape or scotch tape, or may be held up against the face with the person's hand.
A list of the instructions for each group. (Below)

WARNING:
Don't push too hard. This exercise explores some of our most emotionally charged areas. Allow the participants their defenses!

Procedure:
1. Count off by 2's. 1's stay, 2's leave the room without any prior discussion.

2. Briefly, a facilitator joins the half of the group outside the room. Give them the masks. Tell them to put them on. Distribute the handouts with instructions.

   Concurrently another facilitator distributes the handout with instructions to the unmasked group which remained in the room.

   Do not answer any questions — if questions are asked, simply state that all the information they need is on the handout — they are to follow the rules and accomplish the task on the handout.

3. Bring masked participants back into the room. Let them sit wherever they wish.

4. Facilitators now observe and make notes on the process which takes place.

5. After approximately 10-15 minutes, ask the "Masks" to give their masks to the "Unmasks" and then continue the discussion after changing roles.

6. After another 10-15 minutes, ask the current "Masks" to remove their masks. Begin discussion.

Note :
Do not interrupt or be drawn into becoming the arbiter of the rules. Watch all interactions carefully during this game. They will be complex and subtle. Make careful notes. They will be useful in the discussion. Watch for things like: Which group speaks more often? Do the Masks become quieter as things progress? Noisier? What about the Unmasks? Are they acting naturally? Do the Masks start to interact with one another exclusively? This is not uncommon because it is easier to talk Mask to Mask (less socially complicated) than Mask to Unmask. Look at this game closely! The responses are similar to those in many situations with two groups of people ... kids/adults, black/white, men/women, students/teachers, prisoners/volunteers.

Alternative:
Rather than ranking a list of priorities, the group can be given a construction project using Tinker Toys or masking tape and newsprint, for example, building a free standing object at least five feet high. Make this task complicated enough that it cannot be easily completed in a few minutes. Allow the Unmasks to begin planning and working on the project before you bring the Masks into the room.

INSTRUCTIONS TO THE GROUP

You are a problem-solving group. Your task is outlined below. The following rules are in effect during the problem-solving period: (Post these rules on newsprint)

Note:
Some programs choose to have the masked people be the ones with power.

1. Masks may only speak to an Unmask by asking permission from an Unmask.

2. Unmasks may speak without asking permission from anyone.

3. Masks must address all Unmasks formally, i.e., by the title of Mr. or Ms. plus the Unmask's Adjective Name.

4. At any time, Masks may address other Masks informally.

5. Unmasks may address everyone informally.

6. Violation of the rules on a repeated basis may result in a participant being asked to remain silent.

Processing:
- What happened here?
- How well did the task get accomplished?
- Were the rules being followed — what dynamics took place around them?
- How did you feel playing each of these roles?
- What did you feel like when you were asked to switch roles?
- Were you surprised at the way you responded in either of the roles?
- There are ways other than physical masks that keep people in lesser roles. What are some of them?
- What does this exercise show about power, both in its effect on those that hold the power and those who do not hold the power?
- In reality, some people have more power than others in a family or in the workplace. What are some ways that people can reduce the negative impact of that power imbalance in families or at work?
- What Transforming Power guidelines does this relate to?

HANDOUT – PRISON WORKSHOPS

MASKS
Instructions to the Group

You are all representatives of an inmate council selected to improve conditions within the institution. Half of your group are wearing masks. As a group, your task is outlined below. The following rules are in effect:

1. Masks may only speak to an Unmask by asking permission from an Unmask.

2. Unmasks may speak without asking permission from anyone.

3. Masks must address all Unmasks formally, i.e., by the title of Mr. or Ms. plus the Unmask's Adjective Name.

4. At any time, Masks may address other Masks informally.

5. Unmasks may address everyone informally.

6. Violation of the rules on a repeated basis may result in a participant being asked to remain silent.

The Task:
- You have been asked to create an agenda for a meeting with the administration.
- Your group has just completed a brainstorming session and has created the following list of issues.

_____Laundry service	_____Availability of jobs
_____Food service	_____Payment for employment
_____Accommodations for visitors	_____Treatment for addictions
_____Telephone service	_____Noise in housing units
_____Racial Tensions	_____Library services
_____Overcrowding	_____Medical care
_____Educational programs	_____Mail & packages
_____Religious services	_____Communicable disease

- You are now entering the evaluation phase and your task is to rank each of the problems you have identified, numbering the most important as 1 and the next most important as 2 and so on until you reach least important which is marked as 16.

HANDOUT – COMMUNITY WORKSHOPS

MASKS
Instructions to the Group

You are all a problem-solving group. Half of your group are wearing masks. As a group, your task is outlined below. The following rules are in effect:

1. Masks may only speak to an Unmask by asking permission from an Unmask.

2. Unmasks may speak without asking permission from anyone.

3. Masks must address all Unmasks formally, i.e., by the title of Mr. or Ms. plus the Unmask's Adjective Name.

4. At any time, Masks may address other Masks informally.

5. Unmasks may address everyone informally.

6. Violation of the rules on a repeated basis may result in a participant being asked to remain silent.

The Task:
- You have been asked to create an agenda for a community meeting.

- Your group has just completed a brainstorming session and has created the following list of issues.

_____Low Productivity Standards	_____Overpopulation
_____Pollution and the Environment	_____Drug Traffic
_____Disease & Poor Health	_____Addictions
_____Labor-Management Disputes	_____Crime – No Respect for Law
_____Racial Tensions	_____Government Reform
_____Inadequate Housing	_____Inflation
_____Low Educational Standards	_____Sexual Stereotyping
_____Unemployment	_____AIDS

- You are now entering the evaluation phase and your task is to rank each of the problems you have identified, numbering the most important as 1 and the next most important as 2 and so on until you reach least important which is marked as 16.

MAY I SHARE SOMETHING WITH YOU, PLEASE?

Purpose: To become aware of boundary issues in communication; to learn to respect differences in perspective which are not readily apparent; to practice communicating and listening non-violently in a situation which is ambiguous and potentially uncomfortable.

Time: 30-45 minutes.

Materials: Tennis or koosh balls (and/or stuffed toys/animals) for about a third (or more) of the group.

Sequence:

Ask the group to gather into a circle. Explain:

1. There will be no talking in this exercise, except for three phrases:
    1. "May I share something with you, please?"
    2. "Yes, thank you."
    3. "No, thank you."

2. When the exercise begins, I will place tennis/koosh balls (or other "toys") at the feet of several of the participants. Each ball represents either a gift or a burden to be shared with another person. It represents different things to different people; it can also represent different things to the same person at different times.

    Whether a gift or a burden, it is something that the holder wants or needs to share. To the (potential) receiver, it may be a welcome gift or it may be an unwelcome burden.

3. Pass out the tennis balls (or whatever) to about a third (but no more than half) of the participants in the group. (Depending on the size of the group, all but one or two of the facilitators can participate in this exercise.) As the exercise progresses, the facilitator may place more balls (or toys) at the feet of the participants.

4. Explain: Except when initially picking up a ball (or toy) placed at their feet by the facilitator, participants do not use their hands after the exercise begins. You may place the ball under your chin or between your elbows, for example.

    The holder of a ball (or toy) approaches a non-holder of his/her choosing and asks, "May I share something with you, please?" The (potential) receiver responds by saying "Yes, thank you" or "No, thank you," depending on what the ball (or toy) represents to him/her at that moment and whether s/he wants to receive it from the person offering it.

    If the potential receiver says "yes, thank you," the ball (or toy) is exchanged without the use of hands. (A non-participating facilitator can retrieve any loose ball or toy and return it to its owner.) If the potential receiver says "no, thank you," the holder moves on, looking for another potential receiver.

    If possible, the exercise continues in this manner until everyone has had an opportunity to be both a giver and a (potential) receiver.

    Remind everyone of their right to pass before beginning the exercise.

    Note: The less explanation about "the purpose" of the exercise, the better.

Processing:
   Since the exercise has the potential to arouse strong feelings, it is important that the facilitator allow as much time for processing as the group dynamic appears to warrant.

   Issues which will probably arise:
   1. Boundary issues.
   2. Intimacy/sexuality
   3. Male/female interaction.

- How did this exercise feel safe? unsafe?
- Did anyone choose not to receive?
- Did anyone feel "obligated" to offer to pass to a particular person?
- Did anyone feel "obligated" to receive because of the person offering?
- If anyone was not offered an opportunity to receive, how did s/he cope with those feelings?
- How did it feel to be told "no, thank you"?
- What was being shared? Did it change during the exercise? Did it change from person to person?
- If you think about the giving and receiving, not of physical things, but of personal thoughts and feelings, or of concerns and issues that you are in conflict about, what does this exercise show?

MY POTENTIAL

Purpose: To help participants identify the inner strengths and resources that they possess to be successful in life; to allow participants to envision themselves as people who can achieve their highest potentials; as a lead-in to later goal-setting activities.

Time: 20-30 minutes.

Materials: None.

Sequence:
1. Explain to the group: "We are now going to do an exercise which asks us to imagine ourselves as we are when our full potential is realized. This exercise will help us to begin goal setting. Goal setting is a useful way to take direction of one's life. No doubt many times you have set goals for yourself — whether they are simple goals, or more life shaping decisions. No matter whether or not we have succeeded in reaching our goals, all goal setting actions involve forming a mental picture of the 'possible' and then using our inner resources to accomplish our objectives."
2. Instruct participants to sit comfortably with their eyes closed, hands in their laps. Using a relaxed voice, guide participants to relax their breathing, taking slow deep breaths. After about 10 slow breaths, say:
    "Imagine a blank space. Then, in the midst of that space, imagine a point of light that slowly fills the blankness."
    (Facilitator should pace his/her voice with the slow, deep breathing.)
3. Once they have filled up the space with light, invite the group to think of, or create, an image of the person they would like to be. Tell the group to be very free in imagining this person. Facilitator may guide the group to consider the following questions:
    "If you had freedom to be whatever way you want — what would that be? ... (pause) ... What are the characteristics/qualities that you already possess that could help you to become this person?
4. The facilitator invites the group to imagine this person fully.
    "What age is this person?... Where does s/he live? ... What type of work does s/he do? ... What type of people surround this person"?
5. The facilitator asks the group to:
    "Go through the day to day life of this person;... attempt to become this fantasy person ... Once the image is fixed in your mind, hold it for a moment, and become familiar and comfortable with the picture ... (long pause) ... this is the image of you at your winning best."
6. Participants open their eyes. The facilitator passes out paper and pencil for each, and instructs them to take about five minutes to write a description of their "fully realized selves" that they would be willing to share with others.
7. Facilitator asks for a volunteer to read what s/he has written. This continues until all who want to share have had an opportunity to do so.

Processing:
- What are the concrete steps that can be taken to move us from fantasy to reality?
- What are possible barriers we may encounter?
- What can help?
- How can Transforming Power help?

PARALLEL CONSTRUCTION
An Alternative to the Tinkertoy Dog Exercise when there are few sets available.

Purpose: To help participants learn accurate communication skills. This exercise emphasizes the need to give clear and complete instructions, and to listen carefully to instructions given.

Time: 20 to 30 minutes.

Materials: Tinker Toys or Lego Blocks.
If you use Tinker Toys, try to avoid using the wooden wheels with the large center holes as they are too similar to the regular wheels. Other building toys, such as Lego Blocks, are also successful.

Sequence:
1. Set the chairs back-to-back in two rows, about 5 to 7 chairs per row. Count off by twos and ask the ones to sit in Row A and the twos in Row B. The participants in Row A should not be able to see the participants in Row B. Row A will build a construction. The goal is for Row B to build an identical construction by following the verbal instructions from Row A.
   Note:
   With a large number of participants, have several sets of parallel lines at the same time to keep the lines from getting too long.
2. Give the first person in each row an identical set of building toys (in a box or paper bag) to choose from.
3. Instruct the person in Row A to pick out two to four pieces from the box or bag and assemble the pieces. The person is then to describe to the person in Row B behind him which pieces to select and how to join the pieces.
4. The person behind can not speak or ask questions. S/he must do the best s/he can with the directions given. The person in Row B may not ask any questions about the instructions.

   Except for the description of how pieces are being placed, there is no conversation or help from others, except that the person following instructions says "I'm finished" when it is time to pass the construction to the next person.
5. Then both people pass the constructed object on to the next person in line. Again, the person in Row A chooses two to four pieces from the box or bag and describes how they are being added to the construction, with the person in Row B doing likewise as best s/he can.
6. When the end of the line is reached, the roles are reversed so that Row B describes to Row A how they are placing the pieces. Thus, both rows have a turn to describe how to place pieces. The process continues until the construction is passed back to the original pair.
7. When the last people have added their pieces, ask participants to turn their chairs around and form a circle facing each other. Both stand up and show their constructions to the group, comparing results.

Processing:
- Where were the problems in the communication process?
- Ask participants how they felt about the exercise.
- How did it feel to be leaders?
- How did it feel to be followers?
- Did anyone feel frustrated in this exercise?
- Did you learning anything about communication in this exercise?

PERCEPTIONS BASED ON PARTIAL KNOWLEDGE

Purpose: To show how judgments based on partial knowledge of a person can be mistaken; and to explore the factors which influence those judgments.

Time: 40 minutes.

Materials: Newsprint, set of facts about a person, markers, pads, pencils.

1. Put together a list of 15 to 20 facts from the life of a person. It is best if you use a facilitator who is willing to expose him/herself to being judged by partial and negative-sounding facts. Or use a famous person.

   Divide the list into four sets. In deciding the language you use (look at the sample done for Jesus, and which facts go into one set, remember that the facts put into one set should be "weighted": some of the facts should imply that the person is trustworthy; others imply ordinariness; others that the person is unstable or unreliable. Put each set of facts on a separate sheet or card, and label "Character A, B," etc. You should have as many sets of facts as you have groups of participants (usually four).

2. A sheet of paper and pencil for each small group, the paper color-coded so that when you graph each group's responses you do it in a different color. (A brown group, a red group, etc.)

3. A chart prepared on newsprint, allowing for a graph on a scale of one to ten (along the left vertical line) and the four (or whatever number) character-set letters (A. B, C, D,...) spaced along the right horizontal line.

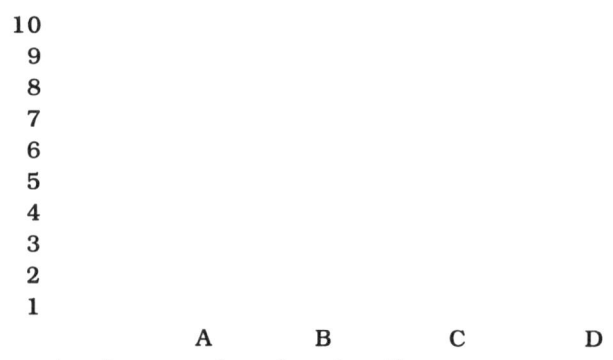

```
10
 9
 8
 7
 6
 5
 4
 3
 2
 1
     A     B     C     D
```

4. A different color marker for charting responses of each group of participants

Sequence:

1. Divide people into 4 groups. Assign each group its "color," and hand out a pencil and sheet of paper to each group.

2. Explain the purpose of the exercise in a way that does not indicate these sets of facts are all about the same person: "In this exercise, we will be examining how we make judgments and decisions about people. Depending on our personal backgrounds and experiences, certain facts will be more important than others when we judge people. Your group will be receiving a set of facts about a real person. You will rank the trustworthiness of that person, basing your rank on the facts you receive. When you finish, you will be given another set of facts about a real person, and do the same."

3. If the sheets of paper have not been color-coded, have the recorder write down the group's assigned color.

4. Explain that each time a group receives a set of facts, the recorder should write down the label for that set (Character A, Character B, etc) so that it is clear which set the group ranking is for.

5. Explain the process the group should follow: "Begin by having one member of your group read the list of facts aloud. Then, take a moment of silence while each person in your group mentally ranks the character (1=Trustworthy ... 5=Untrustworthy.) Then, share and discuss your individual rankings and come to a consensus or note the average score for a group ranking. Have the recorder write down that ranking along with the label for that set."
6. Give each group one set of characteristics. Have them put the "character's letter" on the first line of their blank sheet. Remind them of the process.

    Example: The group that receives characteristics set "C" would write: C and then the group's average (person's rating + person's rating + person's rating ... divided by the number of persons in the group = group average rating.)
7. Collect the slips of paper and pass them along so that each group has a different one. Have them repeat above process. Repeat collecting and passing until each group has had and recorded their assessments of all of the slips.
8. Using a different colored marker for each small group's responses, chart their responses for the trustworthiness of each "character" on the chart with dots and then connect.

Processing:
- Select a character that received widely different ratings from some groups. Read the set of facts aloud and ask the members of the group that rated it high which fact(s) in the set influenced them. (Repeat with the members of the group that rated it low).
- Ask if there were widely different ratings for one character set within a group. Again, read the facts and ask which fact(s) influenced each member of the group.
- Let them know that the characteristics were all of the same person, and give the identity of the person.

Return to a large circle and open up discussion to relate this to real life:
- Which factors influence us in the way we look at people (families? sex groups? experiences from childhood? peer groups? cultures?)
- Did anyone find him/herself looking positively at a fact while someone else in the group saw the same fact as negative?
- We deliberately worded these facts in particular ways to give certain impressions. Why is it that the same words or phrases can be positive to one person and negative to another?
- In what ways can being labeled negatively take away a person's sense of feeling powerful and capable?

Note:
It is preferable to use Jesus only as an example for facilitators to follow in writing their own characteristics, since the use of any figure representing a religion might be offensive to some.

> was an influential teacher — had a good trade — traveled extensively — loved children — cared little for worldly possessions — was not afraid to fight the establishment — had communist leanings — had problems with his parents — was friends with a hooker — enjoyed counseling — sided with women's lib — hung out with fishermen — was known for his magic act — physically demolished a business he disapproved of — was grand marshal of a parade

Facilitators have made the following suggestions for characteristics that require assumptions when judged: Met the president (president of what?), has been in and out of prison (as a facilitator), carried drugs across the border with Mexico (prescription medicines), hangs out with known felons (AVP facilitator), has committed a felony (civil disobedience), moved five times in three years (home, dorm, college apartment?)

PERSONAL SPACE

Purpose: To explore personal space or territory in a nonverbal way. To learn to trust your inner sense of when to act and when to withdraw.

Time: 10 minutes.

Materials: Guides to Transforming Power.

Sequence:
1. Count off by twos and ask the participants to form two lines facing each other, eight or ten feet apart. Each person should be lined up with a partner in the facing line. Once the exercise begins, no one is to talk.
2. One line will be designated as Signal Givers and the other line as Signal Responders. The Signal Givers stand still and give signals to their partners to either advance, stand still or go back, as follows:

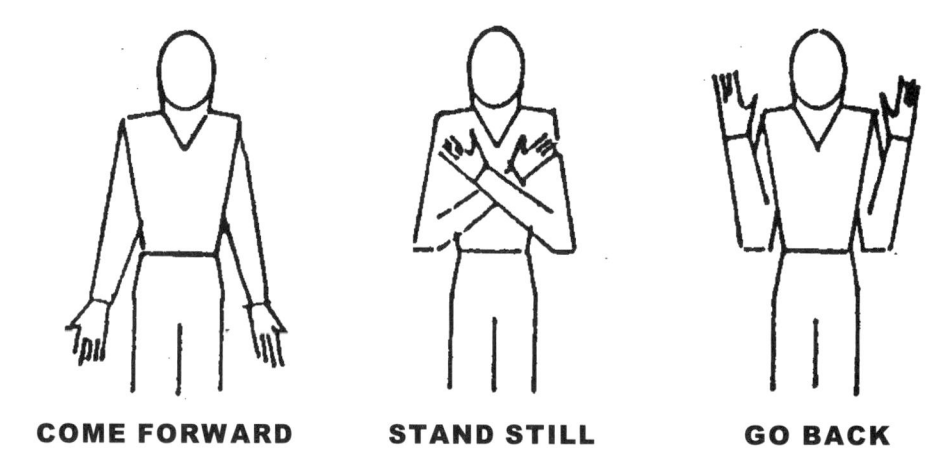

COME FORWARD   **STAND STILL**   **GO BACK**

3. After all pairs have reached a comfortable space, the leader asks them to freeze and then look around to compare the personal space of the other pairs with their own.
4. Everyone is asked to return to their original positions and the Signal Responders now become Signal Givers.
5. You may wish to ask for comments after the exercise.

Note:
This exercise may be used as a gathering or a light and lively. Since it is a fairly light exercise, not a great deal of debriefing is necessary. The experience is the important thing.

A PICTURE PAINTS A THOUSAND WORDS

Purpose: To understand how we form opinions based on impressions.

Time: About 40 minutes.

Materials: Notebook paper, tape, pencils, large numbers of pictures from magazines or newspapers or from the Picture CD available from the AVP Distribution Service.

Sequence:
1. Tape sheets of notebook paper up around the room, one for each participant. Spread out a large number of pictures from magazines or newspapers (at least twice as many pictures as participants).

2. Instruct the group that each participant is to pick one picture they feel a strong sense of affinity or kinship with, and to casually (trying not to attract anyone's notice) take the picture and tape it up on the wall above a sheet of notebook paper.

3. Now have the group walk around and look at the pictures above the notebook paper. At each sheet they are to write one or two lines, answering the following questions (post on blackboard or newsprint):

   a) What might be the adjective name of the person who picked this picture?
   b) How might this person be expected to behave in the group?

   Announce how long the writing period will be (perhaps 10-15 minutes). And emphasize that people are to write about the person who might have picked the picture, and not about anyone who happens to be in the picture.

4. When everyone is finished writing, ask them to bring the pictures they selected and the accompanying notebook paper and sit down. One by one, have participants tell why they chose the picture, and then read their sheet of answers to the questions asked, responding on the answers if necessary.

Processing:
- Were impressions from a picture consistent or mixed? Were they accurate?
- After learning who chose each picture, how did people feel about the assumptions they had made about them?
- What does this exercise show us about our impressions and stereotypes of people.

Note:
1. Be aware if there are participants who cannot writ or who are embarrassed about spelling. Announce that spelling doesn't matter, but if anyone wants help with a word, (facilitator's name) will help.

2. If anyone seems upset by the comments on his or her sheet, make sure to spend sufficient time to help them and others to disassociate the person from the picture comments.

3. If you are going to do the picture gathering it should be done after this exercise with different pictures, or it will taint the experience.

PICTURE PERFECT

Purpose: To deepen the experience after an exercise which has been particularly meaningful.

Time: 30 minutes.

Materials: Newsprint, masking tape, ample supply of markers and/or crayons.

Sequence:

1. After an exercise that seems to have been particularly meaningful, place newsprint sheets, one per participant, joined together side by side with masking tape. Place this long string of newsprint on the floor.

2. Supply participants with an ample supply of felt tip markers and crayons, and have them each choose a sheet to work on. Let them create whatever they wish to express their present state of mind and feeling. Work in complete silence.

3. When the creations are finished, give time for any who wish:

    a. to add to or modify any of the others (silently).

    b. to share what they wish of their work with the whole group.

    c. to reflect on any common themes.

4. Find a place to hang the banner, if possible.

PICTURE SHARING
Can Be Used To Elicit Feelings About A Number Of Subjects

Purpose: To bring to the surface, share, and build on feelings and thoughts that may be evoked by the pictures. Especially useful for focusing both the thoughts and emotions of a group on the theme to be covered by a workshop unit, where the theme is emotionally powerful (such as anger, fear, power, etc.)

Time: 20-40 minutes, depending on the size of the group.

Materials: Pictures, mounted in plastic jackets for handing around.

Each facilitating team should prepare a selection of pictures protected and mounted for passing around. Some of these pictures will be very specifically related to certain themes; others will relate to several possible themes.

(Anger and fear can be shown by photos of angry or fearful people and animals; power can be evoked by photos of people working together, people grown old and strong through struggle and pain. Some nature pictures should always be included — natural phenomena such as mountains, rivers and their canyons, trees clinging to barren cliffs, whatever. Use your imagination.)

The preparation and selection of the pictures is a part of the preparation that the facilitating team may find useful in getting ready for the workshop. A large core group of suitable pictures may be found in many places. Good sources are magazines such as Natural History, Smithsonian, and National Geographic. A CD with 190 suitable pictures is available from the AVP Distribution Service.

Sequence:
1. Place the pictures on the floor in silence. Ask people to select a picture and then sit back in the circle. Ask everyone to comment on their chosen picture and what special meaning it has for them. Then encourage sharing of feelings brought to mind by the exercise.

Note:
This is a good chance for the exercise facilitator to practice some active listening. At the end give a very brief summary of the themes of the pictures shared, as a way of acknowledging the wisdom shared by this thoughtful and illuminating exercise.

Processing:
- Are there further thoughts anyone wants to share?

POWER GAME

Purpose: To help people recognize the dynamics of conflict: the victim, persecutor, and rescuer cycle.

Time: 30-45 minutes, depending on the size of the group and the amount of discussion.

Materials: Large sheets of paper (one for each small group) with the diagram given below. Facilitators should prepare a conflict scenario ahead of time that would involve three people. (Sample given below) Or, begin the exercise by brainstorming scenarios

Sequence:
1. Introduce the exercise by explaining the purpose. Then, define the three roles:
   Persecutor   is someone who puts people down or belittles them;
   Rescuer   is someone who does not believe other people can take care of themselves;
   Victim   is someone who believes s/he cannot take care of her/himself.

   These are roles, and do not apply in a situation where someone genuinely needs help, for example if someone stops to help an injured person in an accident. All of these roles are outside of awareness. No one ever says "I don't believe that other people can take care of themselves," but in a given situation, a person may behave that way without realizing that is what s/he is doing; s/he is responding to the past rather than the present. Often, when people behave in these ways, they then change roles in the situation. Usually these shifts in position are accompanied by bad feelings.

   If we think of most classic stories, like fairy tales, the people in the stories can be charted on the triangle. Little Red Riding Hood – Rescuer to Victim to Persecutor; Grandma – Victim to Persecutor; Wolf – Persecutor to Victim; Woodsman – Rescuer to Persecutor.

   This dynamic can also, and often does, happen in conflicts with just two people.

2. Ask the participants: "Spend a few minutes thinking about times that you have been in conflict situations in which you have been in the persecutor role, the rescuer role, and the victim role."

3. Then, divide into groups of three. Place on the floor in the middle of each group the following diagram drawn on paper, with one person standing on each corner.

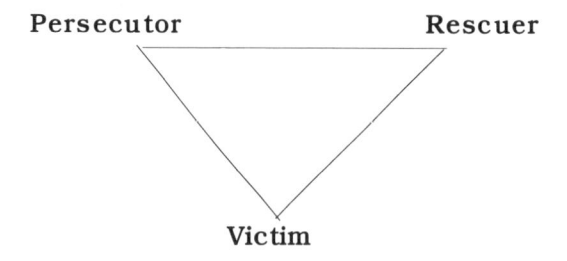

```
    Persecutor          Rescuer
          \            /
           \          /
            \        /
             \      /
              \    /
               \  /
              Victim
```

4. Give each group a scenario which involves three people. Each person chooses a name (and makes a name-tag) for him/herself.

D-138   Power Game

5. Have them act out the scenario for 3-5 minutes; then ask what was said and how each person felt in each group.

6. Have them rotate around the triangle to the next corner, with each person keeping the same character but assuming a new role/attitude.

7. Ask how it felt to be the same person but taking on a different role.

8. Rotate a third time, and repeat the question.

Processing:
- Was one role easier or more familiar for you than another?
- How did your experience change when you changed roles?
- Did you feel more powerful or more in control in one role than you did in the others?
- What observations can you make about the roles people play in conflict situations?
- How does this relate to Transforming Power?

Sample Scenario:

A son breaks the family rules.

Mother (Persecutor) is angry at son (Victim).

Father (Persecutor) gets angry at mother (Victim) for being so harsh, thereby Rescuing son.

Son replies, "Don't get so mad at Mom; it was my fault." (Son Persecuting father, Rescuing mother, father now Victim).

Father (Persecutor) then yells at son (Victim) for not appreciating his intervening. Mother then Rescues son by saying "Let's talk about this outside." (Mother Persecuting Father).

Based on concepts from Transactional Analysis and the work of Nic Fine and Fiona MacBeth

POWER GRAB

Purpose: To demonstrate how losers feel toward winners, and vice versa, after they have been grabbing for power.

Time: 10 minutes.

Materials: Sheets of newsprint (one sheet for each group of five people).

Sequence:
1. Divide into groups of 5. Assign a facilitator to each group.

2. Give each group one sheet of newsprint and explain to them that the sheet represents power. Instruct group as follows: "Each person is to take hold of a piece of his group's newsprint firmly with one hand. When I say `Go!,' each is to try to get as large a share of the power represented by the newsprint as he can. You are to use only one hand." Then say "Go!"

3. When newsprint sheets have been torn apart and each participant holds his respective piece of "power," debrief.

Debriefing:
- How did you feel before I said 'Go!'?
- How do you feel about the amount of power you got?
- To the person who got the largest chunk of power: How do you feel about the others in your group, who got less power than you did? To the people who got the least power: How do you feel about the person in your group who got the most power?
- To everyone: What experience in your own life does this exercise bring to mind?

POWER INVERSION

Note: To be used only in very specific circumstances, (e.g., facilitator's workshop).
Not for usual second level workshops.

Purpose: To deal with power structures in a here-and-now experience within the workshop group. To help people to be aware of their own power, and of how it feels to experience power inversion.

Time: 90 minutes or more. This exercise may arouse strong feelings and should not be rushed or left without closure.

Materials: Paper and pencils for all participants. Two sheets of newsprint with numbers (e.g., 1-15) down the side for the number of participants.

Sequence:
1. Say to the participants: "I am going to give you two to three minutes to think about your own power and influence in this group during this workshop. Please be silent during that time."

2. Ask the participants to push their chairs back to the wall, and then say: "Now, I want you to rank yourselves, by forming a line from one side of the room to the other. The most powerful/influential will be at one end, and the least powerful/influential will be at the other. Please do not talk, but you may motion to or GENTLY direct a person to a place in front of you or behind you." Have a facilitator note the sequence on one of the newsprint sheets. Then, ask the participants to take their seats.

3. Process the experience: The facilitator should explain:
   "Who was ranked where is not important to this exercise. The process (how you made your decisions) is."
   a) How did you make your decision?
   b) Did you compromise yourself and fail to be honest in order not to hurt someone's feelings?

4. At the end of the discussion, ask participants to think about what people said about the reasons for their choices and decide whether they would like to change their rankings or change any other participants' rankings. Then, have them line up again in the original order.
   a) Give each person an opportunity to change his/her own position; then
   b) Give each person the opportunity to change the position of two other people if s/he wishes.
   c) Have a facilitator note the final ranking on a sheet of newsprint, and ask participants to take their seats.

5. Task: Participants are to elect a fair and effective leader.
   a) Pass out paper and pencils. Explain that participants will be given an opportunity to caucus for their candidate. However, the campaign is to be nonverbal, using written messages and body language.
   b) Allow 10 to 15 minutes for caucusing. Then vote by casting ballots. Ballots must show rank order of the person voting and name of the person for whom s/he is voting, (e.g., #2 (my rank); Jane Doe (my choice for a fair and effective leader). No split votes. Facilitators tally votes.

c) Now the facilitator will explain that the weight of each person's vote will be in inverse proportion to their final ranking in the amount of influence credited to the individual — the more power a person has, the less weight his/her vote carries. Thus, the person at the head of the line gets only one vote and the person fifteenth in line gets 15 votes. The purpose is to change the focus of power to allow individuals new behavior in power or lack of power.

6. The elected leader is then to lead a 15-minute discussion with the rest of the participants on the impact of power refocusing, or a similar power-related theme.

7. Process the exercise with emphasis on feelings during each step of the exercise and the personal learning resulting from the experience. Watch closely for residual feelings of resentment or hostility and help participants to vent these safely.

Note:

This can be a very heavy-duty experience, which can arouse correspondingly heavy feelings, and should be used toward the end of a workshop, when considerable trust has been established. It takes careful monitoring not to leave negative feelings unresolved.

PROCESSING ANGER

Purpose: The purpose of this exercise is to help individuals see that experiencing anger is a normal part of living. And that the key to handling our anger is to deal with it not by denying it or suppressing it, but by finding acceptable outlets for it.

Time: About 30 minutes, depending on how much discussion is involved.

Materials: Newsprint and three different colored markers.

Sequence:
1. Put two sheets of newsprint on the wall, one under the other, with the title "Processing Anger."
2. Depending on what has been covered on the debriefing of the "Getting in Touch" exercise, a brief explanation about anger should precede the brainstorm in this exercise. Important points to include are
    a) Make it clear that you are speaking from your own experience (e.g. "To me anger is...").
    b) Anger is neither good nor bad. It is what you do with your anger that is good or bad. We probably could not survive if we did not have the capacity to experience anger.
    c) Anger is a secondary emotion. Usually we have another feeling first: hurt, frustration, fear, grief, jealousy, etc.
    d) To me, anger is to my emotional system what a fever is to my physical system. If I am experiencing anger, I need to find out what is behind the anger and do something about the source of the anger.
    e) Now we're going to brainstorm all the various things that we can think of that we might do when we are angry to help us deal with our anger.
3. Next, get the group to list as many items (just one or two words) as they can think of which are things they might want to do when they are very angry to help them deal with their anger. Do not crowd the items since you will need to leave room for the next step. Stick to brainstorming rules. Do not get involved in discussing items. Make it clear that you are looking for both positive and negative items. If they start listing various sports, suggest a single category "sports." Same with hitting and assaulting, a single category "fighting" etc. This is also important to the next stage. The facilitator should feel free to inject important items that may not be coming out.
4. When it seems the group has pretty much exhausted its ideas, call a halt to the brainstorm but explain other items can always be added later, if desired.
5. Explain to the group that we are going to go down the list and have the group say about each item whether it is a positive or negative way of dealing with anger.

    Now have two distinctly different colored markers in hand and circle the positive ones in one color and the negative ones in another color. If the group can't agree, the item doesn't get circled at all. Do not have a discussion about items on which there is disagreement.
6. When the whole list has been covered, count up the positives, negatives and neutrals and record the numbers. Usually the positives outweigh the negatives and if the neutrals are added, show that there are many more positive ways of dealing with one's anger than negatives.

7. Ask the group to look at the two lists, positive and negative, then ask what do they see as a distinct difference between them? If they don't come up with it, and often they don't, take the colored marker for the negative responses and draw the diagram below giving an explanation as you draw it:

Emotion → **Reaction**

And then the colored marker for the positive responses and draw the diagram below giving an explanation as you draw it also!

Emotion → **Think** → **Action**

Allow for any discussion that seems to want to take place.

Note:
This exercise works best if it is immediately preceded by the exercise "Getting in Touch with Anger."

PROJECTION

Purpose: To retrieve a hidden part of self and own it.

Time: 60 minutes.

Materials: A sheet of paper or several pressure-sensitive name tags for each person, pencils, piece of tape, markers.
One sheet of newsprint with the statement "One behavior/attitude that irritates me is ..."
One sheet of newsprint with the three illustrations on it.

Sequence:
1. Form groups of five, with a facilitator in each group (to participate and guide). Have each person divide his/her paper into three equal pieces and tear at the folds. On one paper, each person is to complete sentence: "One behavior/attitude that irritates me is ..." (3 minutes)

    Participants will read their statements in turn to their group, adding a couple of sentences to clarify their thoughts and feelings. With the help of the group, the person will come up with a word or two that characterizes this behavior: a label — perhaps a character from a movie or book. For example someone who is phony, puts on airs, or acts as if s/he is better than everyone, could be labeled "Prima Donna" or "Major La-di-da." This label is then written in large print with a marker on the second paper. The process continues until all participants have a label. (20 minutes.)

2. Have participants tape their labels to their chests and all mill about in the total group, acting out the behavior of their label as they observe others' labels.
(10 min.)
Return to 3 groups.

3. The facilitator posts the illustrations: "Good me," "Bad me," "Not me," and offers the idea that people sometimes deny or disown parts of what is their "self." Then, the facilitator instructs the participants:
    a) Decide for yourself whether your label is "bad me" or "not me," and take turns declaring your decision to your group.
    b) The group will then help the person look for positive results in the behavior they acted out. For example, the "Prima Donna" or "Major "La-di-da" could become great actors. When you have found a positive result, create a positive label with the help of the group and tape it to your chest. (15 minutes)

GOOD ME   **BAD ME**   **NOT ME**

4. Mill about and act out this positive behavior for 5 minutes. Regroup.

Process:
- Did you learn anything about yourself?
- Is there anything you want to change about yourself?
- What does this have to do with conflict resolution and Transforming Power?

QUERY WRITING

Background: Query writing is derived from a longstanding Quaker practice used for both corporate and personal stock-taking and self-evaluation.

Introduction: In the Second Level Workshops of AVP, query writing is suggested as a way of taking stock of what people have learned, how they have grown and what they still need to work on. It is done at the end of the workshop or in a concluding session for a particular focus unit. It enables each person to focus on what has been learned in the workshop and to integrate those lessons with life experience. Once a body of queries has been composed by the group, it can be used as a basis for in-depth discussion of the workshop experience, and to build the ability to make use of it. These questions are generally open-ended ones, which we can ask ourselves to find out more about our responses to a particular topic.

Materials: A sample set of queries, paper, pencils and newsprint.

Sequence:
1. Post on newsprint or a blackboard a sample set of queries prepared by another group, preferably on another subject than the one under discussion in this workshop.
2. Explain the purpose of queries. Point out the posted set of queries and explain that it is there as a sample only, and that this group is going to write its own queries about its own experiences at this workshop.
3. Pass out paper and pencils for query writing.
4. Ask people to look at the posted queries, to think about the focus of this workshop and to write similar queries that cover:
   a) What specific thing(s) have I become aware of in this workshop that I did not think much about before and that I think I (or we) should be more aware of in the future.
   b) What specific things can I do to improve my contribution to community life? What specific things should we consider or do as a group or a community?
   c) What specific things can I and should I do for my own growth?

   Give the group 15 to 20 minutes to think about and write their queries.
5. Go around the circle and ask people to share the queries they have written that they think are most important. Write these on newsprint.
6. Open free discussion of all queries with a view to coming up with a set of queries that will express the consensus of this workshop about what is important. With the group's help and approval, eliminate duplications or combine similar queries into one. Eliminate any that the group does not agree upon, and add any new queries that come to people's minds after considering those that are already there.
7. If time and facilities allow, the list of queries developed by a group should be reproduced and distributed for people to keep and ponder.

Note:
In the past, queries developed by workshop groups have been preserved and passed out to other groups as guidelines for them to follow. This practice has not been found particularly helpful, however. The benefit to be derived from queries lies in the group process involved in composing them; each group must base itself on and learn from its own experience.

RELATIONSHIP REFLECTION

Purpose: To increase our awareness of relationships and the give and take of life.

Time: 30-40 minutes.

Materials: Questions written on Newsprint.

Sequence:
1. Introduce the exercise: We all have relationships with people: our parents, children, other relatives, friends, people in positions of authority or power. We also have relationships with objects that are important to our way of life: a car, guitar, welding torch, computer. We may also have a relationship with an addiction, like smoking, drugs or alcohol. In this exercise we will reflect on what we give to these relationships and what we receive from them. The answers we find will help us understand the place of relationships in our lives, and how they shape who we are. Think about the relationships in your life, and choose one that is important in your life to focus on during this exercise.

2. Ask the first question: "What have I received from _____ ?" Take 1-2 minutes to reflect on the question and the answers that will come to mind.

3. When 2 to 3 minutes are up, invite people to share thoughts and feelings:
   - What have you received from this relationship?
   - Do you normally take for granted the things you receive?
   - Was there something you hadn't thought about receiving until you had a chance to reflect?

4. Ask the second question: "What have I given to _____ ?" Take 1-2 minutes to reflect on this question.

Processing:
At the end of the reflection, invite people again to share thoughts and feelings:
- What have you given to this relationship?
- Do you think that you give more than you receive, or receive more than you give?
- Does the giving and receiving in this relationship interfere with another relationship? (Even in objects this can be true: spending too much time practicing the guitar can keep a person from reading or from sports)
- Are there any other observations anyone would like to make about this experience?

Note:
Close the exercise by suggesting that asking these questions on a regular basis with respect to relationships in our lives can help us to understand their relative importance to us, and help us in making choices with respect to those relationship and our values.

The sharing part of this exercise may also be done in small groups with the questions posted.

SCULPTING

Purpose: This exercise is a way of dramatizing a moment in time of growing up in one's family or the aspects of conflict in a group. It brings out the fact that persons within a particular group may have different feelings and different perspectives. The same situation may be experienced differently by members of a group. Sculpting is like a symbolic snapshot: it shows how community is nourished or depleted.

Time: 60-90 minutes.

Materials: Chairs or other stage props as needed in order to pose the volunteer "statues."

Sequence:
1. A willing volunteer who will serve as the "sculptor" picks a moment in time (for example, his/her adolescence) or an experience working with a team with which s/he has had some conflict.
2. Without talking, the "sculptor" chooses participants one-by-one to represent the various members of his/her family or a group to be "sculpted." The sculptor then proceeds to pose or arrange these participants physically, as though they were puppets, into a kind of group statue or a posed moment on a stage, capturing the essence of the family/group members as the sculptor sees them. Facial expressions, gestures, and positions in relation to each other should be considered: who's close to whom, who is far away, who facing away, etc. The volunteers posing as the characters should be instructed to be like clay, to be molded as with clay. They passively cooperate as if they were statues or puppets, refraining from using their own interpretations. Each will express the characteristic relationship that the sculptor wishes to show.
3. The sculptor then gives each character a line to speak, a phrase which is characteristic, revealing who that person is and where s/he is coming from in that situation and in that group, typical of their relationship. The phrase may be one that was originally real, or it may be made up by the sculptor; it may represent a spoken phrase or an unspoken thought of the character whose phrase it is.
4. Finally, having arranged the stance, provided the gesture and the statement of each of the characters, the volunteer sculptor puts himself into the group with his/her own position, gesture, and statement.
5. The other participants in the workshop watch without talking, moving silently as they walk around the group while the characters speak their phrases repeatedly, all at the same time as one another, as if the phrase were a broken record or the identifying call of a species of bird.
6. After a few moments the facilitator calls "freeze" and debriefs each person who took a character role, beginning with the "sculptor."

Processing:
- What was it like to be in that position? comfortable, uncomfortable?
- How did you feel when you heard ... ?
- Could you identify with your character?
- What did you learn about what builds or limits positive relationships?
- Ask the circle for their impressions.

Variation: Sculpt your family as you see it when you are released.

SPEAKOUT

Purpose: To help people who feel oppressed to speak out and receive the support of the group. To help participants feel empathy for members of oppressed groups.

Time: 60 minutes.

Materials: Newsprint with list of questions given in No. 4, below, to be posted in view of all participants. (It is not required that you post the questions, but it is important that the same questions be asked each time.)

Sequence:
1. Brainstorm a list of oppressed groups which are targets of stereotyping (e.g. people of color, women, poor, working class, homosexuals, alcoholics, ex-mental patients, AIDS patients).
2. Set up a chair in front of the group, and explain that participants may volunteer to represent the oppressed group of which s/he is a member, or speak out on behalf of a member of a group s/he feels empathy for.
3. If people seem hesitant to be the first, a facilitator should be VERY prepared to do so (this means having gone deep into his/her heart and honestly "feel with" the member of the group chosen).
4. The facilitator leading the exercise should stand close to the person in the chair, perhaps with his hand on his/her shoulder, and ask the following questions:
   - Of which oppressed group are you a member?
   - What do you like about being ...?
   - What is hard about being ...?
   - What do you like about others who are ...?
   - What do you dislike about others who are ...?
   - What do you never want to hear said about or have done to a member of your group again?
   - How can people who are not ... be your friends or allies?

Processing:
Ask people to comment only on their own thoughts and feelings during the speakout, and NOT comment on what anyone said.

Note:
If the facilitators demonstrate an atmosphere of seriousness and concentration from the beginning of this exercise, it will be contagious. It is important to be in control, and if someone laughs, to gently remind the person that we are here to learn and to understand. Some individuals may be taking a great risk in speaking out and it is important for the facilitators to thank the group for their honesty and after the exercise is over, to seek out individuals who may need affirmation.

This exercise should not be done as the last exercise before people are to leave at the end of the day. It would be helpful to have the "Empathy Rap" before doing this exercise so that people who wish to speak on behalf of an oppressed group understand what is required of them.

SYMBOLS OF POWER

Purpose: This is a reflective exercise intended to help participants better understand themselves, through the creation of symbols and concepts of power that are meaningful to them.

Time: 40 to 60 minutes at least. Can run as long as 2 hours if there is no time constraint and depending on the number of participants involved.

Materials:
1. Three simple symbols: an equilateral triangle, a circle, and a square, drawn with dark marker on white letter-size paper. They should be large enough to be visible when posted on the wall.
2. A marker for each participant (have different colors available).
3. Newsprint or a quantity of brown wrapping paper sufficient to supply each person with enough paper to draw on. At least one pair of scissors (some toy stores have blunt tip plastic scissors.)
4. Masking tape.
5. Elmer's glue or other paste.

(The above materials are the minimum necessary. Other useful items: crayons; colored construction paper; watercolors and paintbrushes.)

Sequence:
1. Post the three white sheets with symbols drawn on them, on three separate walls around the room. (The posting on separate walls is important, as participants should be able to concentrate on one symbol without being distracted by others in their line of sight.)

2. Explain to participants that symbols, such as those on the white sheets, can be used by people to discover and express the inner meaning that concepts such as power or love have for each individual. We are going to use the three symbols on the wall to evoke and express such meanings for us. When we are finished, each person will have created out of the materials available, a symbol of his or her own to express something that power means to him or her personally.

3. Distribute to each participant a marker (preferably of a color of his or her choice) and a quantity of wrapping paper. Show participants where other materials (scissors, tape, etc.) are kept and invite them to use these as they feel the need. Some materials will need to be shared, and this should be done, but in silence.

4. Point out the three symbols posted on different walls. Ask each participant to pick the one of these symbols (the square, the circle or the triangle) that happens to appeal to his or her mood at this moment, and to gaze silently at that symbol while meditating or reflecting on the subject of power.

Explain that after a period of this reflection, a person will begin to get an image or an idea or a picture in his or her mind that will express something about power and that can be expressed by creating something — a drawing or a construction — out of the materials at hand. Instruct the group that when such an image or picture comes to each person, s/he is to begin drawing or painting or constructing a symbol to express it.

Emphasize that this is not an exercise in artistic ability, and people are not to worry about their artistic talent or lack of it in creating their symbol. The object is to express a concept or a feeling, not to create an artistic masterpiece.

People may get up and move around to get needed materials, and may share materials where necessary, but there is to be as little talking as possible during this part of the exercise.

5. Begin! Allow about 20 minutes for the group to conceive and construct their symbols; more if possible. Give a time warning about 5 minutes before the end of this period.

6. Call the group together and give each participant a minute to demonstrate and explain to the group the symbol s/he has created and its meaning for him or her.

Note:
> This seemingly simple exercise can evoke surprisingly powerful and meaningful concepts and images about any given subject. The symbols created by the participants can take on a considerable significance to their creators, and they should be allowed to keep what they have created if they wish.
>
> If scissors are not available, demonstrate sharply creasing and tearing along creases.

TANGRAM DOG
(AN ALTERNATIVE TO TINKERTOY DOG)

Purpose: To illustrate the ways communication can be affected.

Time: 40 minutes.

Materials: Enough sets of identical shapes for a sample as well for each small group. These can be made by taking three or four sheets of paper and drawing the shapes on the top one and either cutting or folding and tearing the shapes. It is best if you can prepare these ahead of time and color them or use some method of making shapes so that people don't have to know geometric labels.
Sets of 2 slips of paper (or tape) for each team, on which you have written "engineer" and "supervisor." These will be used to mark the meeting spaces on the floor between the groups and the sample.

Sequence:
1. Divide participants into teams of four. Each team should select one person as architect, one as engineer, one as building supervisor, and one as construction worker.
2. Give each team a set of shapes, while another facilitator uses all of the pieces to make a sample "dog" on a table or floor out of sight of the teams. Place the teams a distance from the sample and from each other.
3. Explain that the task is to create a copy of the sample design. However, the architects are the only ones who will see the sample. The architect will then describe the pieces to be put together to the engineer. The engineer will then describe the pieces to be put together to the building supervisor, and the building supervisor will then describe them to the construction worker, who will put the pieces together. Suggest that they describe only two pieces at a time.
4. After the groups are satisfied that they are finished, let them see the sample, and whether any teams have duplicated the sample.
5. Collect the sets and bring people back into a large circle to debrief.

Processing:
Note: This exercise should reveal that the less personal and more distant we are from people and our goals, the more frustrating life-coping becomes. Use the following questions to help bring this out:
- How is communication affected when the individual cannot see the "whole picture?"
- This exercise set up a hierarchy (top-down structure) — only one person could see the "whole picture" and every other person had to depend on the person above him. Can this kind of a structure of roles work in a family, in a job situation, in society, in government?
- Does this exercise show anything about family roles, or about relationships?
- How do we perceive our jobs/burdens in relation to others in this kind of structure? What mis-perceptions can lead us to resentment?

D-153 **Tangram Dog**

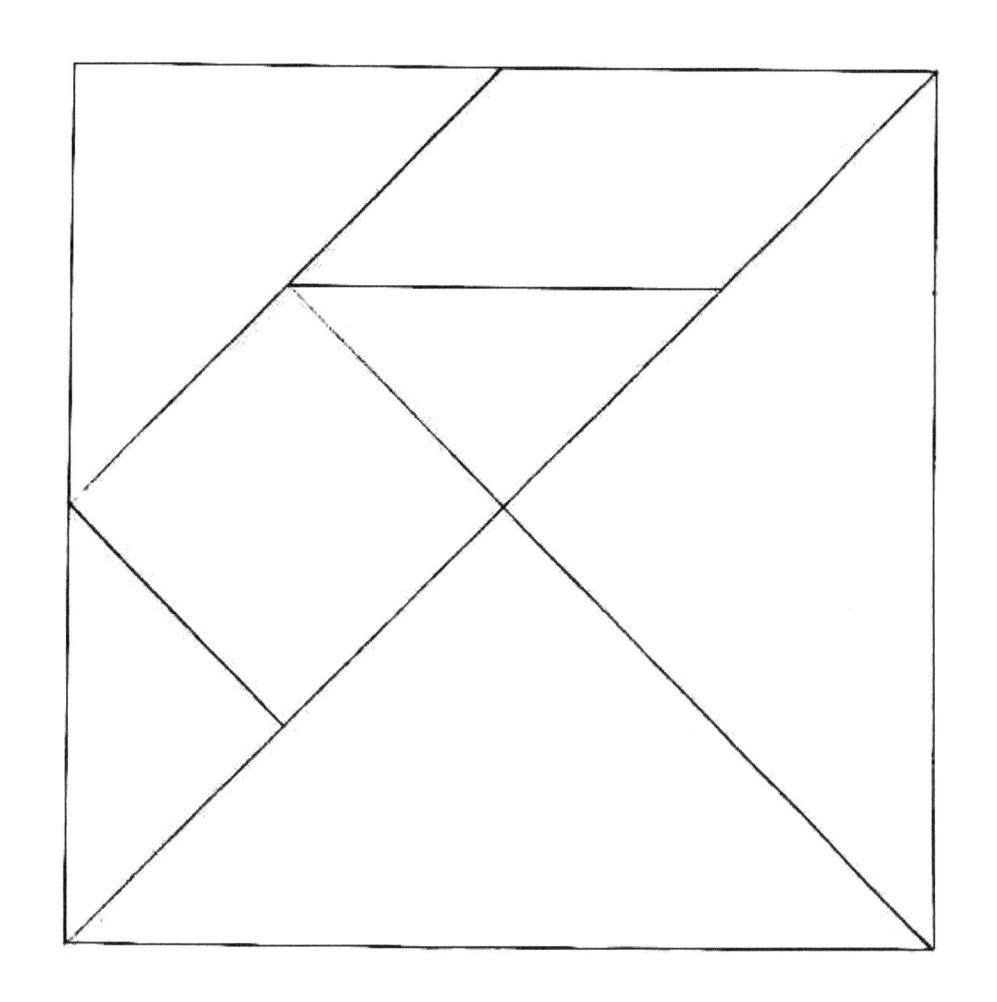

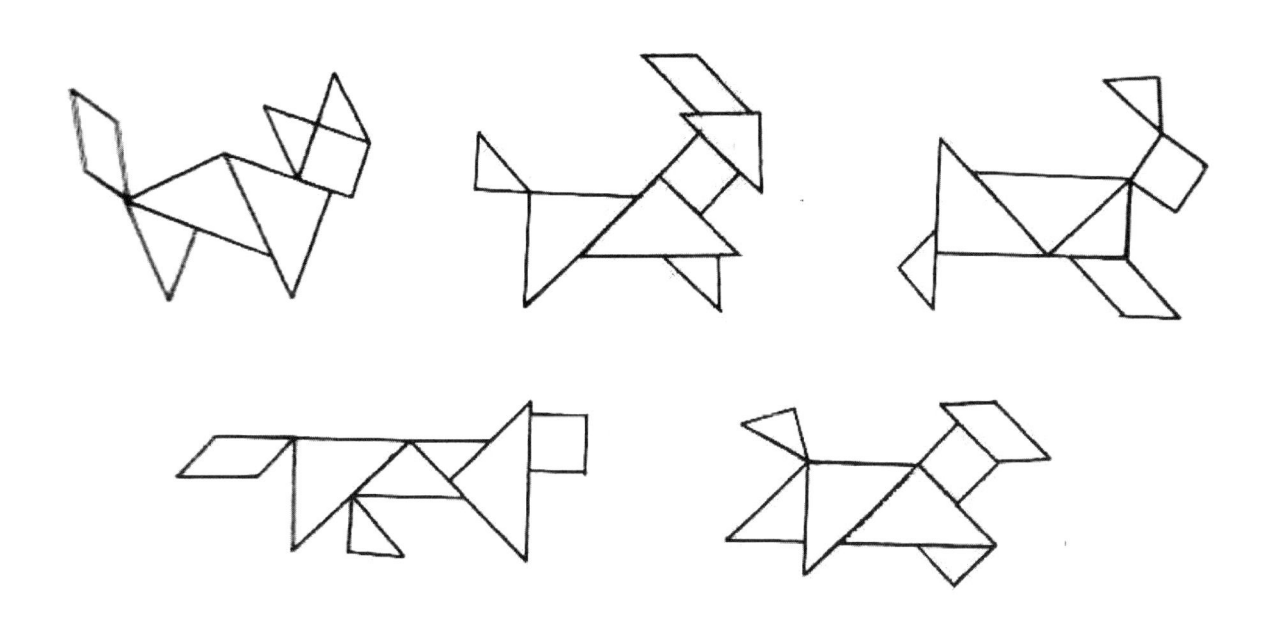

TERRITORY

Purpose: To provide an opportunity to experience various outcomes of conflict, namely, Lose/Lose; Win/Win; Win/Lose; Win/No-Lose; and Compromise.

Time: About 15 minutes.

Materials: None.

Sequence:
1. Explain that this exercise is done in pairs. Once they are in pairs you'll explain the task.
2. Have them count off by half the number in the group. Ask them to find their like number and stand with them, not too close to any other pair.
3. Have them call themselves A and B.
4. Ask each pair to visualize an imaginary line separating them.
5. Explain that the task for all the A's is to have their B come over to the A's side of the line. The task for all the B's is to have their A come over to the B's side of the line. The A's and the B's will be working on their tasks at the same time. (Repeat the explanation at least twice.)
6. Mention that they'll have about two minutes, and you'll call time. Then say that they may begin.
7. After two minutes or so, ask them to return to the circle and sit next to their partner.
8. When they're back in the circle ask for a pair to show what they did. Ask if others did something similar.
9. Repeat #8 until no pair has anything new to show.

Processing:
- Did any of the pairs show a Win/Win (that is, both A and B completed the task — both went on one side and then the other or just exchanged sides)?
- Did any show a Lose/Lose, a Win/Lose, a Win/No-Lose (one person didn't care about the task) a Compromise (they straddled the line in some way)?
- Might another name for a compromise be a Fair/Fair, if both A and B feel good about the outcome?
- In real life is it wise to continually adopt a No-Lose attitude (i.e. to give in to another all the time)?
- If the directions had been "Get your opponent to your side of the line" or "Bring your partner over to your side of the line," might the results have been different?
- Can the use of one word or another affect how we behave in real life? Might that give others control over our actions?

Note:
It is also possible to have the pairs form a long line, similar to "Hassle Lines." In many rooms this places the pairs quite close to each other and one pair may influence another.

It is good to ask co-facilitators to circulate around the room to observe how pairs are interacting.

Co-facilitators might take part in this to even numbers but they may bias the results unless they take quite a passive role.

THINK AND LISTEN

Purpose: For use when a topic has aroused more heat than light and the discussion has deteriorated so that people are not hearing each other.

Time: 20 to 40 minutes.

Materials: None.

Sequence:
1. Break into pairs for a mini-listening session.

2. Explain the rules:
   a) Partners in a pair will alternate between being speakers and being listeners. Each will have five minutes in each role.
   b) The speaker is invited to share his or her thinking on the topic under discussion, BUT
   c) The speaker may speak only from his own experience, and
   d) The listener must pay total attention to the speaker. No interrupting, no conversation of any kind, no looking out the window or at the floor or anywhere but at the speaker. The listener is to give the speaker his/her first-quality attention.

3. Gather into large group. Repeat the rules: Participants may share their own thinking or experience (but only their own) if and as they feel moved to do so. Emphasize that this is not a debate, but a group sharing. After each person has spoken, and so that all may have the opportunity to reflect on what is said, there will be at least one minute of silence before the next person may share. Begin discussion.

THREE QUESTION INTERVIEW

Purpose: To develop community.

Time: 30 minutes, depending on group size.

Materials: Paper and pencils.

Sequence:
1. Imagine you have a group of people to interview, one of whom you will be spending a lot of time with on the basis of his/her answers to three questions. What three questions would you ask in order to learn as much as you could about them? Avoid questions that can be answered with one or two words such as "Where are you from?" or "How long have you been here?" Ask questions that gets them talking about what's important in their lives. Write your three questions on a card.

2. Choose as a partner someone in the group you don't know well. Have you and your partner decide who will go first. When told to begin, ask your partner your three questions. Remember the answers to those questions, but don't write them down. Then change roles and your partner will ask his/her three questions.

3. At a signal, return to the group and have each pair introduce each other to the whole group, using adjective names with the information learned during the exercise.

4. If the group is large and time is too short for each pair to do introductions to the whole group, at a signal, change partners and exchange questions and answers with a new person. This can continue as time permits, allowing many more people to have a one-to-one discussion.

Processing:
- How did you feel about this exercise?
- Did you learn anything new?
- Would you ask different questions if you were to do it again?
- Is this something that might be useful when not in a workshop?
- What might this have to do with resolving conflicts?

THREE QUESTIONS ON OPPRESSION

Purpose: To make oppression real and tangible. To help each person see his/her past in each role, so as to move into liberation.

Time: 40 to 60 minutes.

Materials: The three questions on oppression written on newsprint.

Sequence:
1. Explain that this is a small group sharing, and divide into groups of three.
2. Tell the participants that they will be asked to consider three questions on oppression. Then, define oppression as "the unjust or cruel exercise of authority or power." Name some infamous oppressors (Hitler, Stalin), but then explain that sometimes people who considered quite acceptable by society but who are in positions of authority or power, can become oppressors. The oppression of children by adults is very common, no matter what sex, color or clan we are. It may be a caregiver, a teacher, a religious counselor — even an older or bigger child in the same school or neighborhood — who exercises power or control over the child in an unjust or cruel way.

    QUESTIONS:
    - When was I oppressed?
    - When did I oppress someone else?
    - When did I stand up to challenge oppression?

3. Encourage participants to go to their earliest memory of childhood. (Going to the earliest memory has the most profound effect.)
4. Explain that each person in the group will have three minutes to answer the first question. Then move on to the second, and then the third.
5. Bring the participants back to a large circle for processing.

Processing:
- Would anyone like to share their feelings or observations during the process of sharing?
- Did you find that you looked at some experiences differently when you were asked to share a time you were oppressed? That you hadn't thought of the experience as one of oppression before?
- What is the relationship between stereotyping and oppression?.

TINKERTOY DOG

Purpose: To examine how different roles in a task or situation cause people to perceive an event differently. To examine feelings of trust/competence in a complex working group. To understand how the less personal and more removed we are from people and our goals, the more frustrating life-coping becomes.

Time: 40-50 minutes.

Materials: A box of tinkertoy parts (several sets mixed together) or a large box of assorted collage materials; an animal constructed out of tinkertoy parts (fairly complicated figure) that can be reproduced with parts available in the box of parts, or a collage figure of some animal that can be reproduced with the collage supplies. Do not let the group see the prepared animal.

Sequence:
1. Place the tinkertoy animal in a room other than the workroom (or in a corner that can be blocked from sight). Set the supply box near the door to the room in which the participants will work.
2. Organize the participants into groups of six to eight people. Tell them that there is a tinkertoy animal in the room next door and that the task of each group is to duplicate it, using the materials in the supply box near the door. They must, however, use the following system to gather information and construct the animal.
3. Draw or post a large copy of the diagram

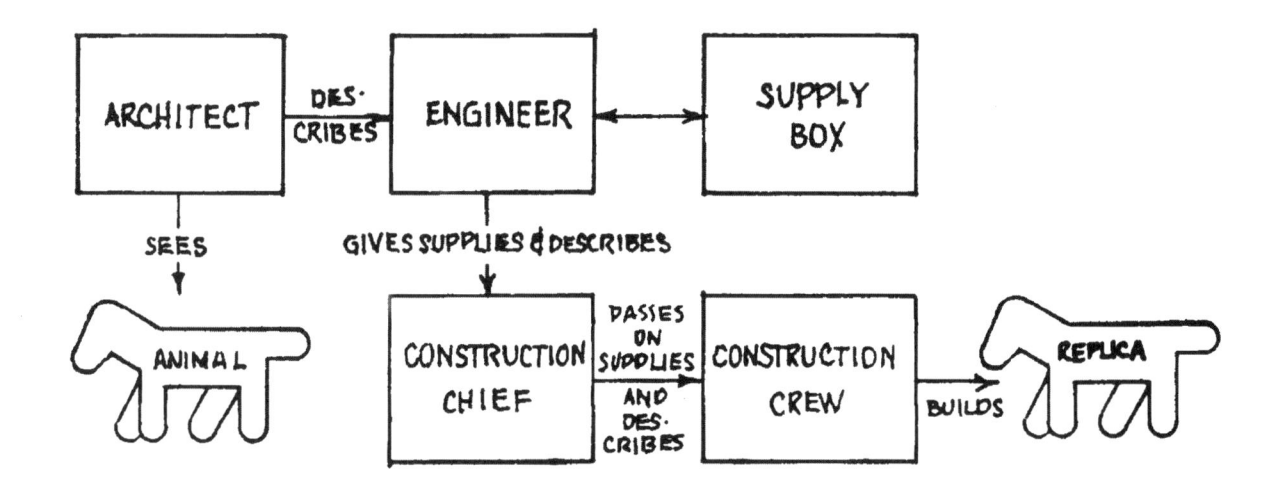

4. Explain that the diagram is a flow chart for making the tinkertoy dog, and that it works according to the following rules:
   a) Each group must appoint an architect, an engineer and a construction chief. Other group members become members of the construction crew.
   b) Once named to a post a person may not be removed from that post.
   c) The architect is the only member of the group who may actually see the animal. The architect may not speak with anyone save the engineer of the same group. The architect may not reenter the workroom once she has left to begin observations. All conversations between architect and engineer must occur outside the workroom.

d) The engineer may speak only with her own architect and construction chief. After getting information from the architect the engineer goes to the supply box, takes needed supplies, and passes them on to the construction chief with needed descriptions. These meetings must take place next to the supply box.

e) The construction chief may speak only to his/her own engineer and construction crew. The construction chief receives materials and directions from the engineer and passes them on to the crew. The chief may not participate with the construction crew in building the replica. The crew receives materials and directions from the chief only, and must attempt to replicate the animal in the other room.

5. When rules are understood, begin. Allow about 25 minutes.
6. Enforce rules strictly. Begin discussion when time or task is completed.

Note:
When people work or live together, they frequently lose track of the burden others carry on their behalf. They perceive themselves as carrying the greater share of the burden because their responsibility or task is the most immediate and intrusive. This mis-perception often leads them to feel resentment, distrust, inappropriate anger, and bitterness. This exercise tries to reveal this phenomenon. It also reveals the effects on communication among members of any group, when individuals can't see the whole picture, or when arbitrary and hierarchical rules limit interaction.

Listen carefully during this exercise to the words that pass between people. Do they indicate dissatisfaction with others' work? Distrust of fellow workers? Frustration? Anger? Are people supporting one another or are they focusing only on the difficulty of their own specific tasks?

Processing
- What kinds of feelings about what your teammates were doing did you have during the task? Architects? Engineers? Chiefs? Crews?
- Did the task get easier or more difficult as you went on? Was it easier to listen and remember, or more difficult? Why?
- Did you find yourself getting frustrated? Angry? Why?
- What or whom did you blame for these feelings?
- This exercise set up a hierarchical structure – top down management. Only one person could see the "whole picture," and every other person had to depend on the person above him. What effect can this have on people's sense of responsibility to the task and to one another?
- How is communication affected when the individual cannot see the "whole picture"?
- Does this exercise show anything about family roles, or about relationships?
- Which Transforming Power Guides relate to this experience?

TRANSFORMING OURSELVES

Purpose: To present the concept of Transforming Power through experiential and group process.

Time: 30 minutes.

Materials: Newsprint and markers, slips of paper for each task. Reproduce tasks on page D-161 and cut into slips for each group. You may choose to write each task on the top of a piece of newsprint to be distributed to the appropriate group.

Sequence:
1. The facilitator briefly defines the words Transform (to change) and Power (energy). Each of us has the power to transform people and situations. Some things are more difficult to transform than others. If we try to transform other people, they may resent it. The best place to start with Transforming Power is to attempt to transform ourselves.

2. Divide the participants into six groups. You do not need the same number in each group. Make copies of the tasks listed below and give each group a slip of paper with one of the tasks. Ask for a volunteer to be scribe and reporter of their project. The scribe will record the suggestions, post the newsprint, and then later will announce the group task (reading aloud from the slip of paper) and its conclusions. When you are finished, there will be six papers on the wall filled with good ideas about how to transform yourself. These may be kept posted throughout the workshop.

Processing:
- What ideas did you get about how to transform yourself?
- How does this relate to the idea of Transforming Power?

Note:
If the group is too small for six groups, eliminate the Ideals group.

IDEALS
Imagine yourself as the most wonderful and fulfilled person you can be.
  Your task: On the top of your paper write   I CAN BE:
  The task of this group is to list some words that describe that ideal person.

SPEECH
Recognize the power of your speech for negativity, such as put-downs, lying and abusive words; but also recognize the power of your speech for good.
  Your task: On the top of your paper, write   I CAN SAY:
  Then list words you can say that encourage others and help to develop good relationships.

BEHAVIOR
How can we act towards others to comfort them in their distress or calm them down when they are angry?
  Your task: On the top of your paper, write   I CAN ACT:
  Then list examples of good behavior you can use in your daily life, or whatever situation in which you find yourself.

USE OF TIME
Use your time and energy in activities that build you up rather than destroy.
  Your task: On top of your paper, write   I CAN USE MY TIME TO:
  Then list examples of good and constructive use of time.

EFFORT
There is energy inside you that can be used, with will power, in a steady pull to achieve a better direction.
  Your task: On top of your paper, write   I CAN ACHIEVE:
  Then list examples of goals you might work on to achieve, how you might encourage help from others, and how you plan to overcome difficulties.

PEACE
Keep your mind tranquil and free from frantic desires, so as to tap inner strength.
  Your task: On top of your paper write   I CAN BE PEACEFUL:
  Then list ways to achieve inner peace.

TRANSFORMING POWER MANDALA EXPERIENCES

Purpose: To develop a deeper understanding of Transforming Power.

Time: 30-45 minutes.

Materials: A large Transforming Power Mandala on display.

Sequence:
1. Explain that this will give participants an opportunity to understand Transforming Power. Point out the mandala and go over the different parts. Point out that each segment is for a thing you can only do for yourself, not something you can do for others, or that they can do for you.
2. Divide the group into pairs. Each pair will chose a segment of the mandala and then come up with a scenario that demonstrates how this principle might be applied in such a situation. Have them plan a role play of this scenario. As with all role plays, make sure they understand that they are not to determine the outcome in advance.
3. Each pair then role plays the scenario they chose.

Processing:
- Do you see any situations that were familiar to you?
- Were you surprised at some of the outcomes?
- What do these role plays help you to understand about Transforming Power?

TRANSFORMING POWER QUARTETS

Purpose: To discuss applying Transforming Power alternatives to real situations; to see if using these ideas in your own way can help with your own choices, and be useful in your personal situation; to provide more one-on-one contact between participants and build trust and the feeling of a community of shared concerns and methods.

Time: 30-45 minutes.

Materials: Transforming Power cards or sheets for each person.

Sequence:
1. Divide participants into groups of four. If possible, have a facilitator join each group once the groups are set. If not, you might wish to write the four topics on four different slips of paper so that you can give the next one to a group that has finished the first without interruption.
2. Pass out Transforming Power sheets or cards and say: "These can be helpful in choosing some alternatives to violence. They can be useful ideas in a situation. Read them over and see if they can be applied to the situations we are about to discuss."
3. Say: " I am about to read a topic. Someone in your group may volunteer to speak from his/her experience about this first topic. The rest of the group will listen and then look on the Transforming Power sheets to see if anything there can be useful in the situation being described. You can also give the speaker your own advice and suggestions about this situation. After you have finished discussing the first person's experience, another member of your group is welcome to share his/her experience and have the group respond. After all have had an opportunity to speak, we will go on to the next topic."

    Discussion Topics:
    A. A situation in my own life which led to violence.
    B. What triggers a violent reaction in me personally?
    C. What if someone is coming at me with violence?
    D. In the long run, is violence ever a good response?

4. Read Topic A. Once the groups start talking, facilitators in the group need to move on to the next topic when the discussion seems to wind down. The other facilitators keep the discussions in their individual groups on track, and give Transforming Power ideas.
    Note: if there are not enough facilitators to have one in each group, have them go around to present the next topic so that the discussion continues in each group, rather than have a group sit quietly waiting for other groups to finish their topic.
5. Call time when all groups seem to have finished.

Processing:
   Note: Don't rush the discussion. Facilitators can add their own Transforming Power suggestions on each subject for a few minutes in each case, if appropriate.
- Can someone from each group tell us a story on any of the topics, and the Transforming Power alternatives they found?
- What other advice did you give in this situation?
- Anyone want to comment on this advice?
- What other topics would be good for this exercise?

TRANSFORMING POWER: REVERSE MANDALA

Purpose: To reintroduce the concept of Transforming Power.

Time: 30 minutes.

Materials: Posted mandala, newsprint.

Sequence:
1. Post the mandala in a prominent place before the workshop starts (along with the other posters of the AVP Philosophy, AVP Building Blocks, Guides to Transforming Power, etc.).

2. On a sheet of newsprint, draw the outline of the mandala and ask the group to agree on the words which are the opposite of each section, e.g. "Caring for Others" becoming "Not Caring for Others." It has the same effect as comparing/contrasting violence and nonviolence, and leads to a larger discussion of Transforming Power

VALUES CLARIFICATION
For Prison Workshops

Purpose: The purpose of this exercise is to help individuals examine what their values have been, what they are now and to consider how you would like to change them for the future. The format described here is for use in prisons but it could be easily altered for use by other groups by changing the designations of the before and after categories to "Previous to Now" and "In the Future."

Time: Approximately 60 minutes.

Materials: Values Clarification Grid Handout, pencils.

Sequence:
1. Pass out the form with the values areas designated or brainstorm the value areas the group wishes to have included. (Often in a Second Level workshop this may not be necessary since the group has already indicated their areas of concern in setting the goals for the workshop.)

2. Explain that individuals working alone will write in the various boxes the values they have had, have now or want to have in regard to each value area listed. They should be as honest as they can with themselves in order to get the most out of the exercise. They will not have to share anything they have written down with others unless they choose to do so.

3. Demonstrate the exercise by going down the various areas and giving examples of values. (This is most effective if it is a shared task between inside and outside facilitators alternating sample responses.) For example, if the category were money, a sample response in the "Before Prison" box might be "Get as much money as I can any way I can." In the "Now" box it might be "Have enough money to start my own business and have a nice house and a new car." And in the "After Prison" box might be "Have enough money to support my family."

4. It is usually helpful to do this with each of the categories as a warm up. Then allow 20 to 30 minutes for the individuals to fill in their boxes. Explain that spelling or the language they write in is not important since they are the only ones who will have to read it. They do not even have to put down complete sentences just so long as they know what it means.

5. Break into small groups. Four is a good size and five is maximum. Have a facilitator in each group to help keep the discussion going. Try to talk about each of the categories but let the group select where to start. Don't ask individuals directly what they put down on their chart but rather ask, "What does anyone want to say about (name the category)?" Let people share whatever they want on the topic and then move on to the next. Facilitators need to keep the discussion moving. It is also important for facilitators to be open and share from their own responses.

Processing:
After about 30 minutes bring the groups back to the large circle and debrief.

Note:
Some of the most frequently used categories have been: Money, Family, Employment, Education, Women, Sex, Drugs & Alcohol, Other People's Rights.

HANDOUT

VALUES CLARIFICATION EXERCISE

Categories	Before Prison	Now	After Prison

Values Clarification Handout

WHAT'S IN MY CIRCLE

Purpose: To clarify and prioritize ones values.

Time: 30 minutes.

Materials: Handout or letter-sized paper, envelopes, pencils, newsprint posted with the questions in #'s 2, 3, 4, 5 below.

Sequence:
Explain that in life we make choices, and those choices are based on our values. This exercise is to help us recognize which are long-term values and which are short-term values that may change.

Part I
1. Pass out the handout and pencils (or a piece of paper on which the participants draw a large circle). Then say: "In this circle, list answers to the question:

    What are some of the things I care about?"
    (give examples: family, being a good father to my son/daughter,
    my future freedom, having a safe space while in prison, money, religion)

2. After four or five minutes, ask them to study their lists and answer the following:

    Which am I willing to sacrifice if I can't have both
    it and another value important to me?
    Mark these with a symbol of your choice.

3. After people seem to have finished this, ask them to study their lists again and answer the following:

    Which am I willing to stand up for?
    Mark these with a symbol of your choice.

4. After people seem to have finished doing this, ask them to study their lists again and answer the following:

    Which am I willing to die for?
    (you may prefer to use "live" instead of "die")
    Mark these with a symbol of your choice.

5. After people seem to have finished doing this, ask them to study their lists again and answer the following:

    Which am I willing to go to prison for, or have my sentence extended for?
    Mark these with a symbol of your choice.

Note:
AFTER they have answered the questions, post the list of questions so that you can refer to them after the next part. Posting the questions before might mean that they spent too little time focusing on each one.

Part II
1. Have the participants fold up their papers and put them in their pockets to have available. Then, divide them into groups of three.
2. Say: "Take time to think of a conflict you experienced that ended in violence, or a conflict or situation you are in now that could end in violence. Give a few minutes for people to think, and then take turns sharing the conflict with your small group."
    (Give 3 minutes per person, approximately.)

Part III
1. Say: "Take out your circles and look at what you have written in them. Think about the conflict you just shared. Did it reflect the values that you have in your circle? During that experience, did you sacrifice a value that you didn't mark in your circle as being willing to sacrifice? During that experience were you — or are you — willing to die for something you did not mark in your circle? Did you stand up for a value you marked in your circle as something you would stand up for? Answer these questions in your own mind. You do not have to share them."

2. Bring people back to the large group. Process with the following questions:
   - Did anyone learn anything you would like to share?
   - If you could do the circle over, would you change some of the values in it? Add to them? Subtract from them?
   - Did you sacrifice one of your values during that experience, or will you have to in the experience you are anticipating? Is it the one you indicated in your circle that you were willing to sacrifice?
   - Will the values you now have in your circle help you to make choices in the future about what actions you take in potential conflict situations?
   - Is there a Transforming Power guide that applies to making choices about values?

   Note:
   You may want to have participants do Part I, and then have them fold up the papers and tape them shut, and then have them put their names on the outside (or, use envelopes). Later in the workshop, have them share in groups experiences that ended violently, and then pass out their circles and continue with the exercise.

HANDOUT

WHAT'S IN MY CIRCLE?

No one but you will read what you have written on this sheet. Try to be as thoughtful and honest as you can be. You may wish to take this with you at the end of this workshop, so that you can refer to it again to see if you would want to change what you put in the circle.

Which am I willing to sacrifice if I can't have both it and another value important to me?

Mark these with a symbol of your choice.

Which am I willing to sacrifice if I can't have both it and another value important to me?

Mark these with a symbol of your choice.

Which am I willing to stand up for?

Mark these with a symbol of your choice.

Which am I willing to die for?
(you may prefer to use "live" instead of "die")

Mark these with a symbol of your choice.

Which am I willing to go to prison for, or have my sentence extended for?

Mark these with a symbol of your choice.

WHISPERED AFFIRMATIONS – FORGIVENESS CIRCLE

Purpose: To learn how we can overcome the barriers to our being our best selves. To get affirmation to counter negative messages. To identify mental blocks to self-forgiveness. To give support to one another To experience validation and improve self-esteem.

Time: About 30 minutes.

Materials: 3x5" cards and pencils. A soft music CD/ Tape if available.

Sequence:
1. Tell the group: "We receive many negative messages throughout our lives. We store them inside ourselves, and they have a powerful effect on us and how we feel about ourselves. They can affect how capable we are of being in control of our lives. It is important to balance those negative messages with positive ones that affirm our goodness and our worthiness so that we become strong, capable and caring people."

    a) Hand out 3x5" cards and pencils. Participants should close their eyes, sit back and think what is blocking their taking the next step to healing, self-forgiveness, change or growth (whatever is appropriate for their particular focus). What messages did they get as children or from life experiences that make those blocks relevant today? (e.g., A parent or a teacher said, "You'll never amount to anything." Or chemical dependency taught you, "You're a drunken failure.") Now, for each negative message you remember, write down a positive message that balances it. (e.g., "You are smart and capable," "You are in recovery and you can do things well.") Remind people that these all have to be positive "you" messages.

    b) Collect all the affirmation cards and shuffle them.

Variation for FORGIVENESS CIRCLE

Have written on newsprint or have read several times the queries:
- What stands in the way of forgiving myself (or another)?
- What would I give up to get forgiveness?

After everyone has written an answer on the 3x5 card, ask them to write an affirmation that contradicts or eliminates the block they have. For example, if I write "Accepting that I'm doing as well as I can" as my block, I might write the affirmation: "You are doing the best you know how" or "You are good enough" or something that counters the old put-down tapes. Collect all the affirmation cards and shuffle them.

---

2. Divide the group into two by counting off by 2s. Have everyone stand and all the 2s pull their chairs into a circle facing inward. Have them sit down and get comfortable. Ask the 1's to stand behind them, one in back of each chair. Hand out the affirmation cards, TWO cards to each one of the 1s.

Explain the process below and then ask for questions. Put on soft music in the background. Check with the group if they are comfortable with hands touching shoulders. Have the 1s close their eyes, and if possible, dim the lights before 2s begin to move around the circle. Tell everyone to do this in a quiet and respectful way so everyone can hear their own affirmation.

Take one card, bend over and whisper the affirmation into the left ear of the person in front of you. Say their name first... e.g. "John, you are a wonderful loving and caring person who has many friends who love you..."

Take the next card and read it whispering into the right ear. Move slowly to the person on the right and repeat the process. Continue until you return to the first person.

Tell the group seated to open their eyes. In silence, ask the 2s to then stand up, trade places with the person behind their chair, and receive that person's two affirmation cards.

Have them read the affirmations now to the seated 1s as was done when they were seated.

Process:
Reconvene in the large circle and invite participants to share what the experience was like for them. This should be kept brief if participants cannot stay at the feeling/emotions level.

WHO SAYS I AM?

Purpose: To explore feelings about being labeled and how people deal with those feelings.

Time: About 20 minutes.

Materials: Newsprint and a marker; a printed poster with questions listed in #2.

Sequence:
1. In the large group, do a brainstorm for labels which participants have heard applied to people — as individuals or as groups — in the prison, in the community or world-wide.

2. Split into groups of three or four to discuss the questions:
   - Have any of these labels been applied to you?
   - What were your feelings about this?
   - Did you think of doing something about it?
   - How did you handle it?

   Choose one of these experiences to share in your group.

   Note:
   These questions should be posted on newsprint for all to see.

3. Return to the circle in groups to share the experiences they've chosen.
   (You may wish to write down strategies people have found successful.)

Processing:
- What did you think of what you heard?
- Was it a surprise to find how many of us believe that we have been labeled?
- Why do people label other people? How does this affect us all?
- What Transforming Power guides apply here?

YOU SAID / I SAID

Purpose: To use listening and assertion skills when conflict or controversy arises, and to see how they can enhance understanding or resolution.

Time: 60-70 minutes.

Materials: Card marked Responder for each group. Newsprint listing suggested topics for discussion. (See #5, below)

Sequence:

This works best with a group of 6 or 8 participants. Be sure that you have a facilitator with each group.

1. Announce the topic. If no topic has arisen from previous discussion, post a newsprint list of those topics suggested under step 4 below, and brainstorm for others that people on both sides of the issue tend to feel very strongly about (e.g., abortion, prison abolition).
2. Divide group into 2 teams along lines of opinion held on the topic.
3. Arrange chairs in 2 rows. Put your teams, facing each other, in the chairs. Ask for a volunteer to start.
4. Explain the steps as follows:

    a) You will have a chance to state your position. One member of the other team will hold responder card.

    b) When you have finished, the person holding the responder card will restate what s/he heard you say, and then give you one opportunity to correct any misunderstanding before s/he states his or her own position.

    c) When the first responder starts to talk, the facilitator will take the responder card away from him or her and give it to someone on the opposite team. That person will be the next responder, and will respond to the first responder, who is now the speaker and giving his or her own position.

    d) Keep this process going until everyone has spoken and been responded to in this way.

    Emphasize that this is not a debate, and that the goal is to find points of agreement or common ground. (For example, if we are discussing euthanasia, we might all agree that the suffering of people who are dying of painful diseases is terrible.)

5. Suggested topics for discussion: (Others may be brainstormed. In brainstorming, facilitator should call for topics about which this group does not agree or is in conflict.)
   - Is abortion ethical when the mother's life is not threatened?
   - Is euthanasia (helping a terminally ill person to die) ethical?
   - Is it ever right to strike a child?
   - Should people be able to play their radios as loud as they want?
   - Power is good/power is bad.
   - Should prisons be abolished?
   - Is there such a thing as constructive criticism?

Processing:
- What influence, if any, did this exercise have in causing people to change their original positions?
- How did the change come about — what caused you to change your mind?
- Was any resolution reached to an existing controversy or conflict?

Note: The experience of those who developed this exercise indicates that the process seems to work best if, rather than being conducted on a theoretical level, participants live through it by assuming roles, such as the attending doctor and the family members of a dying person on life support.

SECTION E

The Boxing Ring

**Role Playing
Variations on a Theme**

THE BOXING RING
A New Approach for Role Plays

Purpose: A scripted role play technique created by LEAP, a London-based AVP program, provides a structured and safe environment for experimenting with alternative ways of responding to potentially violent situations. The title conveys the basic structure: the ring, the rounds, the referee and coaches in the corners.

Time: At least 60 minutes.

Materials: Gummed labels or strips of masking tape for the players in the role play: the principals. coaches, and referee. Other props as necessary according to the scenario.

Sequence:
1. Introduction: Explain the purpose of the boxing ring. In AVP workshops, its primary uses are for skill development (assertiveness, communication) and to provide participants with an experience of conflict resolution in action. It gives participants a real opportunity to slow down, see with more clarity, explore choices, experience different options and to give and receive support from the group. It also allows other members of the group the opportunity to be involved as coaches and monitors rather than just spectators.

2. The Scenario: The whole group will decide on a situation that will test the role players. One way to do this is by brainstorming followed by values voting: everyone can vote as often as s/he wishes and the scenario with the top number wins. In the sample scenario used here, one person is accused by another of stealing his radio.

3. Casting:
   a) **The Players:** Ask for volunteers to take both roles. Give the characters melodramatic stage names and write these names on gummed labels (masking tape) placed on their clothing to distinguish clearly between the role player and the person's real identity as a group member. In this case, "Big Jim" will accuse "Humble Herb" of stealing his radio. Big Jim will be the aggressor and Humble Herb will seek to keep his cool and try to defuse the situation.

   b) **The Coaches:** Both role players will be assigned two volunteer coaches, who will give ideas and tips to the role players between rounds. Each role player has time before the role play begins to prepare with their coach. One or two other group members are asked to be **monitors** to give feedback at the end of the role play about the effectiveness of the coaching.

   c) **The Referee:** This role will be played by a facilitator who will set the scene, designate the coaching corners, explain the rules and ensure that they are honored. Rules are:
      1. No physical contact is allowed. Characters must stay at least a foot apart.
      2. The referee can call "freeze" if the role play becomes too heated. At this point the role players are to stop and the referee may restate the agreed-upon rules, or send players to their corners.
      3. The role players also have the right to stop the action by calling "time out."

4. **The First Round:**
As the role play begins, the two characters eye each other warily as they enter the ring. Big Jim tells Humble Herb that he knows that Herb has taken his radio and he wants it back. Humble Herb says that he doesn't know what Jim is talking about. The temperature rises. After two or three minutes, the ref calls the end of the round. This call should be made when there is enough material for the coaches to work on, or when either player is in need of some support. Ending the round depends on judgment rather than strict obedience to the clock.

In the corner, Humble Herb's coaches make suggestions to resolve the problem. Big Jim's coaches are encouraging him to keep the pressure on. The next round will begin when the referee determines that the coaches have had enough time to do their work. Between rounds, in consultation with the players, the ref may decide to make the next scene an hour or a day later, or in a different location. The ref gives thirty seconds warning before the next round.

5. **The Second Round:**
In the second round, Humble Herb asks Big Jim if they can talk over the problem of the missing radio and come up with ideas of what to do about it. But Big Jim doesn't want to talk; he wants his radio and if he doesn't get it, there will be trouble. Humble Herb tries to be sympathetic about the loss of the radio. Big Jim continues to accuse Humble Herb and the role play is going nowhere. The ref calls the end of the round.

6. **The Third Round:**
Round three begins with no appreciable advance. Humble Herb's coaches have not been able to give him any fresh ideas. Humble Herb maintains his cool but the dispute seems deadlocked. In this case, however, he has a sudden thought. He remembers where he first saw the radio. "It was Bob's radio when I came on this wing. As I recall, you stole it from him in the first place!" Big Jim opens his mouth but can't think of anything to say. He takes the challenge in good humor and shakes Humble Herb's hand.

Processing:
- Begin the debriefing process by carefully removing players from their roles, taking off their name tags and restoring them to their real selves.
- Discuss the role play in the larger group. The discussion should center on elements in the action that either escalated or de-escalated the conflict. One participant suggested that the ending would not have worked out if the accusation had not been true. It was also pointed out that Humble Herb's offer to discuss the problem showed genuine and sympathetic concern.

Note:
The boxing ring structure has demonstrated its value in working with a variety of groups in different settings.

ROLE PLAYING
Variations on a Theme

Role play is a powerful tool, and is central to AVP workshops.

The Basic Manual has a complete section on Role Play. We use those methods in this workshop, but that material is not repeated here. The following additional methods are suggested, to be used as may seem appropriate, perhaps to add variety to the workshop, or because a specific situation seems to call for their use.

However, take care to facilitate well ... these methods can lead into some unexpected depth at times, and make sure that you are confident about processes such as de-roling (transitioning a person out of role and helping them reflect on the similarities, differences and learnings that character has given them), and careful debriefing as a group to acknowledge any strong feelings or sensitivities that may have arisen.

DEROLING:

Deroling is essential, especially if someone has taken on a role into which they have invested some energy. It can be simple (e.g., taking off a name tag) but in many cases it is an opportunity to gain some significant learning from the experience. Also, don't underestimate the power of being in role, even if the role-player hasn't shown it to be so.

Please also make sure that the group does not refer to people by their role name after the role play. One way is to create a 'doorway' from the role play out into the workshop.
- Ask person if they are ready to step through the door and leave their role behind.
- Take off their name tag and stick it on the chair saying "I am no longer ... (role name), I am ... (real name)."
- To further disassociate with the role, ask the role-player to then face the empty chair and, as his/her **real self,** give any advice or comments to the role-play character, as if the role-play character were still sitting in the chair.

Facilitator Interviews
- What was it like being ...?
- How are you similar to ...?
- How are you different from ...?
- What could you, with your experience and wisdom, offer to this character as a way forward?
- Thank the player for all they have shared and taught the group.
- Thank the group for their sharing of wisdom.

ACTIONS SPEAK LOUDER THAN WORDS... VARIATIONS ON ROLEPLAYS

Thought Sculpture

Purpose: Exploring the mind-set of a person (for example, a person offered drugs).

Place an empty chair before the group. Define it as the person in the situation described. People come up, sit in the empty chair, and offer what might be going through that person's mind. Get different points of view. Then have discussion. Or play around. Put people with "do" thoughts on one side and "don't" thoughts on the other. Have them shout at each other all at once. This can be quite effective when done around a major character in the role-play (perhaps an inmate going home for the first time).

Another variation is to be a person in relation to their character who is trying to offer support or counsel, and ask them to do a second round, initially repeating their characters statement or feeling, then sitting in a chair beside the character and offering that advice/statement of empathy.

Confrontation in Triads
- Done in groups of three: a confronter, a confrontee and an observer.
- Confronter confronts confrontee with some failing that the confronter wants corrected.
- Confrontee responds.
- Allow three minutes, then ask observer to report what happened and how each party behaved.
- Confronter and confrontee then reverse roles and repeat; observer again reports. Debrief in large group.

Listening
Get people into pairs. Then use the following sequence, always giving 30 seconds of silence for reflection at the start of each segment. Give 30 seconds for people to think about what they heard and what they said, then take turns reflecting it back to their partner. Then ask for comments from the whole group (staying in place).
1. Tell a story for one minute, a word at a time, alternating the word between them. The story should have a beginning / middle and end. Freeze. While people remain in pairs, reflect in large group about experience —who managed to finish, How did people find it? Easy? Difficult? What made it challenging? What does this have to do with listening? Facilitation?
2. Both talk at once —no pauses. Use simple non-threatening subject, e.g. what I did on my way to the workshop this morning. One minute, then freeze. Take turns at reflecting to your partner what you heard him or her say. Briefly discuss in the large group.
3. Talk in turns; listener has "stony face" (no non-verbal communication, but maintain eye contact). Subject such as "something that gives me great pleasure is..." One minute. Freeze. Swap over. Then process in whole group...
   - What did you notice?
   - How did you feel when someone wasn't responding?
   - Why is that important to you?
   - What did it feel like to not respond?
   - How well did you listen?
   - What does this have to do with listening?
4. Talk with true subject, and follow rules of reflective listening, e.g. "An experience of aloneness was when..." or something about the theme of the workshop. Three minutes. Reflect. Swap. Process about the experience, not the content of what was shared.
5. You could brainstorm a chart listing the attributes of effective listening.

Open Chair
Allows up to three people to play the same role simultaneously.

Place one empty chair for each character involved in the roleplay (at least two chairs) facing each other or in a circle. Label the chairs with the name of the character they stand for. Assign to each chair three volunteers, who will all stand behind the chair and any of whom may speak for the character it represents. (Their statements do not have to be consistent.) Allow a maximum of five minutes for the roleplay, less if it becomes too uncomfortable or plays itself out to a resolution.
Or
Have the characters created by the whole group, labeled onto chairs, and then allow volunteers to come and sit in the seats for as long as they feel they have something to add.
De-role as whole group ...

Continuums

Continuum on Experience:
This is a good way to find the range of experience of a group. Define one end of the room as "1(I am very experienced...)" and the other end as "10 (I have no experience)."

Continuum of Opinions
Facilitator makes a statement which reflects two polarized strongly held opinions e.g., "No-one should ever take mind-altering drugs because they are bad" to "mind-altering drugs have a useful place in our society" (keep the statements simple and unambiguous). Ask people to put themselves somewhere along the line that they think represents either themselves or someone they may be interested in understanding some more. For any category (for example, drug use and culture), ask people to place themselves where they think they belong on the continuum.

Processing:
- Get them to talk to a neighbor first, to get a sense of similarities.
- Ask clusters to say something that represents their choice, with the whole group listening. Then ask someone in a different spot. One way of doing this is to break the group at the half-way mark and then shift the half line along beside the other so that the middle people are talking to the ends. This ensures a good contrast, or you may choose pairs who might benefit from talking together.
- Bring the whole group back together in a circle to reflect on learnings (if it 'went somewhere).

Continuum on Big Wave:
Rather than using "1" though "10" as above, describe an enormous wave coming to shore. Describe the space in the room as a lovely day at the beach, and ask for a volunteer to step into that particular place as you go out on the ocean in a boat, (one end), surfing on water, swimming, paddling, beach-combing, sunbathing, picnic on the dunes or grass, wandering on a hill behind the beach, in the woods on a hill, sitting on a hill-top looking out, or in a meadow beyond the hill (other end).

Then tell them that this enormous wave comes out of nowhere. And ask them to describe how the wave appears to them in their position — what happens to them? Make an analogy to the chosen subject, e.g., the theme of the workshop or other important topic. Have people place themselves (in that same position) in relation to that subject (e.g. "what is it like to nearly 'drown' in a situation of cross cultural conflict?"). They can play themselves or take the role of the person they wish to understand. If too many are bunched together, move them around; ask them to fill missing places. Ask them to describe themselves, then talk to someone in another place.

Process the learnings as a whole group.

Additional Variations
1. **Alter Ego:** In an open-group role play, each participant has someone standing behind him/her, who says what he imagines the participant might be thinking or feeling but has not said aloud. This is particularly useful when the character becomes 'stuck.'

2. **Stop before solution:** This gives everyone a chance to work together on what the best solution might be, either by brainstorming or by a group discussion. Then replay the solution.
   - you can take the two main characters, get suggestions from the group on how to seek a resolution, then split the whole group into pairs and they take on the two roles to try out possible solutions. Some may wish to replay them in front of the whole group.

3. Ask people to come up and model someway that a particular character might be able to talk to another in a tricky or stuck situation in the role play. Let the main 'player' watch from the side and then choose the one that suits them the best and retry it.

4. **Reverse roles:** Do role play twice, reversing roles, with careful directions that it's not to be a caricature, but a real chance to experience a different point of view.

5. **Model role play:** Prepare in advance a scenario to be done by team members or by interested participants to bring out some aspect considered important by them.

6. **Variation on "Hassle lines"** exercise: Ask the whole group to create the opposing character, and then play them through. This can lead into a large group focused exercise, and deepens the experience. Everyone is more focused, and playing the roles all at once overcomes some people's shyness.

Note:
See Sculpting, in the Section D.

SECTION F

Talks - Explanations

Opening Statement
Suggested Points to Cover

Anger

Anger, Fear & Taking a Stand

Communication

Empathy

Fear

Forgiveness

Removing the Obstacles to Forgiveness

Making Friends with Conflict

Power

Stereotyping

OPENING STATEMENT
Suggested points to cover

- The Second Level Course builds on the Basic Workshop and goes deeper into things. It has a different sense of time. We want to spend more time on things that seem important to the group.

- We will be perfecting skills developed in the basic workshop and learning new skills to add to them. Some of these skills will be about relating to people, communicating with them, working with them. We will build on respect and caring.

- We will be focusing on other skills relating to what goes on inside ourselves: how we can free ourselves to be open to creative and transforming possibilities.

- We will take a deep look at some obstacle or problem area that seems important to the group and that gets in the way of conflict management.

- Conflict has roots in our perceptions, attitudes, and expectations of persons and events. We can learn about human behavior from our own conduct; in order to lessen conflict by communicating and cooperating better with one another, choose to make changes in our perceptions, attitudes and expectations.

- Reminder of the AVP guidelines which we used in the Basic Workshop:
  1) Affirm one another.
  2) Give others space. All should participate in discussions but no one should monopolize them.
  3) Give everybody a respectful hearing; no interrupting one another.
  4) No putdowns of ourselves or others.
  5) Everything that happens in the workshop is confidential. Do not repeat anything that is said here.
  6) Volunteer yourself; do not volunteer other people. In the way we say things as well as what we do, use I-Statements.
  7) Everybody has the right to pass.

- Attendance at all sessions is expected. New participants are not admitted to the workshop after the second session, as the need to accommodate new people breaks the flow of the program. Those who want to participate but could not make the first, or second session, are invited to sign up for the next Second Level workshop.

- Announce schedule and times of the workshop and discuss housekeeping details: Location of toilets, meals, sign-up sheets, etc.

- Certificates of completion will be awarded at the end of the workshop to all those who have completed it satisfactorily. If the question arises at any time during the workshop, it is usual to state that the certificates will have no influence with the Parole Board unless changes in behavior are noticed by the authorities.

ANGER

Our culture and our psyches give us 3 different ways to look at anger:

1) Anger is wrong and destructive. It can damage the angry person and others, and it is the major, if not the only, cause of violence. Good people do not get angry.

2) Anger is a feeling, neither good nor bad. It shouldn't be suppressed; great damage is done by suppressing it. Good people do get angry, and they express their anger openly. Anger is not destructive; only violence is destructive.

3) Anger has its rewards and its pleasures, and its very practical uses. You cannot dispense with anger. You do not even want to. You could not survive if you did.

When we are angry, these different messages collide. We are either frozen or frenzied by the internal conflict, and almost anything we do — whether frozen or frenzied — stands a good chance of being the wrong thing. What we need, therefore, is to take a look at anger — at what it really is and how it really functions — so that we can develop our own individual, non-destructive, perhaps even creative ways of coping with it.

Anger is a response to pain or hurt. When we feel pain or hurt, our muscular system mobilizes. The anger emotions are one such response; the anger emotions seek to confront the cause of the pain. There is nothing simple about its effects, starting with the physiological changes that take place as anger escalates, and ending with the destruction it can leave in its wake.

We feel the anger emotions as a rush of feeling upward and frontward to the head and arms, where they are released as increased physical strength and movement of the upper body and/or facial muscles, directed at the source of the pain. The escalation of the anger emotions is:

1. Annoyance (very slight hurt.)
2. Irritation (persistent slight hurt.)
3. Anger (real pain, which is beginning to get to us – the angry person is still in control, and can adjust his/her actions.)
4. Rage (the pain has become an agony; the person feels driven to the wall.)
5. Fury (the pain has become unthinkable, and so all thinking has stopped.)

Anger provides the energy for confronting a problem. When that energy is used by the person to think through the problem so that s(he) can communicate effectively with an opponent, it can lead to positive results. In AVP, a major goal is to help people learn how to communicate effectively about things that make them angry.

Effective communication is not yelling or blaming; it is not sulking in silence. For communication to be effective, it must be stated clearly by the speaker in a manner that does not get in the way of its being heard by the hearer. The speaker must be assertive without being aggressive. The speaker should state a problem and let the blame take care of itself.

It is important to understand what can happen when anger is not resolved. There is a limit to the body's ability to sustain the peak energy brought about by anger. If it is too often repeated or too long sustained, anger can exhaust the body and spirit, causing an individual to burn out. If it is unacknowledged or unreconciled, it can turn into depression. If a bout of anger leads to a resolved conflict, the anger has accomplished its purpose and fades into history. If not, it is likely to bury itself in the psyche, where its specific content will be forgotten but its energy will remain active.

This is how those buttons are installed which later in life can so easily be pushed and reactivate a pattern of anger. Patterned anger of this kind is destructive, because it can no longer be aimed at the pain that caused it – that problem has been forgotten – and is aimed instead at hurts or problems that it cannot solve, because it is not about those problems, really. Such anger, with regard to the external problem, can do more harm than good. The pattern is hard to stop unless the original hurt that caused it is uncovered and worked through. There is nothing simple about exposing and healing the festering wounds caused by anger in our past that has been left unresolved and sometimes is not even remembered.

Since stale and forgotten anger is so powerfully destructive, it is much better to use the anger response as nature intended it to be used – to confront and solve the cause of the hurt when it is fresh, stimulated by the energy of the anger, and using the power of communication which anger at this stage leaves with us.

Whether or not the anger buttons can be disconnected, it is possible to hesitate momentarily when they are pushed, and open the mind to the possibility of another approach to the immediate problem. This momentary suspension has often been known to serve as an invitation for Transforming Power to intervene, when people have been willing and able to try for it.

Note: See also ANGER, FEAR, AND TAKING A STAND

Exercises Pertaining to Anger

Body Imaging	I-Messages	Projection
Buttons	In His Shoes	Rumors
Dealing with Put-Downs	Injunctions of Childhood & Life	Sculpting
Escalator	Masks	Three Questions on Oppression
Exploring Roots of Anger	Processing Anger	
Grief		

ANGER, FEAR, AND TAKING A STAND

The anger emotions are closely related to the fear emotions, which are also a response to pain, and which also have five escalating steps: Apprehension, Anxiety, Fear, Panic, and Terror. The difference is that while the anger emotions seek to confront the cause of pain, the fear emotions seek to withdraw or flee from it. The physical direction of the feelings aroused by the fear emotions is backward and down, centering in the back of the neck; the head will be pulled backward and the shoulders will rise — in other words, the person will cringe. These emotional gamuts and their bodily reactions are opposite faces of the same coin. They both proceed from the physiological state of the person, and so closely are they related that if the characteristic body movements are exchanged, the emotions will change with them. If a fearful person adopts an angry stance and confronts the source of fear, s/he will lose his fear and become angry. If the angry person adopts a cringing posture, s/he will lose his anger and become afraid.

Both the anger and the fear emotions correspond to the "fight or flight" syndrome. There is, however, a third option that can be chosen in the same circumstances that inspire anger and fear. It is the option of taking a stand. It transforms the simple emergency emotions of anger and fear, because it does not merely arise. Instead, it is chosen as a conscious option. The physiological stance of this response is one of physically grounding oneself. The feet are planted firmly, the face is lifted upward and toward the opponent, the hands are at the sides or in a non-threatening position. The emotional effect on the one taking the stand is one of stability, a calming of both anger and fear, and the feeling of being able to cope somehow with whatever comes.

One of the most eloquent expressions of this state of mind was that of the Protestant reformer, Martin Luther, when ordered by the Pope to withdraw his criticisms of the Church or suffer some horrendous medieval punishment: "Here I stand, I cannot do otherwise. God help me. Amen."

This third response to hurtful or frightening circumstances is one that is sometimes brought on by Transforming Power working through people; it is certainly the one that is most likely to invite that Power to work.

Fear is difficult to deal with. One fear that most of us do have is the fear of admitting to fear. Yet, fear is part of living. If we feared nothing, spirit and imagination would be dead.

Fear can be a spur to do our best, keep us at top performance, (e.g., on the job, without fear of poor ratings or job loss, it's easy to get lazy). Fear can give us strength we didn't know we had (to rescue a drowning person, lift a car off a child), can make us add prudence and knowledge to courage. It goes together with hope. To give up hope and fear is to give up the effort to be our best selves.

See exercises on page F-5 pertaining to Anger, and on page F-11 pertaining to Fear

COMMUNICATION
Types of Communication

There are four types of communication. These are passive communication, aggressive communication, passive-aggressive communication, and assertive communication.

These are four general ways in which a person can respond in any situation. It is particularly difficult to respond appropriately in a negative situation that raises a lot of emotions and stress. Responding appropriately, however, is a communication skill that one can learn and the skill has a tendency to improve over time with practice. The following is a description of each type of communication, how it tends to affect others, and how it affects the speaker (the one who is trying to communicate an idea or personal boundary to another individual).

Passive Communication

The speaker involved in passive communication tends to be a doormat and allows others to take advantage. The passive person does not express his/her true feelings, many times because s/he does not feel worthwhile and may believe that what s/he has to say is not important. This kind of communication tends to happen on the part of victims in an abusive relationship and may, on some level, represent a survival skill (for example, a victim in an abusive situation may choose not to speak out for fear of angering the abuser during a tension phase). In other situations, however, a passive person may want to speak out and feel as though s/he would not be in danger in doing so, but may feel unable (not know how) to speak out and express ideas or opinions. The passive person's motto tends to be "I am not O.K., but you are O.K." Therefore, the passive person may tend to give in to the feelings and opinions of others, while "stuffing" their own.

Aggressive Communication

The speaker involved in aggressive communication makes doormats of others and tends to take advantage. The aggressive communicator expresses his/her feelings and opinions regardless of the hurtful effect it may have on others, and may feel entitled to do so. The aggressive person may angrily or forcefully express him/herself at the cost of others and may disregard any objections others may have. The aggressive person takes over completely and does not give any consideration to others' ideas or feelings. The aggressive person's motto tends to be "I'm o.k. but you sure aren't o.k." Therefore, the aggressive person freely expresses his/her ideas, opinions, wants, and needs without any regard for the feelings or opinions of others.

Passive-aggressive Communication

The passive-aggressive person tends not to express his/her true feelings at the moment but works toward "getting back" at the other person at a later time. The passive-aggressive communicator may be resentful and plan some kind of revenge. The passive-aggressive person may feel hurt in some way, but may not believe him/herself capable of expressing this to the other. Therefore, the passive- aggressive person may feel justified in expressing pain or anger in an indirect way by hurting the other individual. Sometimes, the other individual involved may not even realize they are being hurt by the passive-aggressive person. The passive-aggressive person may believe that his/her own opinions are not important and may not feel worthwhile in expressing them directly. Passive-aggressive communication does not. involve direct confrontation, but the passive-aggressive person believes the other "deserves" what they get (in terms of the revenge plan). The passive-aggressive person's motto tends to be "I'm not O.K., but neither are you." Therefore, the passive-aggressive resentments hurts in an indirect way with the goal of hurting the other person back.

Assertive Communication

The assertive person is able to express his/her feelings and opinions without guilt while also allowing the other person to express feelings and thoughts which may differ. The assertive person stays true to his/her own feelings, says what they think in a direct way, and also respects other peoples' rights. Assertive communication allows an individual to be honest and direct with him/herself and also with others. The assertive person believes that it is O.K. to say "no" if s/he is uncomfortable with something or situation, feels good rather than guilty when standing up for him/herself, and communicates a positive attitude to others which respects a differing viewpoint. Negotiation is the key! The assertive person is able to maintain healthy boundaries with others. The assertive person's motto is "I am O.K. and you are O.K.,too." Therefore, the assertive person takes care of his/her own wants and needs and feels good about it — and also allows others to express themselves in terms of their feelings and opinions.

Principles of Assertiveness

- By standing on our rights we respect ourselves and get others' respect.
- Not letting others know how we feel is a form of controlling them.
- Sacrificing our rights can result in training others to mistreat us.
- If we don't tell others how their behavior affects us, we are denying them an opportunity to change.
- When we do what is right for us, we feel better about ourselves and have more authentic and satisfying relationships with others.
- Everyone has the right to courtesy and respect.
- We have a right to express ourselves as long as we don't violate the rights of others.
- Much is to be gained from life by being free and able to stand up for ourselves, and also from honoring the same rights in others.
- When we are assertive, everyone involved can benefit.

Processing:
- Where is assertiveness appropriate and where is it not?
- Discuss vulnerability.
- Discuss the relative degrees of power within a relationship and the effect of these differences on the use of assertiveness.

Exercises Pertaining to Communication:

Acknowledgment Process	Goal-Wish Problem Solving	Listening I Statement Combo
Active Listening	I Want/I Want	Masks
All Aboard	I-Messages	Parallel Construction
Assertiveness	In His Shoes	Perception
Buttons	Inclusion	Personal Space
Carefronting	Injunctions of Childhood & Life	Rumors
Dots		Tangram Dog
Escalator	Let's Go Swimming	Tinkertoy Dog
From Another Point of View		You Said / I Said

EMPATHY

Empathy is different from sympathy, just as compassion is different from pity.

Sympathy comes from the Greek word sympatheia, which means "feeling with or together." Empathy comes from the Greek word empatheia, which means "in a state of emotion." The English empathy means "the power of understanding things outside ourselves."

If you have sympathy, you stand with the other person. You feel/care about their hunger or pain.

If you have empathy, you stand inside the other person. You feel their hunger or pain.

With empathy, you try to understand not only what the other person does, but why s/he does it.

Empathy requires:
- involvement
- imagination
- insight
- identification
- interaction

If you are going to empathize, you must be willing to get involved with another human being, to recognize and honor that person's humanness, even though you may not accept his/her behavior.

If you are going to empathize, you must imagine the experience of what it is like to be that other human being and to feel his/her feelings. This means you leave behind the background and environment that shaped your values and attitudes.

If you are going to empathize, you must work to gain insight into the other person's thought processes — how that person's mind works. You must be able to understand (without judging) what the other person believes and values, and with what attitudes the person faces his/her decisions. A test is whether you can explain that person's beliefs or positions fairly and without demeaning them.

If you are going to empathize, you have to identify with a person's intentions and feelings. This does not mean you have to approve of the behavior. You might identify with the feeling a person has of being so hurt and angry that s/he seeks revenge without approving the revenge.

If you are going to empathize, you have to open yourself up to the other person enough to permit mutual exchange and mutual influence. Interaction requires us to recognize that we are all human beings (and that makes us of equal value).

Exercises pertaining to Empathy:

Anatomy of an Apology	Human to Human
Empathy	In His Shoes
Fairy Tale Theater	Projection
From Another Point of View	Speakout

FEAR

Fear is difficult to deal with. One fear that most of us do have is the fear of admitting to fear. Yet fear is part of living. If we feared nothing, spirit and imagination would be dead.

It can be a spur to do our best, keep us at top performance, (e.g., on the job, without fear of poor ratings or job loss, it's easy to get lazy). It can give us strength we didn't know we had (to rescue a drowning person, lift a car off a child), can make us add prudence and knowledge to courage. It goes together with hope. To give up hope and fear is to give up the effort to be our best selves.

Fear also tears down love. It attracts hate and violence. It can paralyze. Most mean actions can be ascribed to fear.

We often cover fear with anger. Anger manages fear but doesn't deal with it. Fear is flight part of fight/flight. Love/Fear/Control/Hate — an all too natural progression:

If you can't love, you fear. If you fear, you try to control. If you can't control, you hate. "In time we hate that which we often fear." - Shakespeare

How do our emotions work inside us? How do they relate to our personality?

Think of your personality as a series of concentric circles.

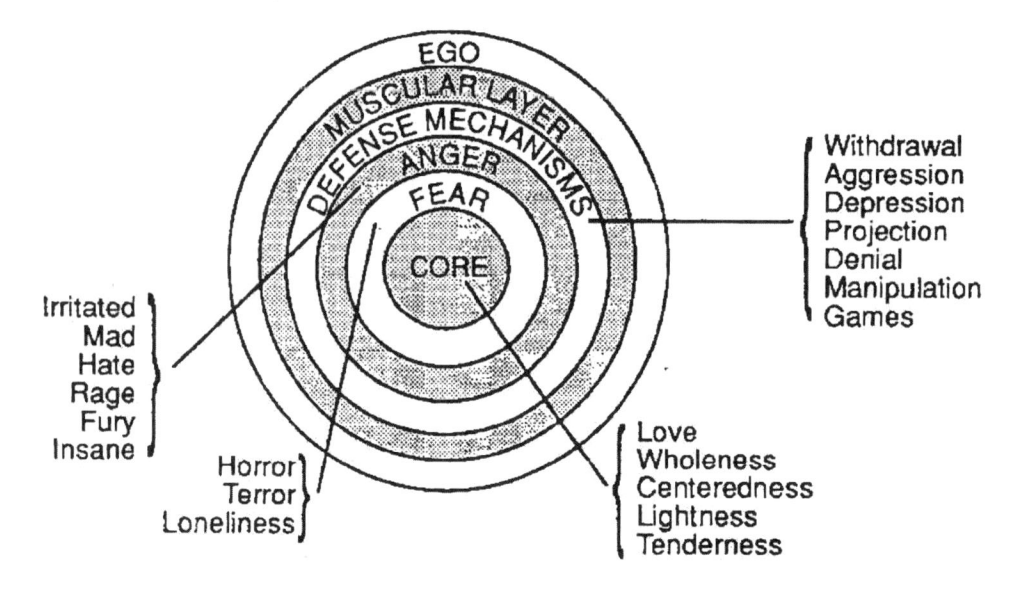

Concentric circles from outside to inside: EGO, MUSCULAR LAYER, DEFENSE MECHANISMS, ANGER, FEAR, CORE.

- Ego / Defense Mechanisms: Withdrawal, Aggression, Depression, Projection, Denial, Manipulation, Games
- Anger: Irritated, Mad, Hate, Rage, Fury, Insane
- Fear: Horror, Terror, Loneliness
- Core: Love, Wholeness, Centeredness, Lightness, Tenderness

The core is the source of our positive feelings: love, caring, authenticity, etc. Sometimes the core is blocked by fear. Some ways this works are:

Fear → Anger → Aggression
Or
Fear (Anger) → Withdrawal → Denial

Feelings get more generalized as one proceeds from the core to the outer rim of this circle. Thus, the initial fear may arise from a specific event or encounter with a specific person. Translated into anger, the feeling may become more generalized to include everything about that person. Escalated to aggression, the anger may become directed at everything about not only that person, but at everything about everyone of the same sex, or race as well, or even at everyone in the whole world.

One goal in exploring fear is to become more aware of what is going on inside us. Ultimately; the hope is to break through all these layers within ourselves and get in touch with the authentic self, the source of love and joy, the source of the spirit.

One can rid oneself of fears by taking a stand, making a statement, claiming a right, taking action, taking responsibility. Use small steps. Let each step, safely made, lead to another step. Get rid of small fears first. Then try working on a larger one. Learn to take charge, to take control. The more control over your fears you take, the more you will dare to take the next step.

Suggestions:
- Learn to relax, to deliberately take hold of your tension and release it.
- Use your breathing to calm yourself down. Count your breaths or silently say "In" with your in breath and "Out" with your out breath.
- Notice what fear feels like in your body and name it — "This is fear." Let yourself know you will live through the fear.
- Stop fearing in advance — stay in the present moment. Much is what we fear is not in the present moment but in some future time
- Do what frightens you, one step at a time.
- Learn to live with fear.

Exercises Pertaining to Fear:
Aliens (using fear)   Getting in Touch
Body Imaging   Personal Space
Concentric Circles

FORGIVENESS

Forgiveness is a growth process, and like other forms of growth, it is often difficult, frightening and painful, involving honest confrontation, risk and vulnerability on both sides.

There are several stages of forgiveness:
- **Hurt:** recognition that there is something that hurts.
- **Hate and anger:** awareness of anger, including a desire for revenge. (Hate is different from anger — anger moves us to action which can be positive. Hate can destroy the hater).
- **Heal:** see the truth of the other person, that they are needy, weak, need our help. They were persons before they hurt us and are persons now.
- **Come together:** forgiveness abolishes an existing barrier to fellowship, reestablishes freedom and the possibility of friendship. To accomplish this, each person must be truthful with the other. The other person must feel your hurt and understand what was done.

These steps have worked for countries as well as for individuals.

In the early 1990's, the system of apartheid ended in South Africa. Apartheid was a legal system of separation of the races and serious discrimination against blacks. Many people were worried that black South Africans would resort to violence in revenge for the terrible wrongs they had suffered.

Instead, the Truth and Reconciliation Commission (TRC), a court-like body was assembled in 1995, headed by Archbishop Desmond Tutu. Anybody who felt they had been a victim of violence could come forward and be heard at the TRC. Its purpose was to offer amnesty in exchange for full disclosure of events in the apartheid years. Perpetrators of violence could give testimony and request amnesty from prosecution. This way the country would know what happened, grieve, forgive, and move on. Without the disclosure, the past could not be put to rest.

The hearings were national and international news and many sessions were televised on national TV. The TRC was a crucial component of the nonviolent transition to full and free democracy in South Africa and, despite some flaws, is generally regarded as very successful. Other countries with violent and painful histories have also used Truth and Reconciliation Commissions, including Sierra Leone and Peru.

Bishop Tutu said at the end of the commission "We will have looked the beast in the eye. We will have come to terms with our horrendous past and it will no longer keep us hostage. We will cast off its shackles and, holding hands together, black and white will stride into the future."

Forgiving ourselves can also be difficult when we know we have hurt ourselves or someone else, but the same process of forgiveness can work for our own forgiveness, and help us to move on and live our lives with more inner peace.

Exercises Pertaining to Forgiveness:

Dealing with Put-Downs	Guided Reflection on	Magic Carpet
Forgiveness	Forgiveness	Three Questions on
From Another Point of	In His Shoes	Oppression
View	Injunctions of Childhood	Whispered Affirmations/
Grief	& Life	Forgiveness Circle

FORGIVENESS
REMOVING THE OBSTACLES TO FORGIVENESS

As human beings, we have a particular way of making sense out of our lives. We have stored up memories for everything that has ever happened to us, almost since the day of our births. Some of these memories are conscious, and others are buried deep in our subconscious. If we have hurtful or fearful things that have happened to us when we were young, we tend to cling to them for judging the past and the future.

It is as though our minds are motion-picture projectors: our memories become the images we project on the screen as we make judgments. When we understand that, we also understand that these judgments are filtered through the lens of our past — they are not without bias.

To prepare our minds for forgiveness, we need to deal with our memories. The "because" section of I-Messages addresses this: When an action (or someone's attitude) bothers us, it is "because" of all the stored memories that have shaped our attitudes, our beliefs — our judgment-making mechanism. When we accept responsibility for our own perceptions and projections, we are able to make new choices. We are better able to forgive, whether it is ourselves or others.

Our judgment-making mechanisms have been a long time in the making, so it is a challenge to take responsibility for the "because" in our responses, reactions and judgments. It is easier to place the blame on others: to believe that the "because" is due to their actions and not the stored up memories that produced our judgment-making mechanism.

But we can remove these obstacles to forgiveness:
- We can recognize our judgment-making mechanism for what it is; we can realize that holding on to unforgiving thoughts is a choice we make — a choice to suffer.
- We can understand that by denying forgiveness to others we punish ourselves with the festering wound of resentment.
- We can take new beliefs into our hearts, ones that allow us to see the value of letting go of self-condemnation and condemnation of others.
- We can overcome fear, shame and blame.
- We can become willing to see other people either as being loving, or fearful and as fellow human beings who may be giving a call for help.

The purpose of forgiveness is to release us from the painful legacy of the past. It is to free us from the grudges and grievances we have with other people.

MAKING FRIENDS WITH CONFLICT

Let's take a little time to explore our attitudes about conflict. Conflict is not the same as violence. Ask the following questions: How many people here like conflict? If you do, please raise your hands. (Usually few participants raise hands.) How many people would like to see a world without conflict? (This generally results in a multitude of raised hands.) How many people watched a television drama in the last week? (Ask the group to raise their hands in response to each question.) ... or saw a movie in the last month...or read a novel recently...or have ever seen a stage play? (Generally, most of the group will raise their hands in response to these questions.)

Would you have watched television, gone to the movies, read a novel or gone to a stage play if they did not involve conflict? Think about it! Would there be a story without conflict? (The reply is generally "No.") Conflict is essential to writing fiction. Conflict is an essential part of life.

What is important about these dramas is not that they involve conflict, but rather, how the conflict is resolved. In the case of the stage play, there are basically two kinds: if there is a negative solution, we call the play a tragedy, and the story generally ends with the death of the hero. If there is a positive solution, we call the play a drama or comedy, and the hero probably lives on, and because of having worked through the conflict in the drama, the hero will be a little wiser and have better skills and more confidence, making him/her better able to reach a positive solution in the next conflict that life offers. Positive relationships are about making friends with conflict.

The question for me is: "What I want to do with my life?" Do I choose a tragedy with a negative ending? Do I choose to make my life a comedy with a positive ending? How can I make my life a comedy and not a tragedy? How can I embrace conflict and use it as an opportunity to learn to make the right choices?

What would the world be like without conflict? How would the world be if it were totally peaceful and harmonious, and if my interactions with others were never questioned or challenged? Would I have any need or desire to grow and change? Hardly! Personal growth is about making friends with conflict! Usually people only change when faced with conflict, because conflicts are vital in providing people with the incentive to grow and change.

Although we may experience conflicts as difficult and painful, they are truly a gift. Each conflict that comes along is a new opportunity for us to grow and change. We need to be thankful for the conflicts that come into our lives. For many people, their dream of "a peaceful world" is a world without conflict. Many people fear conflict and will often go to great lengths to avoid conflict. Some of us grew up in families where we were taught to avoid conflict. Many of us have belonged to organizations that fear conflict. However, often, in the long run, avoiding conflict generally makes matters worse. Although we may wish for a world that is completely peaceful and joyful and without conflict, even if it were possible, I don't think it would be beneficial or healthful for us.

Social change is about making friends with conflict! When Mohandas (the Mahatma) Gandhi was working to gain independence for India, he organized the Salt March to the Sea. The Salt March certainly created a great deal of social conflict, but he was determined to resolve the conflict non-violently. His strategy resulted in the social change that liberated India from the colonial rule. The Mahatma Gandhi was a person who made friends with conflict.

When Dr. Martin Luther King Jr. worked to gain civil rights for all Americans he had a very simple, two part strategy for social change. First, he created conflict to initiate change. He writes in his famous letter from the Birmingham jail:

> "Non-violent direct action seeks to create such a crisis and foster such tension that a community that has consistently refused to negotiate is forced to confront the issue. It seeks to dramatize the issue so that it can no longer be ignored."

The second part of his strategy was to make a commitment to a nonviolent resolution. When he was leading the bus boycott in Montgomery, Alabama, in 1955, he said: "We will not resort to violence. We will not degrade ourselves with hatred. Love will be returned for hate."

He presented America with conflicts that gave it an opportunity to grow and change. Schools were desegregated. Public transportation was desegregated. Restaurants were desegregated. African Americans had the right to vote. America did change and it will never be the same again. Dr. King was completely committed to a win-win solution. Dr. King was a person who made friends with conflict.

Note:
> *If you use this as an opening talk, continue at this point to introduce what you will be doing in the workshop.*

POWER

We all, every one of us, have personal power, inescapably, whether or not we are aware of it. It includes the power to be: to exist, to be alive, to think, to believe in and affirm oneself and to feel one's significance; to appeal for recognition to those around us. It includes the power to change our own lives, to make decisions that will send us into new paths. It also includes the power to influence others and, to make changes in our world. We have all used these powers, and when we might have thought we were not using them or did not have them, we were using them all the same. Conversely, the power of other people has been used to shape us and to shape our world, and even those people who thought they were most powerless have been an essential part of that shaping.

What people in general do not realize is that power is inalienable. Everybody has it. No one can get rid of it. If you choose not to exercise it, that choice is an exercise of power, and may force others to await "the dropping of your other shoe." The "little people" have at least as much power as the VIPs; they can and often do frustrate the plans of their *betters* merely by withdrawing their cooperation. It follows that the VIPs are at least as powerless as the little people, and this may sometimes make them dangerous, when they realize that they do not *have* and cannot *get* full control over others. However this may be, it behooves us all, since we cannot get rid of our power, to acknowledge it and to use it as conscientiously and constructively as we can, knowing that we exercise it in an environment filled also with the legitimate power of other people.

Sometimes power is inherent in a relationship, as with parents and children. To exercise it can be destructive to the *little guy,* but not to exercise it can be just as destructive. Sometimes people do not have the strength to use their inherent power, as when parents have too much else to cope with and cannot exercise just and consistent discipline with their children. Sometimes people feel guilty about exercising their power, fearing to be thought domineering or tyrannical. In such cases, the power may go underground and become poisonous.

In dealing with others, there are several kinds of power. Some of these are listed below as developed by Rollo May.

1. **POWER OVER - Exploitive:** based on force and usually on society's expectations, open or covert. The powerful make use of others for their own benefit. The use of this kind of power is an implicit invitation to an answering violence or threat of violence "exercised by those who have been radically rejected."

2. **POWER OVER - Manipulative:** Power over, based on persuasion. People influence others for the benefit of themselves (often a weapon of the con artist or the weak).

3. **POWER AGAINST - Competitive:** Between equals. A one up, one down situation; on the positive side, it can test our mettle.

4. **POWER FOR - Nutrient:** This power grows from one's care for another, concern for the welfare of another or of a group. The classic example is the power of a parent to nurture a child. Nutrient power may have the negative aspect of paternalism — of doing an deciding things for others that they would be better off doing for themselves.

5. **POWER WITH - Shared or Conjoined:** Comes into being when people join together in a cooperative effort to discover a truth or a path of action to which all can commit themselves sincerely. The effort itself involves honest feedback, sometimes confrontation, and always a sincere respect for the positions of others and a willingness to listen and to be convinced when appropriate. It involves both the use and the self-restraint of individual power. Once an understanding is reached, the group can act on it with a power greater than the sum of the individual power of its members. The consensus process at its best produces this result.

6. **TRANSFORMING POWER - Power that acts through truth, justice and love.** This power transcends "human" forms of power. We cannot use it. If we are open to it, it can use us.

Everyone experiences the first five types of power. The goal is to learn to use these different kinds of power appropriately in a given situation and to allow the sixth kind of power to work through us as it will.

Power can be exerted at different levels:
- Assertion
- Aggression
- Violence

Shared power, nutrient power and assertion can partake of and lead towards Transforming Power. In all forms of power except Transforming Power, people seek to gain control, whether of their own lives and actions or those of others. Only with Transforming Power does one deliberately give up control. With this giving up, something greater is allowed to enter, the good of the other person or of one's true self, the "Power that transforms."

Exercises Pertaining to Power:

Assertiveness	Let's Go Swimming	Territory
Carefronting	Masks	Three Questions on
Contract with Self	Personal space	Oppression
Dots	Power Grab	
Injunctions of Childhood	Power Inversion	
& Life	Sculpting	

STEREOTYPING

Stereotyping is putting labels on people. We all label others, and we are labeled by others. Another way to think about stereotyping is in terms of a solid barrier that hides the real person so that s/he can't be seen. The word "stereotype" comes from two Greek words: stereo, meaning "solid," and typos, meaning "image." We want to break this pattern, because stereotypes prevent us from forming good interpersonal relationships and limit us. We stereotype one another for a variety of reasons. Some of them are:

CONVENIENCE:
It's easier and more convenient to use a handy stereotype. We use some that are negative: "She's a gossip." "He's a bigot." "You're an egotist." "They're all alike."

And some that are positive: "He's my kind of person." "You can drink with him." "She's got such pretty eyes, she must be kind."

COMFORT:
We put down others to make ourselves feel important. We may also stay with thinking patterns that are familiar to us because we are more comfortable with them.

COWARDICE:
"Chicken" — afraid not to use the stereotypes that are demanded by peer pressure. Or we may fear a group of people because we do not know or understand them, so we say they are all alike or put them down to deal with our fear.

CONTROL:
We don't have to deal with the person as an individual, and feel like we can control them by placing them into a "box".

NOT USING STEREOTYPING –

requires a totally new viewpoint about the way we look at others. Some of the steps in developing this new viewpoint about people are:

CREATIVITY:
Am I willing to see people as individuals rather than as members of a group? Am I willing to allow myself new ways of seeing people, and break out of thinking patterns from the past? Am I willing to consider different cultures and ideas as having value, perhaps even for me?

COURAGE:
Am I willing to face my fears of people who may seem different from me, or whose ways I don't understand or agree with? Am I willing to risk judgment myself for doing this?

CARING:
Am I willing to see the good in all people, even those people whom I might have judged in the past? Am I willing to care for myself by allowing myself relationships with individuals from a group I may have judged?

Exercises pertaining to Stereotyping:

Dots	Labels	Power Grab
Fairytale Theater	Let's Go Swimming	Sculpting
From Another Point of View	Masks	Speakout
	Perceptions Based……	Three Questions on Oppression
Getting in Touch	Picture Paints a Thousand Words	
In His Shoes		Who Says I Am

SECTION G

Gatherings

Light & Livelies

Closings/Affirmations

GATHERINGS

Name Games	G-4
Adjective Name with Gesture	G-4
High Five	G-4
My Name Is and I like to ...	G-4
Name Ball	G-4
Board of Directors	G-4
Hat Trick	G-4
Mini News & Goods /Minor Irritations	G-5
"Pop" Song	G-5

CLOSINGS & AFFIRMATIONS

Affirmation Posters	G-18
Affirmation Pyramid	G-18
Gift-Giving	G-18
Head, Heart, Hand	G-19
A Little Help from My Friends	G-19
Namaste Circle	G-20
Rainstorm	G-20
Weaving	G-20
Yarn Toss	G-21

LIGHT & LIVELIES

A What?	G-6
Animal Parade	G-6
Ball Pass	G-6
Big Wind Blows, with an Addition	G-6
Big Wind Blows... Factulance	G-6
Blanket	G-7
Buzz	G-7
By the Numbers	G-7
Car and Driver	G-7
Car Wash	G-7
Cooperative Crocodiles & Frogs	G-8
Cooperative Musical Chairs	G-8
Cows and Jello	G-8
Dollar Fifty	G-8
Earthquake	G-8
Elephants, Palm Trees & Skunks	G-8
Face to Face	G-9
Fire on the Mountain	G-9
Gibberish	G-9
Hand Slap	G-9
Hello Train	G-10
Here I Sit	G-10
Hot and Cold (Listen to the Universe)	G-10
Hot Potato	G-10
Howdy, Howdy, Howdy	G-11
I'm Going on a Safari	G-11
Jack-in-the-box	G-11
Leader	G-11
Line-up 1	G-11
Line-up 2	G-12
Mountains and Valleys	G-12
Mrs. Mumbley Gets Serious	G-12
Nigerian Applause	G-12
Name That Tune	G-13
Pattern Ball	G-13
Pizza Pizza	G-13
Pretzel	G-13
Red-Handed	G-14
Rumors 1	G-14
Rumors 2	G-14
Scream	G-14
Slow Boat to China	G-14
Speed Pattern Ball	G-15
Stand Up	G-15
Stop the Music	G-15
Tire Ball	G-15
Tossing Heads	G-15
WBLS, The Quiet Storm	G-15
What Cha Doin'?	G-16
What If?	G-16
Winkers	G-16
Wink'um	G-16
Wizards Giants and Elves	G-17
Yes and No	G-17

GATHERINGS

Gatherings are used at the beginning of each session to "gather" the energy of the workshop after an extended break. They set the tone for the session and, if possible, reflect the themes that will be explored during the session.

Remember when you start these, set an example of what you are hoping will happen in your own sharing — brief, long, deep, playful etc. And when it comes back around the circle to you, give some reaffirming-type comment — a summary of themes, an expression of gratitude for the wisdom of the group, a touching into the spirit of the sharing — it's an opportunity to deepen the sense of listening and respect and affirmation in the workshop. *Concentric Circle Topics in Section D have many potential gatherings, including many on common focus topics.*

Gathering Themes

- Something I've told my family or a friend about AVP since my Basic workshop is…
- What I think about this workshop so far is…
- What I think about the group at this point is…
- Something I became aware of about myself in this workshop is…
- An incident that's part of the reason I'm in this workshop is…
- What I have left behind to be here this weekend is…
- What I think my role in a community can be is…
- We are going to build a new community and I am going to bring…
- A gift I received from my family that I use today is…
- Something most people don't know about me is…
- When I feel I am not appreciated…
- What I do when I am uptight, angry, upset is…
- My idea of a beautiful person is…
- What I most enjoyed doing as a child was…
- What I most enjoy doing now, by myself is…
- A time I needed more self-control was…
- Something I would like to do if I had the courage is…
- Something I have done that I wish I hadn't is…
- A relationship I would like to heal is…
- The most important thing I've ever done for someone, accidentally or on purpose, is…
- One area I would like to explore to help myself be more peaceful is…
- My secret wish is…
- My greatest regret is…
- A time someone abused my kindness or good will as a sign of weakness was when…
- If I could invite three people (or one or two, depending on the time) to dinner, living or dead, real or fictional, they would be… because…
- If I were to come back in my next life as an animal, bird or fish, I would chose to be what animal, bird or fish… because…
- If life were a poker game, do you believe you have been dealt a winning, losing or even hand, and why?
- I often stereotype other people in the following ways… And, I think others stereotype me as…
- I think that people look up to me, down on me or as an equal. Why?
- If you were in an accident and thought you wouldn't survive, of all the things that went through your mind, what would be of the greatest importance to you?
- Someone I'd like to mend fences with is… Because…
- Think of a person or an object that is important in your life and answer the following question: What do I receive from ____? What do I give to____?

NAME GAMES

ADJECTIVE NAME WITH GESTURE

This is a variation on the adjective name game. Participants give their adjective names and accompany it with a gesture that describes or emphasizes the adjective name. For example Smiling Steve might lift the corners of his mouth with his/her fingers as s/he says his/her name, or Thinking Theresa might tap one finger on her head as s/he says her name. After each person says his/her name, the entire group repeats back the name and gesture three times. (Often people like their gestures enough that they repeat them with their names throughout the workshop.)

HIGH FIVE:

Leader asks everyone to stand in a circle. Leader starts by looking at someone across the circle, calling his name and saying "High Five" (for example: "Jazzy Joe, High Five"). The two then raise their right hands, exchange places and slap right hands as they cross in the center of the circle.

MY NAME IS AND I LIKE TO ...

Participants sit in a circle. The leader begins by introducing him/herself by name and then pantomiming a thing that s/he likes to do. The action continues around the circle. The group guesses what the action is. As always, it is all right to pass.

NAME BALL:

(This requires at least two soft, large balls.) Players stand in a circle. Each person learns the first name of the person to his or her right and left. A large rubber, nerf or soft soccer ball is then passed around the circle to the right, the passer calling out the receiver's name as the ball is passed. Another ball is then started to the left with the passer calling out the receiver's name as the ball is passed.

Then everyone changes to a new place in the circle. One of the balls is to be thrown to the person who was formerly on the right as that person's name is called. When this is underway, the other ball is thrown to the person who originally was on the passer's left. If a ball is dropped or goes outside of the circle, anyone can pick it up and resume the game. For added chaos/fun, more Right and Left balls can be added.

OTHER GATHERINGS

BOARD OF DIRECTORS:

Give each person an index card and ask them to draw a long table on it. Explain that this is a Board of Directors' table, and the Board is responsible for shaping the policies and actions of a Company or Organization. Ask them to put around the table the Board of Directors of their lives — the people who have had the most influence in shaping their lives, in good or bad ways. Then go around the circle asking each to share something about one person on their board and what influence that person had.

HAT TRICK:

Ahead of time, make a slip of paper with each participant's name on it and put them in a hat or cup. Pass the hat around, everyone selecting a piece of paper, putting it back if they pick their own name and getting another slip. Then, as they go around the circle, each person says something positive about the person whose name they selected.

MINI NEWS & GOODS/MINOR IRRITATIONS

This gathering gives people an opportunity to talk and be listened to about how they feel as they enter the workshop. After these brief minis people are better able to listen and participate. Divide into pairs and have each person speak on each topic. Each person can be given 2 to 4 minutes. Three minutes generally works.

a) New & Good Things — in my life today, this week.
b) Minor Irritations — which can lead to major irritation.

This is an active listening exercise. Questions of clarification can be asked but it is not a time for discussion or conversation.

Note:
Consider using this at the beginning of each day of the workshop after the gathering. (It is especially important in prisons because prisoners may have been hassled and have not had an opportunity to talk with anyone else that day.)

"POP" SONG:

As the group sits in a circle, have participants close their eyes and think of the first song that "pops" into their heads. Then go around and have each person say the song, and share some of the words and something they connect with the song. Then they may pass, sing the song, or lead the group in singing the song.

LIGHT & LIVELIES

A WHAT?
Select any two different objects, such as a pen and a shoe, or two different tinkertoy pieces.
- Have the group sit or stand in a circle with two facilitators opposite each other, each holding an object, representing something, like the "cat" and the "rat."
- Pass a "cat" to the person on your right, saying, "This is a cat." Ask that person to say back to you, "A what?" You reply, "a cat; pass it on." Let them pass it on using the same dialogue. Let the group pass it to three or four people. After people have the idea, ask that the "cat" be returned to you.
- Go to your left saying, "rat." Hopefully the person on your left will say, "A what?" and you'll say, "a rat; pass it on."
- Explain that your co-facilitator will also be passing out "cats" and "rats." Each facilitator will pass out "cats" and "rats" alternately. The challenge is to see if we can keep things straight.
- If there are no questions, begin. Let the passing continue until everyone is receiving both "cats" and "rats" at the same time.
- *Variation:* Rather than use objects, facilitators can pass A Handshake and a High Five, using the same method, or depending on the closeness of the group, a Handshake and a Hug.

Note: The facilitators should pass out the "cats" and "rats" at approximately the same rate. The rate should be fairly quick for the activity to be a challenge.

ANIMAL PARADE
Sit in a circle on chairs, with one person standing outside the circle.
- The outside person begins making an animal noise and movements, and starts walking around the circle behind the group,
- Once they have got their animal established, the parade leader lightly taps the shoulder of people sitting in the chairs at random, and they come up and join the parade, making the same noise and actions,
- When the leader decides, they go into a seat and everyone has to continue around the circle in the same direction to find an empty seat. The last one begins the next round as parade leader, as a new animal.

BALL PASS
Sit on the floor in tight circle and extend feet toward center. A ball is placed on one player's lap. The idea is to move the ball around the circle as fast as possible without using hands. *Variations:* vary the size and number of balls, reverse the direction of the ball. If it doesn't work the first time, try again. *(Some take in large blow-up beach balls.)*

BIG WIND BLOWS, with an addition
This is the same "A Big Wind Blows," with one person in the middle and with one less chair, and the person calling out "A Big Wind Blows for anyone (wearing green, who has brushed his teeth in the past two weeks etc)." When "Hurricane" is called, everyone has to get up to find a new seat, BUT BEFORE TAKING THAT SEAT, must shake someone's hand and say "Howdy, howdy, howdy."

BIG WIND BLOWS... Factulance
Everyone who calls something out in the middle has to make it true for themselves, so it is a mix of play and deepening familiarity with one another.

BLANKET

Place two chairs facing each other in the middle of the room. Divide the group into two. Have two volunteers hold up a blanket between the two chairs, with the two "teams" on either side of the blanket. Motion one person from each team to sit in their chair. When the volunteers lower the blanket, the people in the chairs try to call out the opposite person's adjective name. The person who "misses" must go over to the other side. The blanket goes up and another person takes the seat on each side.

(Either bring in a good-sized blanket or sheet or tape together 3 or 4 pages of newsprint.)

BUZZ

Players sit or stand in a circle and count off, except the word "buzz" is substituted for the number seven, any number containing seven, as well as any multiple of seven. Thus, seven is "buzz," seventeen is "buzz," twenty-one is "buzz." Players count as fast as they can. Anyone who misses sits down and is out of the game.

BY THE NUMBERS

This is similar to the Gibberish Light & Lively except that it is done with numbers. It is also a way to have fun doing role plays. Ask for two volunteers, and then ask them to go out of the room and decide on a conflict situation. Then they are to come back into the room and act out the situation using gestures and numbers only. For example one may say questioningly, "One ...two three four... five six seven!" while the other replies emphatically, "Eight nine ten eleven twelve!!!" etc. Judging from their body language and vocal intonation, the group tries to guess the subject or the conflict.

CAR AND DRIVER

Ask everyone to stand and move the chairs against the wall. Divide into pairs. Explain that one of participants in each pair will be the car and the other person will be the driver. The car doesn't know where it is going so cars put one hand over their eyes and extend the other hand out in front of them to serve as a bumper. The drivers are to stand behind the cars and place their hands on the shoulders of the cars. The drivers are to guide the cars around the room and avoid any collisions. After a few minutes, ask the cars and drivers to exchange places.

(This L&L is an experience in trust and leadership. If you are doing this exercise in a Training for Trainers, you may debrief the exercise. Ask the drivers how it felt to be a leader and whether they felt any responsibility for the cars who were participants. Then ask the cars how it felt to be a participant and trust their leaders to keep them safe.)

CAR WASH

(Works well as a tension-breaker after a heavy or serious exercise. Best if done in a room with a carpet.) The object of the exercise is to create a Human Automatic Car Wash (without water); everyone gets a back rub in the process.

Ask the group to form two rows facing each other with about a three-foot space in between. Ask both rows to kneel down. The pairs of people at the front of the line are designated "water squirters," then come the "washers," the "wipers," and finally the "driers," to complete the car wash. The exercise begins as the leader becomes a "car" and crawls through the car wash. Participants tap, scratch, rub and brush with their hands as appropriate. The leader is followed by the "squirters" in single file; the "washers" become "squirters," the "wipers" become "washers" and the "driers" become "wipers": At the end of the line the "cars" become "driers." The Car Wash continues until all participants have gone through.

COOPERATIVE CROCODILES AND FROGS

This is the cooperative version! Use large sheets of paper. Kraft paper is preferred since it doesn't tear as easily as newsprint. Let the participants know that the object of the light and lively is for no frogs to get eaten by the crocodile. Of course, players will need to find ways to help one another to get as many people on each sheet as possible. Start out with half a dozen sheets of paper and gradually reduce the pieces to one or two.

COOPERATIVE MUSICAL CHAIRS

We all know the game of musical chairs, but this is different. This is a cooperative game. The rule is that the game ends if there is one person that can't find a seat. Chairs are arranged in the center of the room, back to back, facing outward. The participants march around the chairs and when the music stops, everyone must find a place to sit. One chair is removed each time the music is played. Of course, people will need to find ways to sit on one another's laps, shoulders, etc. You may not get down to one chair, but ending up with four chairs is quite an achievement.

COWS AND JELLO

(similar to Elephants, Palm Trees and Skunks.)

When "cow" is called, the middle person holds arms in front and interweaves fingers together with palms facing self [point fingers of one hand at fingers of second hand; keep fingers straight and slide together like plugging an appliance into a wall socket]. Then turn palms out, which leaves thumbs hanging down separately. Person on each side grabs a thumb and milks the cow.

When "jello" is called, each side person holds arms out like a bowl [like the elephant ear lying flat] and middle person wiggles like jello!

DOLLAR FIFTY

Each gender (or something characteristic of at least half the group) is given a monetary value — e.g. one dollar or fifty cents. The caller then calls a sum of money — e.g. six dollars — and the groups of that value need to be made up.

EARTHQUAKE

Ask everyone to divide into groups of three. All participants should be in a group of three except the leader. Ask two members of each group to form a "house" by facing each other and raising their arms above their heads and joining hands. The third member of each group is the "tenant" and stands in the middle inside the "house." The leader, who is the odd person out, may call one of the three following commands.

Tenants – In this case the houses stay in place and each tenant must move to a new house. The leader tries to find a new house and the person that is left out is the new leader.

Houses – In this case the tenants stay in place and each house must move to find a new tenant. The leader tries to find someone to make a new house with.

Earthquake – In this case all the houses are destroyed and everyone must change. New pairs make houses and tenants jump in to occupy them.

ELEPHANTS, PALM TREES AND SKUNKS

The person in the center of the circle points to someone and says "elephant." That person bends over and puts hands down to make a trunk. People on either side of him or her put their arms up to make his elephant ears. If the person in the center says "Palm Tree," the person pointed to holds hands straight above his/her head. People on either side make branches going out from the tree. After trying this a few times, the leader says "skunk," the person pointed to turns around with a hand behind for a tail. People on either side turn away holding their noses. As the pace picks up anyone hesitating becomes the person in the center. *When first introducing this game, you may wish to postpone adding "skunk" and wait for another time when an energizer seems appropriate. At that time, replay and add the "skunk" challenge.*

FACE TO FACE

Ask everyone to stand and move the chairs against the wall. Divide into pairs. The leader is the odd person who does not have a partner. The leader calls positions rapidly such as "Face to Face" or "Back to Back" and the pairs follow the positions. The leader can also call "Change" and everyone must change partners and maintain the previous position. At this point the leader can find a partner and the odd person becomes the new leader. The positions may be varied such as, "Toe to toe, elbow to elbow, shoulder to shoulder, knee to knee, head to head" etc.

FIRE ON THE MOUNTAIN:

Players, in couples, stand in two concentric circles fairly close to one another, all facing the center. One of the couple stands in front of the other. Hands are at sides. When the Leader calls "Walk," the players on the outside of the circle walk around to the right. At the same time the players on the inside raise their hands above their heads. When the Leader calls "Fire on the Mountain," players on the outside find a place in front of a player with raised hands, who then puts his/her hands on the shoulders of the person in front. At this time the Leader tries to get a place in front of someone, and if s/he succeeds, the displaced player becomes Leader. (After each round of the game the circles will have to move back a step or two to maintain the size of the circle.)

GIBBERISH:

1. Participants are seated in a circle. The Leader says a short phrase in "Gibberish" (sounds that are not part of a known language) to the person on his/her right. This continues around the circle. At any given time a participant will say only two phrases — the one that s/he receives and his/her own that s/he passes on. (The idea is to use Gibberish and not to try to find words in another language that might be offensive — if an accident happens, it's good for a laugh and maybe discussion.)
2. Ask volunteers (two or three) to carry on an argument in Gibberish, not telling the group what the argument is about, only whether it is to be resolved or unresolved. The group can then briefly discuss what happened in terms of body language, tone of voice, etc. Try to make time for all who wish to volunteer.

HAND SLAP

A rhythm game which brings the group into wakefulness or focus —is fun and quite fast.

- Sit in a circle on chairs, with knees close together, so that you can reach your partners knees on either side of you.
- Slap your own palms on your own knees twice.
- Reach across to your right and slap your palms twice, one on your right knee and one on your neighbor's left knee.
- Back to your own knees — slap twice.
- Across to your neighbor on left and as with above, slap your left knee and their right knee twice.
- Slap own lap twice.
- Clap hands twice.
- Click fingers twice.
- Jerk knee up once.
- Call out "hey!" or something similar.
- Repeat slowly to get everyone into it, then getting faster until everyone is doing it together.

HELLO TRAIN

All participants but one are seated in a circle, with space around the outside of the circle. The leader walks around the outside, making appropriate train noises and gestures (arm up and down to ring a bell or back and forth like the wheels), and taps someone on the shoulder. That person stands up and faces the leader. The leader says, "Hello, my name is ____" and the person replies with, "Hello, my name is ____" Each of them repeat this three times, and end with a big cheer for each other. This is all done loudly and enthusiastically. Then, the person takes his/her place on the outside of the circle in front of the leader, becoming the new leader. The people behind the leader put one hand on the shoulder of the person in front, and they go around the circle making train noises and gestures until the new leader taps someone in the circle on the shoulder. Eventually, everyone is in the Hello Train, with the train going entirely around the circle and ending with a cheer.

HERE I SIT

This Light & Lively begins with all participants seated in a circle with one empty chair. Either of the people sitting next to the empty chair may move into the chair and say, "Here I Sit." This leaves an empty chair vacated by the first person and the person next to the chair moves into it and says, "In this chair." This leaves an empty chair vacated by the second person and the third person sitting next to it moves into it and says, "With my friend (and names a person on the other side of the circle)." The friend from the other side of the circle then moves to the seat vacated by the third person, leaving an empty seat on the other side of the room where the process repeats itself.

HOT AND COLD (aka LISTEN TO THE UNIVERSE)

- Explain that in this L&L a volunteer will leave the room for a minute while the group chooses a spot in the room for the volunteer to find. The volunteer will find the spot by listening to everyone slap their thighs.
- If the volunteer is going near the spot or "getting hot," everyone will slap loudly. If the volunteer is far away from the spot or "cold," the slapping will be soft. If there are no questions, ask for a volunteer and have him/her step out of the room.
- Ask someone to pick a spot and then have the volunteer come back into the room.
- After the first volunteer finds the spot, ask for another volunteer to step outside the room. Continue... .

Note: This can be made more challenging by having the volunteer do something when they find the spot. For example, you might have the volunteer go to a table and pick up a book.

HOT POTATO

Players stand in a loose circle. The "Hot Potato" is a lightweight scarf. This is "hot" and cannot be held by anyone, but must be passed or thrown to anyone else in the circle as soon as it is received. One person is "It." "It" tries to catch the scarf in midair or to touch the person who has it. The last person to touch the "Hot Potato" is "It."

HOWDY, HOWDY, HOWDY

Ask participants to stand in a circle shoulder to shoulder, facing the center. One person who is "it" walks slowly around the outside of the circle in a counter-clockwise direction, and then taps one of the people in the circle on the shoulder. The person who is tapped must quickly turn and run around the outside of the circle in a clockwise direction as the person who is "it" runs around in a counterclockwise direction. As they meet on the opposite side of the circle they must stop, shake hands, and say "Howdy, Howdy, Howdy" and then race onward to get into the empty space in the circle. The person who is left out of the circle then becomes "it" for the next round. (Active — not recommended in smaller rooms where there isn't much space outside the circle. Some ask participants to "walk quickly" to avoid injury caused by runners colliding.)

I'M GOING ON A SAFARI

Imagine that you are going on a safari and you can take anything you want from a teddy bear to a dozen purple elephants. The more outrageous the object, the better.

This Light & Lively works in a way that is similar to the Adjective Name Game. However, instead of repeating all the previous adjective names, each participant must repeat the items named by the previous members of the group. Thus, the last person must remember every item named by the entire group. It is more fun than a barrel of monkeys or a pool full of seals.

This exercise is a sure way to lighten up tensions after a heavy exercise.

JACK-IN-THE-BOX

Start by asking participants to form a circle. Then ask the members of the group repeat this little rhyme:

"Jack-in-the BOX! Jack-in-the BOX! I move like THIS, I move like THAT, I balance WELL, I balance WELL."

Then the leader steps into the center of the circle following the beat and with the words "I move like THIS" the leader makes a slow gesture or "cool move." All participants in the circle then repeat the gesture or move. With the words, "I balance WELL," the leader turns around and returns to the outer circle. Then another person steps into the center and shows off another "cool move." Continue until everyone has had a chance to show off a "cool move."

LEADER

Players stand or sit on chairs in a circle. "It" stands in the middle, and closes both eyes. Facilitator points to one person, who becomes the leader. Everyone must match the body movements and facial expressions of the leader, trying not to give away who it is. *(It helps to watch the person across from you rather than the leader.)* Leader, when caught, becomes the new "it." Old "It" picks new leader, while new "it" keeps eyes closed.

LINE-UP 1

Explain that this L&L challenges everyone to cooperate in silence. They may, however, use gestures.
- The group's task is to arrange themselves in order, according to the month and day of their births.
- If there are no questions, they may begin. If they ask, "Where is the beginning of the line?" say that they'll have to figure that out in silence.
- When movement ends, ask if they all feel comfortable with the arrangement. If not, they can continue. If they are comfortable, ask them to state the month and day of their births in order.

    Note: Sometimes one or two people may end up slightly "out of order." Affirm the group nonetheless. It's not an easy task in silence. Sometimes even when we speak, we don't fully understand what another is saying.

LINE-UP 2

Explain that this L&L challenges everyone to cooperate without talking. Humming is allowed because people will have their eyes closed. Females may wish to keep one arm across their chests.
- Say that you and another facilitator or two (arrange this beforehand) will watch so that no one goes too far astray or walks into something.
- Ask everyone to stand and push their chairs back so there's plenty of room.
- Ask everyone to close their eyes so you can state the task. Then say, "Without talking and without peeking, arrange yourselves in order by height. Remember, you may hum."
- When movement ends, ask if they all feel comfortable with the arrangement. If not, they can continue for a while. Finally, have them open their eyes and see how they've done.

Note: *As in Line Up 1, total success is definitely not critical. The trust shown in doing this exercise is the important thing. You may wish to congratulate them on this.*

MOUNTAINS AND VALLEYS

This originally was a values-clarification exercise and isn't super active, but it gets people moving and thinking.

Everyone stands up. Make one side of the room Mountains, and the other side Valleys. With the additional questions, name each side of the room. Leader invites them to move to the side of the room that they prefer. Ask them: Would you prefer to be a Mountain or a Valley? They go to the side they want to be. Some won't choose, so they can be in the middle. Ask those on each side why they chose that side. A quick go round is all that is necessary. Then, proceed to other questions, indicating which side for which.

- Are you more an island or a wave?
- Picture window or a screened porch?
- Countryside or city?
- Clothesline or kite string?
- Filing cabinet or liquor cabinet?
- Bubbling brook or placid lake?
- Then, you could do four corners with four seasons...

The awareness that comes from the reasons and who chooses which contributes to any group looking at differences or building community.

MRS. MUMBLEY GETS SERIOUS

Sit in circle. Leader turn to next person, ask, "What do you know about *the focus of the workshop*: fear, anger, forgiveness, whatever. Person gives mock-serious response, then turns and asks the same question of other neighbor. It then continues around circle. As in standard Mrs. Mumbley, no one may show teeth or laugh.

Sample Responses:

Forgiveness: I know all there is to know about forgiveness. I wait until the person is dead, and then I forgive them.

Anger: I never get mad. I'll bust you in the nose if you say I do.

Power: Yea, though I walk through the valley of the shadow of death, I will fear no evil, for I am the biggest SOB in the valley.

NIGERIAN APPLAUSE

Group stands in a circle and people whom the group wishes to acknowledge step into the middle, one at a time. *(May happen at any time in the workshop by starting the cadence).* The group claps in the cadence: Clap, Clap, Clap, Clap... Clap ...Clap. Then the group extends their hands toward the person being acknowledged and the person being acknowledged crosses their arms over their chest to receive the applause.

NAME THAT TUNE
(also can be used to break into groups)
- Have folded slips of paper ready on which you have written names of very familiar songs such as Old McDonald; Twinkle, Twinkle, Little Star; Row, Row, Row Your Boat; Happy Birthday; London Bridge. You will need one song for each group to be formed. There must be as many slips of paper for each song as the number of people you want in each group.
- Put slips in a small container. Everyone draws a slip and reads without letting the others see. Without talking, have people stand and move around while humming their song until they find others with the same song. They will then remain standing together.
- As the groups quiet down, ask each small group to hum its tune for everybody.

Note: This is good for dividing into groups for Broken Squares. Be sure that songs are divided to match the count you want. Be sensitive in choosing which songs to use. Participants not raised in the United States where these songs are common, might not be familiar with some of the songs.

PATTERN BALL
Use 6 to 8 Koosh balls, soft balls or small socks sewn in ball-like shapes. Have the group stand in a circle. Say that we'll be gently tossing a ball around the circle to form a pattern. It is important to remember the person to whom you throw the ball, and the person from whom you receive the ball. The first time the ball goes around, people will cross their arms over their chest to show that they have already received the ball. After the ball has come back to the beginning, send it through the same pattern one more time to be sure everyone has remembered the pattern. Then slowly add more balls, all following the same pattern. See how many you can get going without the group getting confused. Once the pattern is established, see if you can reverse it.

PIZZA PIZZA
Ask participants to name ingredients they like on their pizza. You can ask for outlandish ideas if you want. Write these quickly on a posted piece of newsprint as a memory aid. The facilitator then goes around the circle and assigns everyone an ingredient, usually in the order of the list. Then, with one chair out of the circle, call out items and those people have to move to a new seat. Calling "Pizza, Pizza" causes everyone to move.

PRETZEL
Explain that we are going to have a circle of people holding hands turn their circle into a pretzel puzzle. It will be the task of two volunteers to untangle the pretzel and put it back into a circle. Ask for two volunteers to leave the room. Standing in a circle, have everyone take hands, holding each other's wrist. Stress that they cannot break their handclasp and change the way they are attached or they won't be able to return the same way. One person leads his/her part of the circle across and under the arms of a pair on the other side. They people-twist and duck until the circle is tied into a knot. Call in the volunteers and let them try to untangle the circle.

Variation on "Pretzel":
In a circle of no more than 10 people, each one puts his/her right hand in the center and makes a fist with it. Then, everyone reaches his/her left hand into the center and grasps the fist of someone across the circle, changing to holding hands. When everyone is ready, the entire group figures out how to untwist their group without letting go of the hands. In reality, it doesn't always end in one perfect circle, but it gets everyone involved in the problem solving process.

RED-HANDED

Players stand in a circle, facing the center. Hands are in front, fists closed and facing down. One person in the center of the circle is "It." One or more small objects are passed from hand to hand around the circle. "It" must guess who has the object(s). The first person caught holding an object becomes "It."

RUMORS 1

Have 5 people leave the room. Have someone tell a short story with a moderate amount of detail. Have one person come into the room and have a volunteer tell him or her the story as accurately as s/he can remember. Have that individual tell the next person who comes in, and so on until all have heard the story. Each tries to be as accurate as possible. Tell the audience to try not to laugh at gross inaccuracies.

RUMORS 2

Announce that you will begin a rumor by whispering it in one person's ear. Each person in turn is to whisper it in someone else's ear — the same story, only allowing additions which "improve the story." Those who have already heard the story and passed it on should sit down in the circle. The last person should tell what they heard and compare this to what the first person heard. *Rumors 1 & Rumors 2 can both be a L&L, or they can also be processed like an exercise with some of the following questions:*

- How does this make you feel about rumors?
- Can rumors have power?
- How would it have affected you if you'd been told this in real life — not as an exercise?
- Do rumors seem believable?
- How are rumors empowered by what truth they do have in them?
- How did the story change?
- Was everyone making a good-faith effort?
- Can word-of-mouth distort things even when we have no bad intentions?
- What kinds of things block clear perception/hearing?

SCREAM

Participants stand in a circle, looking down toward the floor. Leader calls "Go!" and everyone looks up and looks at someone. If the person you are looking at is looking back at you, you both scream. The leader then directs everyone to look back at the floor and do it again. Sometimes no one will scream, sometimes many people will. Do this over and over until it feels finished. This is a great L&L if time is limited, because it can be a lot of fun in just 2 or 3 minutes.

SLOW BOAT TO CHINA

This is similar to *I'm Going on a Safari* except that there's a catch. The items named must begin with the first letter of your adjective name. However, the participants are not told about the catch. The leader gives an example such as: "I'm Mellow Mike and I'm going on a slow boat to China and I'm going to bring some music and some money." Then the question moves around the circle as follows: "My name is___and I'm going on a slow boat to China and I'm going to bring ___. Can I get aboard?" The leader responds "yes" or "no" depending on if the first letter of the items match the first letter of his/her adjective name. The participants begin to catch on as the question moves around the circle.

SPEED PATTERN BALL
Get the pattern set up as usual. Clock the time it takes for the ball to go around the sequence and back to the start. Then ask the group for ideas on how to make it even faster. Keep brainstorming and trying out the ideas and timings until you have it down to a few seconds. Good creative thinking and group building.

STAND UP
Divide group into pairs. Each pair sits on the floor, back to back. The pairs then link arms. Their knees are to be bent with their feet flat on the floor. Then the pairs just Stand Up!

Once you've mastered the game in pairs, then try it in groups of three or four. It becomes more difficult as the size of the group increases. With larger groups, it is important to sit in a circle close together, with shoulders and hips touching.

STOP THE MUSIC
This is a little like Pattern Ball. Ask all the participants to stand in a circle. Then take a koosh ball (or equivalent,) and begin to toss it around the circle in a random pattern. The leader then stands outside the circle and faces away from the group so s/he cannot see who has the ball. The leader then begins to sing a song. It can be any kind of a song that the person chooses. The leader then stops singing, perhaps in the middle of a phrase. The person in the circle that has the ball at the time the music stops is the next leader. The new leader then steps out of the circle, turns away from the group and sings another song.

TIRE BALL
(Requires a large ball and at least one old tire or inner tube). People lie close together on their backs. Heads are resting on a tire or inner tube — legs are out straight like spokes of a wheel, hands are down at their sides. The object is to pass a large ball (soft soccer ball size) around the circle of bodies without using arms or hands. (The game is best for about ten to twelve persons. Others can take turns. It's more fun to do than to watch.)

TOSSING HEADS
This is similar to the Elephants and Palm Trees light and lively. Participants stand in a circle. One person makes eye contact with another person across the circle, puts hands to his/her head and makes a tossing motion with his/her hands. The other person makes a catching motion. The people on either side must put one hand to the ear that is nearest the catcher to avoid being hit. Anyone who makes a mistake must sit down. The game continues until there are only four or five players left.

WBLS, THE QUIET STORM
The participants stand in a circle and the leader explains that when it is your turn you need to give the name of a musical performer or group without hesitating. Anyone that hesitates is out. The leader starts by saying, "This is station WBLS, the quiet storm where you hear the sounds of _____ (name of performer)." The person next to him/her immediately names another performer and the game moves around the circle. Names of performers or groups cannot be repeated in the same round. If someone misses, that person is out and the person next to him/her starts a new round saying, "This is station WBLS, the quiet storm where you hear the sounds of _____."

WHAT CHA DOIN'?

Participants stand in a circle, facing in. The leader makes some action, like pretending to dig a hole. The next person in the circle says, "What cha doin'?" The person pretending to dig a hole responds with some different action, such as "I'm playing basketball." The person who asked the question begins to pretend to play basketball. The next person is line asks, "What Cha Doin'?" and is given a new action to do, such as "I'm brushing my teeth" or "I'm doing the 'Funky Chicken.'" The game continues around the circle. When the circle is completed, you take a second round in the reverse direction.

WHAT IF?

Hand each participant a 3"x 5" slip of paper with the words "What if" written on the upper left corner. Each participant is asked to complete the statement in whatever way s/he wishes, such as: "What if all prisons were closed," or "What if an elephant moved into the house next door." Then each slip is handed to the person on the right and that person is asked to turn the paper over and complete the statement on the front. This might be: "Inmates would have to look for jobs." or "He'd have to buy a cast-iron sofa." Then each slip is handed to the person on the right. Each person is asked to read their slip, reading the answer first and then the question, which sounds quite funny.

WINKERS

(renamed "Sniper" by many prisoners)

Have as many slips of paper as participants. On two or three, put an "O." On the rest, put X's. Fold all the slips twice and put into a container. Take the container around and each participant in the circle picks one and opens it without letting anyone else see it. Only the two or three people holding the O's know that they are the winkers. Their object is to try to get people "out" by winking at them. Someone who is winked-at must turn his chair around. At any time, someone may raise his hand and try to guess the winker. If s/he is correct, that winker must turn his chair around. If s/he is wrong, that person must turn his chair around. The game is over when everyone but one person is facing the outside of the circle.

WINK'UM

Divide the group into two, with one extra person. Half the group sits in chairs around a circle, with the other half standing behind them, with their hands behind their backs. The extra person, the "winker," stands in front of an empty chair. The winker tries to catch the eye of someone in the chairs with a wink. That person tries to quickly rush away to sit in the empty chair, before the person behind them takes hands from behind their back and (gently) slaps them on the shoulders to keep them in the seat. If they successfully "get away," then the person with the empty chair is the new "winker."

WIZARDS GIANTS AND ELVES:

Similar to "Rock, paper, scissors"

Explain the characters and movements:
- Wizards —arms stretched out in front, and fingers "zapping" a spell.
- Giants — hands above head, clenched fists, stomping feet.
- Elves — bending down, hands with palms upright, fingers wriggling, trying to grab the treasures from someone's pockets.

Explain the relationship between them (may be useful to post on newsprint).
- Wizards can zap giants and need to run away from elves.
- Elves can grab wizards, but need to run away from giants.
- Giants can stomp on elves, but need to run away from wizards.

The Group is split into two halves. They go to opposite ends of the room, and each group huddles to choose their character. Be sure everyone knows the actions and who they can capture or flee from.

When ready, line up along the ends of the room, or a defined home line, stomp into the middle of the room and stand face to face with other team.

Count/chant all together One! Two! Three! And then make the sign for your character. If the other group is the same as you, you all hug and swap sides.

If they are different you either flee or pursue, and try to capture others who then join your group.

Repeat until you have had enough, or everyone is in one group!

YES AND NO

Print the names of well-known people — athletes, movie stars, leaders, historic figures, etc. on enough cards for all participants. Ask all participants to stand. Then tape the cards on the backs of all participants without allowing them to see the names. The object of the exercise is for each person to find out what name is taped on his/her back by asking other people questions about themselves. Participants may look at the names on the person's back but may only answer their questions with a "yes" or "no." The light & lively continues until all participants have discovered their names.

CLOSINGS & AFFIRMATIONS

AFFIRMATION POSTERS

Purpose: This affirmation leaves a permanent record. It is especially suitable for the last session of a workshop.
Time: 30 to 60 minutes.
Materials: For each participant, a large piece paper or newsprint, a marker (or crayon or heavy flair pen — have an assortment of colors), masking tape.
Sequence:
1. Give each person a marker and a blank piece of newsprint.
   Version A: Paper is attached with masking tape to person's back;
   Version B: Each person writes his adjective name on the paper or newsprint and tapes it to the wall along with others around the room at a level where people can reach to write on it.
2. Explain that people are to mill around the room, and that they are to make Affirmation Posters of each others' newsprint by writing on each poster anonymous, positive, affirming comments about its owner. There are two rules:
   a) Only positive, affirming comments are to be written. This is not a time for jokes or for criticism, however constructive.
   b) No one is to write anything that s/he does not believe to be true. Insincere flattery is not acceptable.
3. If desired and if time permits, when people have all written on every one elses poster, call them back to the large group and have each person share with the others a comment from his poster that is especially appreciated. (People are often considerably moved by some of the comments written on their posters.)
4. Let people take their posters to keep, as a souvenir of the workshop and a record of what wonderful people they all are.

AFFIRMATION PYRAMID

Purpose: A quickie, to build or repair community.
Time: **No more than 5 minutes.**
Materials: One outstretched hand per person.
Sequence:
Have group make a circle to build an affirmation pyramid, starting with the facilitator's own outstretched hand. Each person placing a hand on top of the other hands must say something positive about the group. Facilitator begins. When all have joined the pyramid, lower the hands slowly, then raise them rapidly with a (Texas) yell.

GIFT-GIVING

Purpose: To confirm that we can be a caring community. To let people know that their individual needs and aspirations are perceived and cared about.
Time: 30 minutes.
Sequence:
1. Call the group into a large circle. Explain that beginning with the facilitator, we are going to give each other gifts of the human spirit — imaginary gifts, which if we had the power, we would make real. Each giver will give the one gift that s/he feels the receiver would most appreciate and that will most help him or her to fulfill his or her needs and aspirations as the giver sees them. The recipient will pass the gift along to the next person, changing it to fit that person's needs as s/he has expressed them or as the giver sees them.
2. If appropriate, process the exercise. Ask people how they felt about receiving their gifts, and why did they give the gifts they did?

HEAD, HEART, HAND

Purpose: An alternative evaluation technique, or a closing.
Time: 10 minutes
Materials: Newsprint & 3 different colored post-it note pads.
Sequence:
1. Instead of doing a regular evaluation, try this as a combo evaluation/closing.
2. Draw a large "person" on newsprint. Have three different color "post-it" notes — blue, yellow and pink.
3. Say that the blue "post-it" notes will contain thoughts and will be placed near the person's head; the yellow ones will contain feelings and be posted by the persons heart; the pink ones will contain tools and will be placed near the person's hands. As you say this, write "thought," "feeling" and "tool" on their respective colors and place them on their respective spots.
4. Give each participant one of each color "post-it." Ask s/he to write a thought they have about the AVP workshop on their blue "post-it," a feeling they've had during the workshop on their pink "post-it," and a tool they learned and might use on their yellow "post-it."
5. As they finish writing have them place their "post-it" notes by the head, heart and hands of the "person."
6. When everybody is finished read the results aloud and thank everyone for their input. You might ask those who wish, to read their own "post-it" notes.

A LITTLE HELP FROM MY FRIENDS

Purpose: To help build and strengthen close ties of the kind that can, for instance, help people conquer their fears. Especially appropriate for use after the unit on Fear.
Time: 40 minutes.
Sequence:
1. Explain that this affirmation is centered on a possible fear or handicap that each of us might be willing to share with the group. Ask each participant to think of one such fear or handicap that might trip him/her up in dealing with the realities to be encountered in the present or the future.
2. Explain the procedure:
    a) We will start with a given participant and have him/her share with the group his fear or handicap.
    b) Then the person on that individual's left will provide him/her with the most helpful and sincere direction and advice possible, to aid in overcoming that fear or handicap.
    c) Now the group at large will volunteer quick statements of their positive feelings about the person with the handicap. Emphasize that after the person beside the handicapped person has given direction, the other participants are to supply positive feelings, not further advice.
    d) **Give an example.** John says, for instance, "My greatest fear is that I will not be able to get a job." Jim on his left might say, "You persist, keep trying; you're never licked until you quit," etc. Others in the group would then provide John with positive feelings about him: "You are strong," "You will succeed," etc.
    e) Explain that we will continue this process around the circle until everyone who wishes has shared a fear or handicap. Reiterate that, as always, everyone has the right to pass. If anyone does pass, the whole group should quickly provide positive comments about that person.
3. Give the group a moment to think about this; then begin.

NAMASTE CIRCLE

1. Have the group stand in a circle. Mention briefly a couple of ways people greet each other, e.g., shaking hands or giving a "High 5."
2. Explain that the Hindu people from India greet each other saying the word "Namaste" *(Nah-mah-stay)*. First one person holds his/her hands palms together and says, "Namaste," bowing slightly. Then the other does the same in return.
3. The greeting "Namaste" means: **The good which is in the deepest part of me greets the good which is in the deepest part of you.**
4. This closing circle will give everyone a chance to first return this greeting and then to initiate this greeting.
5. Explain that you will start going around the circle to your left, giving this greeting to everyone in turn. As you move on to the fourth person to your left, the second person will start going around giving the greeting to the first person to his or her left. You might want to have a teammate be the first person to your left so s/he can model this.
6. If there are no questions, begin. The circle will turn in on itself and then open again after you get back in place.

   Note: This closing would be fitting for a Second Level Workshop's 6th Session. If you have done "A What?" with Handshake and High 5, this closing is a nice follow-up.

RAINSTORM

1. Have the group stand in a fairly tight circle with you in the middle of it.
2. Explain that this closing doesn't involve talking but it does involve making some sounds using our hands and feet. Ask everyone to mimic what you do as soon as you make eye contact with them and continue to do it until you come around to them again.
3. Start with one person and go around the circle eight times doing the following: Circle 1: Rub hands together; Circle 2: Snap fingers; Circle 3: Pat thighs; Circle 4: Pat thighs and stamp feet; Circle 5: Just pat thighs; Circle 6: Snap fingers; Circle 7: Rub hands together; Circle 8: hold both hands palms down indicating quiet.
4. Lastly, step back into the circle and say something like, "My wish for you is that all the storms in your life will pass as quickly."

   Note: Don't mention the name of this closing either verbally or on the agenda sheet.

WEAVING

1. Explain that in this closing, everyone will be standing in a circle, holding hands and weaving arms together.
2. Ask everyone to join in a circle where they feel comfortable touching the people on either side.

Instructions:

3. Place your left hand, palms outward, in front of the stomach of your neighbor to your left.
4. Then, put your right arm OVER the left arm of your neighbor to your right, and take the hand of the person on his/her right.

   The facilitator should have BOTH the left arm and the right arm OVER his/her two neighbors' arms.

5. Introduce the words of the song and have people sing it a few times before beginning the weaving:

Weave, weave, weaving together,
Weaving together in harmony and love

[Musical notation: Weave, weave, weave us to ge ther, weave us to ge ther in har mo ny and love,]

6. The facilitator lifts his/her LEFT arm and s/he and the person holding on to the facilitator's left hand lift their joined arms over the head of the neighbor who is standing between them. They leave their joined arms behind the middle neighbor.
7. The person to the left of the facilitator does the same with the person attached to his/her left hand, lifting their joined hands over the person between them.
8. This "weaving" continues around the circle, while people continue singing. When it comes back to the facilitator, the facilitator starts the weaving to the right.
   Repeat several times.

YARN TOSS
(To be used as gathering on last day or as closing)

Purpose: To strengthen and grow in awareness of the bonds between us, to give us a bodily metaphor for them. Very moving.
Time: About 20 minutes.
Materials: Ball of yarn.
Sequence:
1. Start with ball in your hand. Explain that each person is to throw it to another person and state the connection s/he feels between them. The ball must not be thrown to someone who has already received it, and the last person will throw it to you. Demonstrate by doing it.
2. When the web is complete, ask them to pull it a little, and feel the tension of the connection to the whole. Note that even though they are connected to only two people, they are connected to everyone else through that connection. The prison and the world are also connected. Talk about interdependency, and that violence breaks the whole of the web and affects many people. Remind them that there are such webs connecting them even to total strangers, and that we all have these invisible connections all the time.
3. Now, to undo, go backwards, throw the yarn ball to the person who last threw it to you, saying the connection you feel to that person. Continue in this way, winding as you go, until the ball is wound again.

Note: Some people become uncomfortable with exercise because often the quiet people are the last ones chosen. To make this less likely say: "Throw the ball of yarn across the circle and think about any connection you might have made with that person".

Section H

List of Resources

Index

RESOURCES

BOOKS

Apsey, Lawrence S. et al.. *Transforming Power for Peace.* Plainfield: AVP/USA & FGC, 2001.

Arrien, Angeles. *The Four-Fold Way: Walking the Paths of the Warrior, Teacher, Healer, and Visionary*, San Francisco: Harper, 1993.

Avery, Michael. et al. *Building United Judgment: A Handbook for Consensus Decision Making.* Madison: Fellowship for Interaction, 1999. Bennett, Lerone. *What Manner of Man: A biography of Martin Luther King, Jr.* Intr. Benjamin E. Mays. Chicago: Johnson, 1968.

Beer, Jennifer. *Mediators' Handbook.* Philadelphia: New Society 1997.

Bigelow, Albert. *The Voyage of the Golden Rule.* New York: Doubleday, 1959.

Bondurant, Joan V. *Conquest of Violence.: the Gandhian Philosophy of Conflict.* Princeton: Princeton University Press, 1988.

Brown, L. *Raising Their Voices: The Politics of Girls' Anger.* Cambridge: Harvard University Press, 1999.

Buscaglia, Leo. *Loving Each Other.* Freehold: Slack, 1984.

Coover, Virginia, ed. *Resource Manual for a Living Revolution.* Philadelphia: New Society Press, 1985.

Crum, T. *The New Conflict Cookbook: Parent/Teacher Guide for Helping Young People Deal With Anger and Conflict*. Aiki Works, 2000.

Cooney, Robert and Helen Michalowski, eds. *The Power of the People: Active Nonviolence in the United States.* Philadelphia: New Society Press,, 1987

Crane, Mary. *Rape Avoidance and Resistance: A nonviolent approach.* San Francisco: Peace and Gladness Press, 1982

del Vasto, J.J. Lanza. *Warriors of Peace: Writings on the Technique of Nonviolence.* New York: Knopf, 1981.

Desai, Narayan. *Handbook for Satyagrahi.* Philadelphia: Philadelphia: New Society Press, Press, 1980.

Dreikurs, Rudolf. *Coping with Children's Misbehavior.* New York: Dutton Adult, 1972.

Erikson, Erik H. *Gandhi's Truth: On the origins of militant nonviolence.* New York: WW. Norton, 1993.

Fischer, Louis, ed. *The Essential Gandhi.* New York: Vintage, 2002.

- - - .*Gandhi: His life and message for the world.* New American Library, 1954.

Fisher, Roger. *Getting to Yes.* New York: Penguin Books, 1991

Freire, Paulo. *Pedagogy of the Oppressed.* New York: Continuum Press, 2000.

Fry, A. Ruth. *Victories Without Violence.* Ocean Tree 1986.

Gandhi, Mohandas K. *An Autobiography: My Experiments with Truth.* Boston: Beacon, 1993.

- - -.*Gandhi on Non-Violence: Selected texts from Gandhi's Non-Violence in Peace and War.* Shambala, 1996

- - - . *Non-Violent Resistance.* Dover, 2001

Garbarino, J. *Lost Boys: Why Our Sons Turn Violent and What We Can Do To Help Them*. Anchor, 2002

Hare, A. Paul and Herbert H. Blumberg. *Nonviolent Direct Action: American Cases, Social-Psychological Analyses.* Cleveland: Corpus Books, 1968.

Hersch, P. *A Tribe Apart: A Journey Into the Heart Of American Adolescence.* New York: Ballantine Books,1999.

Hope, Marjorie and James Young. *The Struggle for Humanity.* Maryknoll, NY: Orbis, 1977.

Hunter, Allan A. *Courage in Both Hands.* Nyack, NY: Fellowship of Reconciliation, 1962.

Judson, Stephanie, et al. *Manual on Nonviolence and Children.* Philadelphia: New Society, 1977.

King, Martin Luther, Jr. *Strength to Love.* Fortress Pub, 1981.

- - - . *Stride toward Freedom: The Montgomery Story.* New York: Harper, 1958.

- - - . *The Trumpet of Conscience.* New York: Harper Collins, 1968.

- - - . *Where Do We Go from Here? Chaos or Community?*. Boston: Beacon, 1968

Kreidler, W. J. .*Conflict Resolution in the Middle School: A Curriculum and Teacher's Guide.* Educators for Social Responsibility, 1984.

- - - . *Creative Conflict Resolution: More Than 200 Activities for Keeping Peace in the Classroom.* Goodyear Books, 1984

- - - .*Teaching Conflict Resolution Through Children's Literature.* Scholastic, Inc. 1999.

Kreidler, W.J. & Furlong, L. *Adventures in Peacemaking: A Conflict Resolution Activity Guide for School Age Programs.* Educational Media, 1996.

Kreidler, W.J. & Whittall, S.T. *Early Childhood Adventures in Peacemaking.* Educators for Social Responsibility.1998.

Lewis, David L. *King: A Biography.* Chicago: University of Illinois Press, 1978.

Lieber, C.M. *Conflict Resolution in the High School: 36 Lessons.* Educators for Social Responsibility, 1998.

MacBeth, F. and Nic Fine. *Playing With Fire: Creative Conflict Resolution for Young Adults.* Philadelphia: New Society Press, Press,1995.

May, Rollo. *Power and Innocence: a Search for the Sources of Violence.* New York: Norton, 1998.

Merton, Thomas. *The Nonviolent Alternative.* New York: Farrar, Straus & Giroux, 1998.

Miller, Alice. *For Your Own Good: Hidden Cruelty in Child-rearing and the Roots of Violence.* New York:Farrar, Straus & Geroux, 1990.

- - - . *Prisoners of Childhood.* New York: Harper Collins, 1996.

New Games Fellowship. *New Games Book.* Main Street Books, 1976.

- - - . *More New Games and Playful Ideas.* Main Street Books, 1981.

Oppenheimer, Martin, and George Lakey. *A Manual for Direct Action.* Chicago: Quadrangle Books, 1965.

Peck, James. *Underdogs vs. Upperdogs.* New York: AMP&R, 1980.

Polland, B.K. *We Can Work It Out: Conflict Resolution for Children.* Tricycle Press, 2000.

Porro, B. & P. Todd. *Talk It Out: Conflict Resolution in the Elementary Classroom.* Association for Supervision and Curriculum Development, 1996.

Pransky, J. & Carpenos, L. *Healthy Thinking/Feeling/Doing From the Inside Out: A Middle School Curriculum Guide for the Prevention of Violence. Abuse and Other Problem Behaviors. Brandon:* Safer Society Press, 2000.

Prutzman, P. *Friendly Classroom for a Small Planet.* Philadelphia: Philadelphia: New Society Press, Press, 1988.

Rogers, Carl. *On Personal Power: Inner Strength and its Revolutionary Impact.* New York: Delta, 1978

Rohnke, Karl, *Silver Bullets, Project Adventure*, Beverly: Project Adventure, 1984.

Rosenberg, Marshall B. *A Model for Nonviolence and Communication.* Consortium Book Sales, 1983.

- - - .*Nonviolent Communication - a Language of Compassion. Encinitas:* Puddle Dancer Press. 1999.

Sharp, Gene. *The Politics of Nonviolent Action.* Boston: Porter Sargent, 1973.

Sheeran, Michael J., S.J. *Beyond Majority Rule: Voteless Decisions in the Religious Society of Friends.* Philadelphia: PYM, 1983.

Smedes,Lewis B. *Forgive and Forget: Healing the Hurts We Don't Deserve.* San Francisco: Harper, 1996.

Tavris, Carol. *Anger: The Misunderstood Emotion.* Touchstone 1989.

Thich Nhat Hanh. *Peace is Every Step: The Path of Mindfulness in Everyday Life.* New York: Bantam Press, 1992

- - - . *Anger: Buddhist Wisdom for Cooling the Flames.* Rider, 2001.

Woodrow, Peter. *Clearness.* Philadelphia: Philadelphia: New Society Press, 1976.

TAPE/CD

AVP/USA, *AVP/USA Video*, AVP Distribution Service, 844 John Fowler Road, Plainfield, VT 05667. $30.00

AVP/USA, *Picture Sharing CD,* AVP Distribution Service, 844 John Fowler Road, Plainfield, VT 05667. $10.00

Desai, Narayan. *Growing Up with Gandhi.* (Order from Theodore Herman, Cornwall Manor, Cornwall, PA 17016.)

WEB-SITES

http://www.genuinecontact.net/genuine_contact_workshops.html . The Genuine Contact Program. This is a training program that helps organizations and communities achieve health and balance.

www.esrnational.org . A source of curriculum materials and teacher training programs that focus on issues of peace-making and conflict resolution.

www.teachingtolerance.org . Provides a magazine subscription, videos, teacher guides free to teachers and organizations working to reduce prejudice.

INDEX

A Little Help from My Friends G-19
A What? G-6
Acknowledgment Process D-3
Active Listening D-4
Addiction to Grudges D-5
Adjective Name with Gesture G-4
Affirmation Posters G-18
Affirmation Pyramid G-18
Affirmations G-18
Agenda Worksheet B-5
Agenda Planning Guide B-7
Agendas Section .... B
Agenda Writing Guidelines B-4
Aggressive Communication F-6
Aliens D-7
All Aboard D-8
Anatomy of an Apology D-9
Anger D-38
Anger Talk F-4
Anger, Fear & Taking a Stand (Talk) F-6
Animal Parade G-6
Apology, The Anatomy of (Handout) ... D-10
Assertive Communication F-7
Assertiveness D-11
Assertiveness (Handout) D-12
Bag (The) D-14
Ball Pass G-6
Bargaining with Values D-15
Basic Human Rights (Handout) D-13
Bean Jar D-42, D-44
Big Wave (continuum) E-7
Big Wind Blows, with an addition G-6
Big Wind Blows... Factulance G-6
Blanket G-7
Board of Directors: G-4
Body Imaging D-16
Books H-3
Boxing Ring E-3
Brainstorming D-17
Brainstorming and Web Charts D-18
Brainstorming– Eruption of Violence ... D-22
Brainstorms Suggestions for Topics D-19
Break Through D-23
Broomstick D-49
Bumper Stickers D-24
Buttons D-25
Buzz G-7
By the Numbers G-7
Car and Driver G-7
Car Wash G-7
Carefronting D-27
Change (Ways I Want to) D-19
Choices D-31
Choosing Focus Topic Goals/Priorities .. D-32
Choosing Focus Topic with Gathering .. D-34
Choosing Focus Topic by Consensus ... D-34
Claremont Dialogue D-37

Closings G-18
Colored Dots .... (see Dots)
Communication Talk F-7
Concentric Circles D-38
Concentric Circles/Listen–Reflecting ... D-41
Conflict (Making Friends With) F-14
Conflicts in Workshop A-12
Confrontation in Triads E-8
Consensus Bean Jar D-42, D-44
Consensus (Choosing Focus Topic) D-34
Consensus Five Exercise Process D-44
Consensus Flagpole D-49
Consensus Flower D-45
Consensus Octopus D-49
Consensus Perfect Day D-47
Consensus Picture Sharing D-48
Consensus Secret Spot D-50
Consensus Short Exercises D-49
Consensus Triangles D-51
Consensus Using TP D-52
Consensus You Have to Have a Heart. . . D-53
Continuums E-7
Contract with Self for Future D-55
Cooperative Crocodiles and Frogs G-8
Cooperative Musical Chairs G-8
Cows and Jello G-8
Creative Solutions – Brainstorming D-19
Crossover D-56
Dealing with Put Downs D-58
Decrease Violence (Brainstorm) D-19
Definitions D-60
Differences D-29
Dissolving Anger D-61
Dollar Fifty G-8
Dots D-62
Earthquake G-8
Elephants, Palm Trees and Skunks G-8
Empathy D-63
Empathy Talk F-9
Eruption of Violence D-22
Escalator D-64
Escalator Story D-65
Escalator Variation – Anger D-67
Escalator Variation – Fear D-69
Exercises/Techniques Section .... D
Exercise Approximate Timing B-9
Exploring the Roots of Anger D-71
Face to Face G-9
Facilitated Conflict Resolution D-73
Facts/feelings Person D-74
Fairy Tale Theater D-76
Fear D-19, D-40
Fear Talk F-10
Feedback A-10
Five Exercise Process D-44
Fire on the Mountain: G-9
Fishbowl D-78

H-5   Index

Flagpole	D-49	Human to Human	D-97
Flower (Consensus)	D-45	Human Rights, Basic (Handout)	D-13
Forgiveness	D-39, D-80	I Messages Another Approach	D-99
Forgiveness Circle	D-163	I Messages — Don't Give Up!	D-101
Forgiveness Quadrants	D-81	I Statements/Listening	D-119
Forgiveness Talk	F-12	I Want / I Want	D-109
Forgiveness - Removing the Obstacles	F-13	Identity - My Self	D-39
Format of Second Level Workshop	B-3	I'm Going on a Safari	G-11
Four Part Listening	D-83	Impediments to Communication	D-103
From Another Point of View	D-84	In Common	D-44, D-104
Gatherings — Gathering Themes	G-3	In His Shoes	D-105
Getting in Touch	D-85	Inclusion	D-107
Gibberish:	G-9	Injunctions of Childhood and Life	D-108
Gift-Giving	G-18	Introduction Section - Preface	A-3
Goals/Priorities (Choosing Focus Topic)	D-32	Jack-in-the-box	G-11
Goal-wish Problem Solving	D-87	Journal Writing	D-110
Grief	D-88	Labels	D-111
Group DaVinci	D-90	Leader	G-11
Grudges, Addiction to (Handout)	D-6	Let's Go Swimming	D-112
Guided Meditation	D-91	Letter to Myself	D-114
Guided Reflection: AVP	D-92	Life Beliefs	D-115
Guided Reflection: Forgiveness	D-93	Life "Bios"	D-116
Guided Visualization	D-28, D-30	Lifelines	D-117
Guidelines (Workshop)	D-44	Light & Livelies	G-6
Guidelines to Agenda Writing	B-4	Line-up 1	G-11
Guidlines for Consensus	D-54	Line-up 2	G-12
Guides–Being Open to TP	C-13	Listen to the Universe (Hot & Cold)	G-10
Handout: Addiction to Grudges	D-6	Listening	E-6
Handout: Anatomy of an Apology	D-10	Listening/I-S Statement Combination	D-119
Handout: Anger, Stages of Worksheet	D-65	Little Help from my Friends (A)	G-19
Handout: Assertiveness (Principles of)	D-12	Magic Carpet	D-123
Handout: Basic Human Rights	D-13	Making Friends With Conflict	F-14
Handout: Consensus	D-43	Man Woman Relationships	D-39
Handout: Consensus Flower	D-46	Masks	D-124
Handout: Consensus, Have to Have Heart	D-53	May I Share Something With You	D-128
Handout: Consensus, Guidelines for	D-54	Mini News & Goods/Minor Irritations	G-5
Handout: Facts/Feelings Person	D-75	Mountains and Valleys	G-12
Handout: Forgiveness Quad. Worksheet	D-82	Mrs. Mumbley Gets Serious	G-12
Handout: I Messages—Don't Give Up	D-102	My Name Is and I like to … :	G-4
Handout: In His Shoes	D-106	My Potential	D-130
Handout: Reflective Listening,Principles	D-122	My Self	D-39
Handout: Masks — Prison	D-126	Namaste Circle	G-20
Handout: Masks — Community	D-127	Name Ball:	G-4
Handout: Stages of Anger	D-68	Name Games	G-4
Handout: Stages of Fear	D-70	Name That Tune	G-13
Handout: Values Clarification	D-156	Nigerian Applause	G-12
Handout: What's In My Circle	D-169	Obstacles to Forgiveness	F-13
Handout: You Have to Have Heart	D-54	Octopus (Consensus)	D-49
Hand Slap	G-9	Old Woman in the Forest	D-77
Hat Trick:	G-4	Open Chair	E-6
Head, Heart, Hand	G-19	Opening Talks	F-3
Hello Train	G-10	Opinions	E-7
Here I Sit	G-10	Parallel Construction	D-131
High Five:	G-4	Passive Communication	F-6
Hidden Agenda	D-95	Pattern Ball	G-13
Hot and Cold (Listen to Universe)	G-10	Perceptions Based Partial Knowledge	D-132
Hot Potato	G-10	Perfect Day	D-47
How Do You Feel When …	D-96	Personal Space	D-134
Howdy, Howdy, Howdy	G-11	Picture Paints a Thousand Words	D-135
How My Family Put Me Down	D-58	Picture Perfect	D-136

H-6   Index

Picture Sharing	D-44 D-48 D-137	The Way We Do Things	A-4
Pizza Pizza	G-13	Therapy and AVP Workshops	A-5
Planning Guide	B-7	Think and Listen	D-155
Pop Song:	G-5	Thought Sculpture	E-5
Power	D-38	Three Question Interview	D-156
Power Game	D-138	Three Questions on Oppression	D-157
Power Grab	D-140	Times for Exercises	B-10
Power Inversion	D-141	Tinkertoy Dog	D-158
Power Talk	F-16	Tire Ball:	G-15
Preface to Manual	A-3	Tossing Heads	G-15
Pretzel	G-13	Touching as Part of AVP Training	A-6
Processing Anger	D-143	Transforming Ourselves	D-160
Projection	D-145	Transforming Power	D-40
Put-Downs (Dealing with)	D-58	TP Guidelines	C-13
Query Writing	D-146	TP Guidelines Related to the Mandala	C-10
Rainstorm	G-20	TP in This Workshop	C-3
Red-Handed	E-14	TP Indicators	C-12
G-14Reflecting	D-41	TP Mandala	C-9
Reflective Listening Handout.	D-122	TP Mandala Experience.	D-162
Relationships – Man/Woman	D-39	TP On Violence	C-4
Relationship Reflection	D-147	TP Quartets	D-163
Removing Obstacles to Forgiveness	F-13	TP Reverse Mandala	D-164
Resolution of Conflicts in Workshop	A-12	TP Section	C
Resources	H-3	TP Short Talk	C-6
Rights & Equity	D-28	TP Talk	C-5
Role Playing Section	E	TP Talk Using Mandala	C-11
Roleplaying—Variations on a Theme	E-5	TP Using	D-52
Rumors 1	G-14	TP What Makes it Work	C-8
Rumors 2	G-14	Triangles (Consensus)	D-51
Scream	G-14	Triggers	(see Buttons)
Sculpting	D-148	Values (Bargaining with)	D-15
Sculpture (Thought)	E-5	Values Clarification	D-165
Secret Spot (Consensus)	D-50	Violence (On)	C-4
Self-Esteem, Enhancing	D-38	Violence (Decreasing)	D-19
Short Exercises on Consensus	D-49	Violence (Eruption of)	D-22
Slow Boat to China	G-14	Violence/Nonviolence (Brainstorm)	D-20
Society Promotes Violence	D-19	Violence (Society Promotes)	D-19
Speakout	D-149	Ways to Prevent or Decrease Violence	D-19
Speed Pattern Ball	G-15	Ways Society Teaches/Prom. Violence	D-19
Stand Up:	G-15	Ways I Want to Change	D-19
Stereotyping Talk	F-18	WBLS, the Quiet Storm	G-15
Stop the Music	G-15	Weaving	G-20
Symbols of Power	D-150	Web Charts	D-18
Talk – Anger	F-4	Web Sites	H-4
Talk – Anger, Fear & Taking a Stand	F-6	What Cha Doin'?	G-16
Talk – Communication	F-7	What If?	G-16
Talk – Empathy	F-9	What Is a Man (Brainstorm)	D-20
Talk – Fear	F-10	What's in a Word? (Brainstorm)	D-20
Talk – Forgiveness	F-12	What's in My Circle	D-167
Talk – Forgiveness-Remove Obstacles	F-13	Whispered Affirmations.	D-171
Talk – Making Friends with Conflict	F-14	Who Says I Am?	D-173
Talk – Opening	F-3	Wink'um	G-16
Talk – Power	F-16	Winkers	G-16
Talk – Stereotyping	F-18	Wizards Giants and Elves:	G-17
Talks/Explanations Section	F	Working as a Team	A-8
Tangram Dog	D-152	Workshop Conflicts	A-12
Tapes/CD	H-4	Yarn Toss	G-21
Testers Waders Plungers	D-112	Yes and No	G-17
Territory	D-154	You Have to Have a Heart	D-53
The Bag	D-14	You Said / I Said	D-174